VIENNA
1815-1848

VIENNA
in the Biedermeier Era
1815-1848

Edited by Robert Waissenberger

With contributions by
Hans Bisanz, Günter Düriegl,
Regina Forstner, Ernst Hilmar,
Renata Kassal-Mikula,
Selma Krasa, Walter Obermaier,
Peter Parenzan, Hans Urbanski
Robert Waissenberger,
and Reingard Witzmann

RIZZOLI
NEW YORK

German language edition: *Wien 1815–1848: Zeit des Biedermeier*
Copyright © 1986 by Office du Livre S.A., Fribourg, Switzerland
English translation: Copyright © 1986 by Office du Livre S.A.
Fribourg, Switzerland

English translation published in 1986 in the United States of America by:
RIZZOLI INTERNATIONAL PUBLICATIONS, INC.
597 Fifth Avenue/New York 10017

Library of Congress Cataloging-in-Publication Data

Wien 1815–1848, Zeit des Biedermeier.
  Vienna in the Biedermeier era, 1815–1848.

  Translation of: Wien 1815–1848, Zeit des Biedermeier.
  Includes bibliographies and index.
  1. Arts, Austrian–Austria–Vienna. 2. Biedermeier
(Art)–Austria–Vienna. 3. Arts, Modern–19th
century–Austria–Vienna. I. Waissenberger, Robert.
II. Title.
NX548.A1W513 1986 700'.9436'13   85–43524
ISBN 0–8478–0715–0

Printed and bound in Austria

CONTENTS

INTRODUCTION

Among the cultural epochs that have left their mark on Vienna, a prominent place is occupied by the period between the Congress of Vienna in 1814–15 and the outbreak of the revolution in March, 1848. These were years during which the city grew rapidly and was subject to a rising tide of change, particularly with regard to its social structure.

It is important to draw a clear distinction between two terms that are applied to this period: "Biedermeier,"* which stands for a primarily bourgeois-oriented culture of domesticity, and "Pre-March," which is employed generally in the German-speaking world to characterize a particular form of political life and, in Austria, is colored by the "Metternich system," often cited as the outstanding example of an authoritarian state. One is also right, however, in assuming that the two terms are interrelated.

In the aftermath of the Napoleonic Wars, which were seen as a consequence of the French Revolution, this era was a period of restoration in which rulers were concerned to mobilize all conservative forces capable of resisting change and innovation and, in particular, to stamp out all revolutionary elements—regarded as evil. However, since it was more or less common knowledge that ideals of renewal were at work everywhere (even if circumstances dictated that that work must go on underground), a comprehensive surveillance system had to be in operation at all times to keep the government informed of any revolutionary or otherwise subversive movements that might appear among the populace.

This exercise of governmental authority took a variety of forms; and police power, the use of informers, denunciation, and censorship were typical features of the system. As always in such political circumstances, the principal victims were intellectuals of all categories—writers, theater people, journalists, students, schoolteachers, and the like. There was a particular "climate" in other words, and it was this that placed its special stamp on the Biedermeier or Pre-March era.

The "culture of domesticity," as the Biedermeier style has—not incorrectly—been designated, was probably influenced by the general state of mind of the period. The dwellings in the houses built during those years were relatively small. Consequently the furnishings also tended to be small. All the greater were the love and enthusiasm lavished on the design of household utensils, items of furniture, and tableware, whether metal or porcelain. Sumptuous glassware was highly prized, and so, above all, was the *veduta*, a predominantly small-format picture that afforded a glimpse of a lovelier world—the world, principally, of landscape and the beauties of nature, which people were increasingly beginning to discover and appreciate.

Summer holidays, excursions, and walks in Vienna's Prater and Auergarten parks became more and more fashionable. People took great delight in parties and festivities, particularly at *Fasching,* Vienna's carnival time. A dance culture emerged and indeed came to typify the era, for these were the years that saw the birth and popularization of the waltz.

Light music, the cultivation of home decor, and the emergence of a certain popular culture constituted the essence and typical identity of Biedermeier style. Indeed it was in this respect that the term acquired meaning: neither literature, nor serious music, nor architecture can be said to have possessed a typical Biedermeier character in this sense. They were simply manifestations, among others, of a particular period—on which, however, they failed to place an unmistakable stamp.

The onerous political pressure that the system imposed on people could not be sustained indefinitely. Time could not be made to stand still. Social conditions were in flux. The changeover from small-scale manufacturing to industrial operations led to decisive shifts in the social structure of the population. Industrial plants, which the government had obstructed for a long time, could not be kept out of the city for ever. The new production processes brought social tensions in their wake and led to the emergence of an industrial proletariat and to a totally new social situation. The circumstances demanded change. In a context of revolutionary upheavals all over Europe, Vienna too saw the beginning of a revolution in 1848, a revolution that miscarried at first but eventually did usher in a new era.

Robert Waissenberger

---

* Originally "Biedermaier," the term was borrowed from the imaginary author of *Poems of Gottfried Biedermaier* (an artless Philistine), which were actually written by A. Kussmaul and L. Eichrodt. They appeared in 1855–57 in the humorous weekly *Fliegende Blätter*, which was published in Munich. [Translator's note].

I THE CONGRESS OF VIENNA

The Victors in Paris

He had defended himself like a lion against fivefold superiority, exploiting the disunity of the Allies, each of whom wished to be the first to enter Paris. But by March 31, 1814, it was all over; on that day Marshal Marmont surrendered Paris. Napoleon was all for fighting on, but his marshals refused to obey orders. They wanted a time of peace in which to enjoy, at last, the wealth and honors he had heaped upon them. On April 11, 1814, Napoleon abdicated at Fontainebleau, leaving not only France but virtually the whole of Europe without a master.

Nearly all the allied monarchs made their entry into Paris—first among them, of course, the principal figure, the youthful Czar Alexander I of Russia, and, following modestly in his wake, King Frederick William III of Prussia. Emperor Francis, not wishing to gloat over the misfortune of his daughter, Marie Louise, Napoleon's second wife, had himself represented by Prince Schwarzenberg, the victor of the Battle of Leipzig.

The world's destiny sometimes treads surprising paths and takes delight, for example, in placing the future of a continent and the well-being of the coming century in the hands of an inexperienced young ruler to whom the awesome complexities of the old Europe must of necessity be fundamentally alien. The czar came of a German mother; he was married – unhappily – to a German wife, and his tutor, the liberal Swiss Frédéric César de La Harpe, had crammed him with a great many half-understood liberal ideas without managing to form a firm character. Alexander I alternated between exalted states of high-minded Utopianism and periods of coarse sensuality and crude selfishness, reverting in between to moods of remorse and mysticism.

He entered Paris in one of the most exalted states of his entire life. Had Alexander's ardent flights of fancy not come together, in a unique instance of political cross-pollination, with the shrewdly calculating planning ability of Prince Talleyrand, the golden mists enveloping the would-be world-liberator would probably have evaporated. In defiance of Napoleon's instructions (Talleyrand was a member of his regency council), the prince had remained in Paris. As early as 1808, at the Erfurt Congress, he had established contact with Czar Alexander behind Napoleon's back with a view to discussing the rearrangement of Europe after the latter's fall, which Talleyrand was already predicting at that time.

On entering Paris, Czar Alexander wished to take up residence in the Elysée Palace. However, he was handed a note warning him not to move in there because the building was mined. Talleyrand promptly offered the czar his own palace in the Rue Florentin (now the American embassy), and the invitation was accepted. It later emerged that no bombs had been planted in the Elysée Palace. The writer of the warning letter was never traced, but the paper employed was found to bear a strong resemblance to that ordinarily used by Talleyrand.

The Concept of Legitimacy

It is not true that politicians create the principal currents of history. They only recognize them in time, with a greater or lesser degree of perception; measure their strength; and then, with varying degrees of skill, guide them a little; and perhaps prevent them from overflowing their banks.

The same was true of the concept of legitimacy, which has been regarded as Talleyrand's great idea, or in Austria—with a dash of local pride—as Metternich's. It was by no means a new invention, a new historico-philosophical system, a long-awaited political panacea, nor even what it was frequently denounced as, namely an attempt to justify the reactionaries' restoration of an old and obsolete order. In fact, it was no more and no less than the conviction, gained from the most minute observation of all psychological and political factors, that revolution, having failed twice over, could never form the basis of any lasting rearrangement of the international political scene. Revolution was seen as having failed twice over not only because it had been reduced to absurdity in domestic affairs by Robespierre's bloody Reign of Terror, but also because it had now failed in the field of foreign policy as a result of the no less bloody defeat of its latter-day champion, Napoleon. Only the authority of ancient kingship, founded on a centuries-old legal tradition, was thought to offer any guarantee of political stability.

However, such arguments, advanced with all possible acumen, initially met with a stubborn "No" from the czar, for in the course of negotiations among the Allies, the restoration of the Bourbons had never been considered as a serious option. Least of all by Alexander, probably for the very personal reason that it is easier to forgive an injustice suffered than an injustice one has administered oneself: Alexander had not behaved too well toward the Bourbons when, fleeing from Napoleon, they had arrived at Mitau in Kurland (now Jelgava in Latvia). After Alexander had made his peace with Napoleon on the celebrated raft on the Neman (Memel), the Bourbons became an embarrassment

to him. He began by reducing their meat rations, which given the legendary Bourbon appetite hit them particularly hard. Eventually they removed themselves to exile in Britain.

Talleyrand argued rightly that, if anyone from Napoleon's circle was to rule France, in the eyes of the Bonapartists it could only be Napoleon's son, the three-year-old king of Rome. He was a possibility, however, only with his mother Marie Louise as regent, which would guarantee a large measure of Austrian influence. Britain was agreeable to anything that promised to weaken France, tending, because of its own parliamentary system, to favor a republic. Prussia had no opinion whatever beyond a desire to secure the greatest possible terrritorial gains for itself. So, in the end, the czar had to accept the return of the Bourbons on the basis of the legitimacy principle.

On one point, however, there was unanimity from the outset: the monarchy could only be restored in France in conjunction with a constitution that guaranteed the opposition free speech, for that too was a basic requirement for the legitimacy of a state. A further consequence of enormous importance for France arose out the legitimacy principle itself. The Allies had been at war with Napoleon or even, it might be said, with the French Revolution, but they had never been at war with the legitimate rulers of France, the Bourbons. If the latter renounced all the conquests of Napoleon and of the revolution and returned to the frontiers of 1792, then everything was in order: the country could not even be asked to pay reparations.

The incredible—unfortunately it was also incredibly rare—had happened. The wisdom that Talleyrand had distilled from his long experience of political and human affairs, coupled with the bold idealism of the czar at his most high-minded, had brought peace without producing either victor or vanquished. Together the two men had brought release from the fear that had dominated Europe for a quarter of a century. After the cruel destruction of the utopias of the revolution and the Napoleonic Empire, hope was reborn, a hope of justice and hence of

1   P. Gros, after Jakob Gauermann: *Wounded Frenchman Receiving Attention in the Landstrasse Suburb of Vienna after the Battle of Aspern,* 1809. Aquatint, colored; plate 24.7 × 34.3 cm, sheet 35.5 × 52 cm. Historisches Museum der Stadt Wien. Following the Battle of Aspern-Essling (1809), large numbers of wounded French soldiers were brought across the Danube and cared for by the people of Vienna.

Grauermann del.

Gros sculp.

Les Habitans de Vienne distribuent des secours aux blessés François qui reviennent par la Land-Straße.

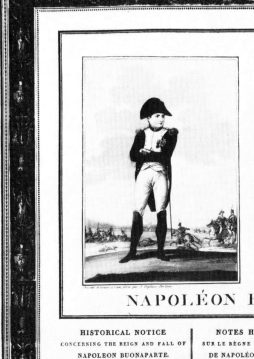

2   *Napoléon Buonaparte: Historical Notice Concerning The Reign and Fall Of Napoleon Buonaparte,* ca. 1815. Copperplate engraving, colored, 66 × 49.3 cm. Printed in Paris by Bance. Historisches Museum der Stadt Wien.
"...The foreign powers form a new coalition; they unite their efforts and Providence declares itself in their favour, guiding by its powerful hand their warlike bands under the walls of Paris. After twelve hours fighting, they enter triumphant in the city, on the 31 of March 1814, not as enemies but as deliverers."

3 K. Ponheimer, after Johann Nepomuk Höchle: "*The Allied Powers Enter Paris on March 31, 1814*." Copperplate engraving, colored; plate 37 × 55.5 cm, sheet 44.5 × 63.5 cm. Printed by "Jos. Eder & Comp." Historisches Museum der Stadt Wien. Following the defeat of Napoleon's army near Leipzig, the allies managed to press on to Paris and to occupy the city.

building true freedom. As far as France was concerned, then, everything was settled in an unbelievably short time and sealed with the Peace of Paris on May 30, 1814. Thanks, again, to the high-minded generosity of Alexander, the fate of Napoleon was decided in a similarly elegant manner. He was granted sovereignty over the island of Elba, kept the title of emperor, was allowed to retain an army of 1,000 men, and was allocated a pension of 2 million francs—though Louis XVIII never paid it.

However, Napoleon's fall had left not only France but almost the whole of Europe without a master and needing to have its future rearranged. To discuss these problems, the Allies agreed to meet for a congress in Vienna within three months. Right at the end of these preliminary discussions, almost incidentally, Talleyrand slipped in what sounded like a quite innocuous stipulation, to the effect that the congress should reach its deci-

sions "on the basis of existing international law and with due regard for the European balance of power." It was through this loophole that Talleyrand gained access to the congress, for in principle France had no business in Vienna—its future having been settled by the Peace of Paris. However, with regard to the European balance of power, France's presence in the Austrian capital was not merely justified but extremely important.

The fact that the legitimacy principle did not mean the restoration of the old state of affairs that had existed before Napoleon and the revolution—in other words that the wheel of history could not simply be turned back—became apparent in France immediately. If France was to continue to be a great power, or rather regain its great-power status, it needed the army. Louis XVIII was shrewd enough to know this, and much to the disgust of the returning emigrants, Napoleon's marshals were confirmed in their possession of all the titles, pensions, and possessions that they had all too often acquired at the expense of the exiled aristocrats. And of course the *Code Civil*, Napoleon's magnificent summary of civil law, remained in force.

The Peacemakers in Vienna

On September 23, 1814, Emperor Francis met Czar Alexander and King Frederick William at the Tabor Gate in Vienna, and the three sovereigns paraded through the city on their prancing horses to the cheers of the enthusiastic Viennese, to whom peace was more than welcome. A certain amount has been written about the diplomatic preparations for the Congress of Vienna and about the intrigues that, of course, began to be woven at this stage. What is usually overlooked entirely is the enormous task of organization and improvisation that inevitably preceded an event on this international scale in what was, in fact, a tiny city—virtually equivalent to the center of today's Vienna. While Metternich's influence on Austrian history in general may have been somewhat overrated, his achievement in putting the accent, during the Congress of Vienna, on the city in which it was held and in making the congress one of the highlights of Austria's past may not have been sufficiently praised. The most difficult obstacle he had to surmount in the process was probably Emperor Francis himself, to whom any kind of ostentation and display was deeply repugnant and who, particularly since the distressing national bankruptcy of 1811, had made thrift a top priority. However, when Austria's standing in the world and the glory of the dynasty were at stake, the Hapsburg monarchs, who were otherwise tightfisted for the most part, were prepared to spend up to the hilt.

The costliest item was undoubtedly putting up the visiting rulers in the emperor's Vienna palace, the *Hofburg*, and maintaining their households at the emperor's expense. The emperor also paid for the major entertainments: costumes, harnesses, sleighs, bands, and hospitality. At the great *Redoute*, or masked ball in the Spanish Riding School, gentlemen

dancers had to pay only for the sashes they gave their partners. Small wonder, then, that the emperor's outlays for the congress were estimated at 22 million gulden—between 7 and 8 billion Austrian schillings in today's currency. Yet seldom can money have been better spent.

The organizing committee had another brilliant idea. They issued an appeal to the Austrian, Hungarian, and Bohemian nobility to move into their town houses earlier than usual that year and so contribute toward showing off the Austrian capital at its best.

4 Woltener, after Eugen Lami: *Czar Alexander I of Russia.* Copperplate engraving, 21.5 × 13 cm. Historisches Museum der Stadt Wien: Wurzbach Collection.

5   Friedrich Loos: *View of
Vienna from the Bisamberg,*
1845. Oil on canvas, 112 × 146
cm. Historisches Museum der
Stadt Wien.
According to tradition this painting once belonged to Emperor
Ferdinand I of Austria. It provides
a view of the imperial capital (in
the distance), which was not
often painted.

Triumph Einzug.
Seiner Kaiserlichen Majestät Franz I. in Wien den 16ten Juny 1814.

6 *Emperor Francis I Enters Vienna on June 16, 1814.* Etching, 20.5. × 32.5 cm. Printed by "Jos. Eder & Comp." Historisches Museum der Stadt Wien.

Feyerlicher Einzug Ihro Majesteten des Kaisers von Rußland, Alexander der 1te und Friedrich Wilhelm des III.ten Königs von Preußen den 25.ten September 1814. Mitags 1. Uhr, durch die Jägerzeil Leopoldstadt, in die Residenzstadt Wien, begleitet von Sey: Maj: Franz des 1.ten Kaisers von Österreich, und villen hohen Offizirs.

Wien) b. Anton Leitner Spitalberg Gaße No 228.

7 *Czar Alexander I of Russia and King Frederick William III of Prussia enter Vienna on September 25, 1814.* Copperplate engraving, colored. Published by A. Leitner. Historisches Museum der Stadt Wien.

The hostesses were distinguished by that rather striking beauty which a happy blend of German, Magyar, Slav, and Italian blood often managed to produce in such circles. They were without exception great ladies, which is to say that they did not concern themselves with politics, had nothing to do with the web of intrigue that reached into every corner of the city, and led absolutely irreproachable lives—none of which could be said of the female members of the foreign aristocracy visiting Vienna at the time. This conferred a special prestige upon the whole Viennese social scene, giving it great inner strength and a kind of cheerful seriousness. The great ladies of Viennese society have gone down in history, each with her own particular commendation. Princess Gabriele Auersperg, née Lobkowitz, was known as *La beauté sentimentale*. She was the favorite of the czar, but when he attempted to become too familiar on one occasion, she not only treated him to a sharp rebuff, but there was even some discussion as to whether he should be challenged to a duel by a relative or by the emperor himself. Countess Julie Zichy, née Festetics, was called *La beauté céleste*. The king of Prussia adored her because she reminded him of his late, unhappy wife, Queen Louise. Countess Sophie Zichy, née Széchenyi, was *La beauté triviale*; Princess Maria Therese Esterházy, née Thurn und Taxis, was *La beauté étonnante*; Countess Caroline Széchenyi, née Clanwilliam, was *La beauté coquette;* and Countess Gabriele Saurau, née Hunyady, was *La beauté du diable*. These sobriquets were simply intended to describe the humors and caprices of the ladies concerned and were not in any way meant to cast aspersions on their virtue.

The chief task of the congress was to reallocate Napoleon's conquests. These covered a vast area that included Spain, Portugal, Belgium, Holland, Hamburg, Danzig, the left bank of the Rhine, the former kingdom of Westphalia, Switzerland, Piedmont-Savoy and virtually the whole of Italy, Istria, Dalmatia, Carniola, and much else besides. Perhaps equally important was the task of reorganizing some kind of German political community,

since Emperor Francis had laid aside the crown of the Holy Roman Empire in 1806. Certain questions had settled themselves in accordance with the legitimacy principle before the congress opened. The hereditary sovereigns had returned to Spain and Portugal, the pope to Rome, the Dutch king to Holland, and many of the German princes to the lands from which they had been expelled.

Austria, too, had reoccupied most of the territories it had lost with two striking exceptions: Belgium was not reclaimed, but instead united with the kingdom of Holland – a surrender that is probably best explained in terms of the psychology of Emperor Francis, who for twenty years had been the sparring partner of the greatest military genius of all time. The emperor had finally had enough of defending possessions that were so distant and constantly in danger; to say nothing of being forced, through those possessions, into the role of defender of Germany. Moreover, Belgium, with its privileges and despite its wealth, had never brought in much money; while in return for giving it up, Austria gained the vitally important alliance with Britain, which felt it could sleep easy only if Belgium were not in the hands of a great power. For much the same reason, the so-called Austrian *Forland* extending up to the Rhine was not reclaimed either.

Just as the individual finds it difficult in his own life to adhere unswervingly to a principle he acknowledges to be right, so at the level of international politics, it proved difficult to apply the highly productive legitimacy principle in every case.

The worst thorn in the flesh, as far as legitimacy was concerned, was Murat in Naples. Joachim Murat was a Napoleonic cavalry general who, thanks to his marriage to Napoleon's sister Caroline, had been elevated to the throne of Naples. He repaid his brother-in-law poorly in that, when Napoleon began losing, Murat left him and joined the Allies, who guaranteed his throne in return. Furthermore, it is important to know that Metternich, as ambassador in Paris, had had a stormy love affair with Caroline Murat, and that he had recently once again confessed to

his wife that his feelings for the lady had not yet cooled completely.

Meanwhile, across the water in Sicily, sat the man who had been driven out of Naples, namely King Ferdinand, a Spanish Bourbon, the son of Marie Caroline, a Hapsburg princess, one of Maria Theresa's daughters – the one, it is said, who most resembled her mother. Marie Caroline was the mother-in-law of Emperor Francis (who had married her daughter, his cousin), and she was now living in exile at Schönbrunn, the emperor's palace near Vienna. The sight of Marie Caroline must have been a scarcely tolerable daily reproach to Emperor Francis.

The next problem in Italy concerned the Papal States. The pope had returned to Rome from his French confinement, but Murat was occupying part of his territories in the south and was not prepared to withdraw until the pope recognized him. In the north, Austria was holding certain territorial pledges simply to be on the safe side. Cardinal Consalvi, the representative of the Holy See, came to Vienna with major demands and expectations. In medieval fashion he threatened the diplomats (and even the pious Emperor Francis) with excommunication if the pope was not given back all his lands, including the long-lost city of Avignon.

8 Jean-Baptiste Isabey: *Session of the Congress of Vienna,* 1819. Line and stipple engraving, 66 × 88 cm. Historisches Museum der Stadt Wien.
The scene is the conference hall of the congress in the former Ballhaus, seat of the state chancellery. Pictured are the principal negotiating partners.

18

Milan and Venetia naturally reverted to Austria, and in Tuscany and Modena the Hapsburg dynasties reestablished themselves. Parma, Piacenza, and Guastalla had, at the suggestion of Czar Alexander, been promised to Empress Marie Louise in the Treaty of Fontainebleau. Because a collateral Bourbon line had ruled there, Talleyrand put up strong opposition until a compromise was found, by which Empress Marie Louise ruled the dutchies during her lifetime, but at her death they reverted to the Bourbons, for it was felt that Napoleon's son must never be allowed to occupy a throne anywhere for fear that, if he were, his claim would immediately be extended to France as well.

Switzerland is the only country that still retains the boundaries bestowed on it by the Congress of Vienna. As far as Germany was concerned, on the one hand, there was the problem of what should replace the deceased Holy Roman Empire, and on the other hand, the need for some redistribution of the territories that were involved. Substantial circles in Germany, and even within Prussia, foremost among them the idealistic patriots of the Wars of Liberation, were in favor of asking Emperor Francis to reassume the venerable crown of Charlemagne. The German princes, including the king of Prussia, would have accepted and even welcomed this solution, but were not prepared to grant the new emperor any more power than the quite powerless former emperor had possessed. On that basis, however, Emperor Francis was unwilling to resume the burden of the imperial crown.

This largely sentimental question aside, the main problem for Germany lay in Prussia's very extensive expectations with regard to acquiring an additional 8 to 10 million "souls"—though one cannot escape the impression that Prussia was less interested in the souls of its new subjects than in using their legs as soldiers. The shy Prussian King Frederick William III, who was wholly under the influence of the czar, nevertheless managed to impose his possessive policy on his ministers, Prince Hardenberg and Baron von Humboldt, who were also amenable to other considerations. Prussia was probably the country that had suffered most

under Napoleon; no one begrudged it a substantial increase in territory which, furthermore, was in line with Britain's policy of securing a balance of power in Europe.

There was one problem that seemed almost insoluble, however, and that was the problem of Saxony. King Frederick Augustus I of Saxony had neglected to "jump" in time. While the Bavarian, Württembergian, and other German troops formerly aiding Napoleon had gone over to the Allies at the crucial Battle of Leipzig, thus sealing Napoleon's defeat, the Saxons had stood by the French emperor till the bitter end. Their king had to pay for that now.

He was not allowed to take part in the congress. In fact, he was held in virtual imprisonment in Pressburg (Bratislava), and Prussia laid claim to his entire kingdom. In this it received the full backing of Czar Alexander. In return, the czar had extracted a promise that Prussia would surrender the territories it had acquired at the time of the partition of Poland. Russia was already occupying these—as well as the greater part of Poland that had formerly been Austrian provinces—and was insisting on right of conquest. Alexander dreamed of restoring Poland as a kingdom, at least in name, with himself as king and with a liberal constitution in line

19

with what his tutor, La Harpe, had taught him.

There were several deadly perils for Austria in all this. To start with, this would make Prussia Austria's immediate neighbor again, which would reawaken all the ghosts of the Seven Years' War; secondly, it would bring Russia disturbingly close; and thirdly, a liberal constitution in a country bordering on Austria would seriously challenge what, for all its paternalism, was the highly autocratic conception of government entertained by Emperor Francis.

Furthermore, to proceed thus would be to ride roughshod over the already sorely tried legitimacy principle. How could a king, who after all was wholly above the law, lose his entire country simply because he had not changed sides in time? Was it not the sacred doctrine of the legitimacy principle that conquest alone could not establish a legitimate claim, but rather that the more or less voluntary cession of the ruler was also necessary? Thus the Saxon question carried with it the additional danger that its solution along Prussian/Russian lines might undermine all the principles on which the congress was based. Being farsighted, Talleyrand feared too great an increase in Prussian, and also in Russian, power, which put France entirely on Austria's side. Together, he and Metternich managed to convince Castlereagh, the British representative, of the grave dangers that a Prussian/Russian solution of this problem would bring in its wake. Positions hardened progressively, with Prussia and Russia showing themselves increasingly intransigent, until it became necessary to contemplate the possibility of war breaking out over the Saxon issue. Thus it was that on January 3, 1815, Austria, France, and Britain concluded a secret alliance against Prussia and Russia, an alliance to which Holland and all the minor German states soon acceded. (It is interesting that, however much gossip flourished at the congress, secrecy regarding really important political facts was very nearly perfect.)

The inflated system of informers operated by Baron Hager, chief of police, which had its origins in a highly personal directive from the good emperor himself, had something almost patriarchal about it. There was not a single great house or embassy where the domestic staff had not been infiltrated by spies. Virtually all landlords and landladies were in the pay of the police. Even some people of standing had made themselves available to the intelligence services, often without remuneration. The art of opening letters and seals without leaving traces now reached its zenith. The contents of most wastepaper baskets of any importance found their way to a room in the police station where they were pieced together to form legible *chiffons*, as they were called. The fruit of such labors was never the exposure of important secrets or the unmasking of a conspiracy, and only occasionally—and then very sketchily—some intimation of a dangerous school of thought. What generally emerged was no more than the most banal kind of village gossip—which the informers then usually contrived to misunderstand.

Nor was Hager's spy network the only one. Most embassies had their confidential agents, indeed their own despatch departments, for the privilege of diplomatic secrecy was almost wholly unprotected. Espionage appeared to thrive better than counterespionage: it proved impossible, for example, to prevent Eugène de Beauharnais from maintaining contact with the Bonapartes, or Marie Louise from communicating with Napoleon, enabling the latter to receive news that was to have a decisive effect on the history of the next few months.

The Congress Dances

Opinions differed widely with regard to the parties and festivities for which the "dancing congress" became famous. There was an awareness, of course, that these were not organized purely for the sake of entertainment. People were able to salve their consciences by reflecting that they were put on for an excellent purpose, in that they helped to achieve peace and to manifest Austria's joyous lifestyle.

The first great occasion was the *Redoute*, the masked ball at the Spanish Riding School, where horsemen in magnificent costumes tilted at rings and "Turks' skulls" at full gallop and paraded their noble mounts in figures of supreme elegance. This was followed by a ball for 3,000 guests in the *Hofburg*. The ushers resold the tickets as fast as they were given up, so that the ball guests eventually numbered some 6,000—not all of them, apparently, from the best court circles since the next day 1,500 of the new silver-gilt spoons were missing.

Prince Andreas Rasumovsky, a descendent of Cossack chieftains, one of whom had been the secret consort of Czarina Elisabeth and another rewarded with immeasurable wealth by Czarina Catherine for his special qualities, had, it was said, "transformed a barren stretch of the Landstrasse district, by the power of his immeasurable wealth, into the paradise of a princely residence." The palace housed one of the largest private art collections of the day, and the exotic gardens extended deep into the Prater, with a special bridge leading thence over the arm of the Danube that is now the Danube Canal. New Year celebrations were planned there to outshine everything that had gone before. The Russian pastrycooks, determined to excel themselves, fed their ovens with anything that would burn. The ballrooms had been decked out with yards of material, ribbons, and glitter. A spark escaped from the overheated modern heating pipes, and in minutes the whole place was ablaze. The fire brigades did their best, helped by detachments from the army. Emperor Francis rode out to the scene of the disaster at midnight and attempted to console Rasumovsky. When told of the probable cause of the fire, the emperor opined, "So much for your modern contraptions!"

Talleyrand, possibly sensing that only the admixture of some seriousness made so much pleasure-seeking tolerable, suggested that January 21, the "day of horror and dismay" on which Louis XVI had been beheaded in 1793, should be commemorated in a dignified ceremony. Sigismund von Neukomm, his private

musician and a pupil of Haydn, had written a Requiem for the occasion; the French priest from St. Anna's read from the moving testament of Louis XVI, and in the black-draped church of St. Stephen there was many a genuine tear on the cheeks of the assembled congress.

Next morning, however, the tears were forgotten in the excitement of an already much-postponed sleighing excursion, which can probably be regarded as the social highlight of the congress and one of the most sophisticated festivities Vienna has ever seen. Hundreds of carriage-makers, woodcarvers, and gilders had been busy constructing the thirty-five or so sleighs that stood sparkling in the winter sun. Hundreds of upholsterers had sewn the gold-tasseled cushions of red velvet. Hundreds of tailors had worked on the dresses and capes of the sleigh queens. The czarina and the czar's sisters wore ermine—their privilege—with their green or crimson covers, tall fur caps, and diamond brooches. The men were resplendent in magnificent uniforms, while the horses, draped with tiger skins to protect them against the cold, wore ostrich-feather headdresses. The procession assembled in the Josephsplatz before gliding slowly through the city so the people could enjoy the spectacle. Behind a rousing band came the first sleigh with the master of ceremonies, Prince Trauttmannsdorf; then came Emperor Francis with the czarina, Czar Alexander with Princess Auersperg, the king of Denmark with the grand duchess of Weimar, sister to the czar, the king of Prussia with Countess Julie Zichy, *La beauté céleste*. Twenty-four pages in medieval costume preceded the Hungarian Guard, the remaining sleighs, and another band.

It was the first manifestation of the new and unaccustomed luxury that was shown to the people, and the people were delighted. They felt proud of their court, but—Vienna being Vienna—some mocking criticism was inevitable: income tax having been raised by 50 percent just three weeks before, on January 1, 1815, the golden sleighs were quickly dubbed "50 percenters." After the slow progress through the city, the sleighs dashed off to Schönbrunn, where a ball was being held for the guests. A British skating champion inscribed the names of the sovereigns on the surface of its frozen pond with the blades of his skates.

The *Dramatis Personae* of the Congress

Emperor Francis is currently undergoing a process of rehabilitation in the history books, where (in contrast to Metternich) he has hitherto been cast as a stately supernumerary. He was constantly overshadowed by his mighty opponent, Napoleon. But if Francis was forced to acknowledge the latter's intellectual superiority and quite exceptional energy, the Austrian emperor's belief in his mission as something quite apart from himself and in the mission of his house was so unswerving that, in the ebb and flow of war and diplomacy, Francis remained throughout the solid rock that could serve as the foundation of the new order. It also appears that Metternich, for all his often brilliant use of the arts of diplomacy, was in fact no more than the executive instrument of the emperor's basic ideas. The surrender of Belgium and the Austrian *Forland*, the renunciation of the German imperial crown in order not to be burdened with unfulfillable German obligations, the unconditional preservation of Saxony, the irreproachable behavior of the imperial family, and probably also—unfortunately—the exclusion of his talented brothers Charles and Johann from politics, all bear the unmistakable stamp of Francis's will and rule out any question of his having been a mere stately supernumerary.

Emperor Francis's refusing to become involved in the day-to-day affairs of diplomacy and his remaining aloof from all intrigue gave him a very special kind of prestige and, when called for, a peculiar effectiveness. When the czar, who fancied himself as the arbiter of Europe, suggested settling the Saxon question, which the diplomats were unable to solve, in personal talks with Emperor Francis, he was not only dealt a sharp rebuff but given a lesson in the way to go about things under international law—with the result that the Saxon question was quickly cleared up, albeit not along the lines the czar had suggested.

Metternich, the loyal paladin, was as good an Austrian as probably only a Rhinelander who had chosen Austria as his home could be. His emperor and he, seizing upon exactly the right moment, had brought the great Napoleon down; and now he had placed Vienna at the hub of the new world of peace. Metternich almost bankrupted himself with the splendor of his parties. Indeed, what except his colossal debts could ever have forced him to sit down at dinner with his Jewish banker Arnstein—a meal that may, with some justice, be seen as the prelude to the emancipation of the Jews, or at least of Jewish bankers, in the world of high finance. But Metternich was reproached—probably also with some justice—with wasting too much time on these festivities, with calling off conferences of state in order to stage *tableaux vivants* (literally "living pictures"), and with allowing his love affairs—a necessary ingredient of fashionable life at the time—to keep him from his desk too long. Those amours took on a positively historical dimension when they brought him into conflict with the czar, who gave Metternich a fearful dressing down and demanded that Emperor Francis dismiss him.

It is extremely difficult to characterize possibly the greatest figure at the congress, the enigmatic Prince Talleyrand. He was immensely proud of his noble lineage, not without justification since his ancestors had had a hand in elevating Hugues Capet to the throne of France, and people felt about Talleyrand all along that, as he saw fit, he could either raise up or depose the rulers he served—petty souls equating the latter course with treason. Talleyrand was truly cynicism itself, evil personified, yet in such a curious way that what he brought about was very often good. Talleyrand defies any kind of conventional moral judgement. For example, in 1795 he ousted the French foreign minister, Delacroix, and took up that office himself. He then dispatched his predecessor to an embassy post abroad in order to be able to pursue an undisturbed love affair with the latter's wife. When their union produced a son (whom Talleyrand naturally refused to acknowledge), the son received the Delacroix name—and grew up to become the greatest painter of early nineteenth-century France. Traditional moral concepts are undermined by such events, and one hesitates to pass sentence on the man concerned.

In Vienna Talleyrand lived in some seclusion in the Kaunitz Palace. His musician Neukomm was required to play to him for an hour each day while he sat and meditated in an armchair specially made for him. It was doubtless from those hours that he took the strength that lifted him above the other diplomats, obsessed as they were with their pleasures. Talleyrand's venality knew no bounds: he was offered large sums of money by the king of Saxony, by Murat and simultaneously by the Bourbons in Naples, and finally by Napoleon after his return from Elba.

Talleyrand had come to the congress with one basic idea: Prussia should not be allowed to obtain total control in Germany, nor Austria in Italy, nor Russia in the east. He may have had the intention of putting a curb on British power too. Scarcely noticed by the congress, yet possibly of greater historical importance than all its dealings put together, the final peace treaty between Britain and the United States of America was concluded on January 1, 1815. It was Britain's first setback on her apparently unstoppable way to becoming a colonial world power, and France, after all, had made a major contribution to the United States' struggle for freedom.

The soul of Czar Alexander embraced everything that made up the greatness and the wretchedness of Russia, where tyrannicide was the only workable democratic institution. Alexander, too, owed his throne to the trauma of patricide, though he bore no guilt for it himself. An eyewitness described his coronation procession as follows: "In front went the great lords, the men who had murdered his grandfather; then came his father's murderers, and then the men who will probably one day murder him." Anyone who has read Tolstoy's *War and Peace*

will be aware of how the czar, officially all powerful, was the prisoner of his bureaucracy and of society, which accounted for Alexander's deep inner insecurity. Moreover, he was evidently seized by some kind of erotic party frenzy in Vienna. After the official festivities he almost invariably repaired to some place of popular entertainment, there to dance the night away. In fact he is believed to have danced more than sixty nights away in the 1814–15 season. In that condition, it was not possible to practice politics on the basis of hard work and reasoned argument.

As a result of the firm stance adopted by Austria, France, and Britain, and not least in consequence of the personal intervention of Emperor Francis, the question of Saxony and Poland was settled along European lines and in accordance with the legitimacy principle: the king of Saxony had to surrender a great deal of territory, but he returned to his throne. Prussia and Austria retained the greater part of the lands they had held since the last partition of Poland.

Nationalists of a later age sought to reproach Metternich with having paid no heed to the voices of awakening nations. When someone spoke to him of the Italian people, he made the famous reply, "Italy is a geographical expression!"—and in a sense he was right. His job as a statesman was to gage the prevailing forces. In this respect, the nationalist camp in Italy (of a liberal, Napoleonic persuasion) was reduced, after the convulsions of France's revolution and Empire, to a tiny stratum of ambitious aristocrats and intellectuals quite simply too feeble to be included in anyone's political calculations.

A rather more complicated case was that of German nationalism. This was a movement that, though scarcely thought out and even less articulated, had ridden high on the fine wave of elation that accompanied the Wars of Liberation against Napoleon, complete with its bards (such as Ernst Moritz Arndt) and its martyrs (such as Theodor Körner). At heart it was thoroughly pro-Austrian, and it was bound up with the Romantic notion of the revival of the German Empire, which at that time was still only conceivable with a Hapsburg at its head. No doubt Metternich had in mind to play up this aspect as well, especially when it was a question of sowing some alarm among the German princes, who placed the most amazing difficulties in the way of reestablishing any kind of German unity.

When Emperor Francis refused to reassume the German imperial crown, the German patriots were automatically driven into the Prussian camp. The Prussian delegate, Humboldt, recognized this at once. "German and national Germanity is on the increase, and Austria will not be able to keep pace with it," he wrote. "Genuine German institutions are impossible there!" Thus it was that, while still in embryo, German nationalism became a Prussian weapon against Austria, the weapon that Bismarck eventually wielded with such success. However, the true unity of all Germans, together with their thousand-year-old mission of peace (the very core of the Austrian Monarchy) to permeate the East with civilizing ties, drawing its peoples together, was increasingly a matter for Austria rather than for the narrow-minded Prussian delegation.

The Man from Elba

The festivities were becoming burdensome. People were beginning to see through them and to feel a certain irritation. The discussions and intrigues went on and on, yet nothing was decided. There was a growing feeling that only some major external event could prevent the collapse of the congress. Yet when it came, it came from a totally unexpected quarter.

In the night of March 5–6, 1815, the talking had gone on—fruitlessly—until 3 o'clock in the morning. Metternich left insructions that he was not be woken. Nevertheless, at around 6 o'clock, a lackey disturbed him with what was marked as an extremely urgent dispatch from the consul in Genoa. Metternich was furious. What urgency could there be about anything coming from Genoa? He laid it aside, unopened. Unable to get back to sleep, however, he did eventually open it

to read that a British warship had appeared in the harbor, inquiring whether anyone had heard anything of Napoleon, because he was no longer on Elba! By 9 o'clock the delegates had reassembled. No one had seen this coming, except possibly Talleyrand who had written to King Louis XVIII months before to the effect that the annual pension Napoleon had been promised ought to be sent to him on Elba, otherwise there might be complications. (The letter had never been dealt with.) The delegates' response was immediate and unanimous: none of them wanted to see Napoleon back at the head of the French nation. A general ban was pronounced, though Emperor Francis toned down Talleyrand's harsh version considerably.

Napoleon, in an unparalleled triumphal procession that was dubbed *l'invasion d'un homme* ("the one-man invasion"), had marched straight to Paris. His eyes, of course, were on Vienna, for he must have known that the congress held his fate in its hands. He did three things that almost shook the congress to its foundations. Firstly, he wrote to his wife, Marie Louise, telling her to hurry back to him with their son, for his throne was now solidly reestablished. Had she gone and not been detained, in the dynastic climate of the time his throne would indeed have become virtually unassailable. Secondly, he sent the treaty of January 3, 1815, between Austria, France, and Britain, which did not rule out a war against Russia and Prussia—Napoleon had found a copy of it, which the king had left in a desk when he fled—to the czar in Vienna. In the meantime, however, agreement had been reached over the main points at issue, and in an access of magnanimity, the czar threw the treaty on the fire in the presence of a badly embarrassed Metternich. Thirdly—and possibly his most dangerous move—Napoleon sent a confidential agent to see Talleyrand in person and offer him the release of his confiscated assets in France plus 10 million francs if the prince would return to his side. But Talleyrand merely replied: "Too late!"

The witticism of Prince de Ligne—*le congrès ne marche pas, il danse*—may

10 Anton Kothgasser: Drinking glass with a portrait of the Duke of Reichstadt, son of Napoleon and Marie Louise, Vienna, 1832–33. Clear glass with transparent painting; H. 11.2 cm, Diam. 8.6 cm. Historisches Museum der Stadt Wien.

have been true of the first few months but was certainly true no longer. The congress had stopped dancing and started working hard at the reorganization of Europe in lofty disregard of the return of Napoleon. This even made some things easier—the Neapolitan question, for example. Fearing that the congress might deprive him of his crown after all, Murat had once again sided with Napoleon and opened hostilities with Austria. His decisive defeat at Tolentino left the throne of Naples free for the legitimate Bourbons. Italy was now finally settled, agreement having been reached with regard to Parma as well, which Empress Marie Louise was to receive for her lifetime and which was to pass on her demise to that branch of the Bourbon family from which the last Austrian empress, Empress Zita, was descended.

The lamentations of Cardinal Consalvi had resulted in the Papal States being returned to the Holy Father *in toto*—except, of course, for Avignon.

Amid all its other preoccupations, the congress had agreed on a resolution that was possibly more beneficial than all its political decisions put together; it had decided to ban the slave trade. Not that this by any means brought an end to the appalling practices associated with a traffic for which the white man is still paying, but it was a noble act of human self-examination that raises this congress far above others that were devoted exclusively to political wrangling.

Once the Swiss Confederation had been restored in its old form (without the Val Tellina, but with the canton of Geneva), the German problem was the only one left on the agenda. Here, too, the Napoleonic adventure helped bring the perpetual French threat home to the German princes and so furthered the idea of German unity, although some of them would still have preferred dependence on France to any kind of German unity. The eventual solution—the "German Confederation"—was imperfection itself. The small states were not prepared to surrender any of their sovereign rights, so that no true unity could be achieved. The German Confederation had no proper head and no army. Its supreme organ was

the Federal Diet, in which Austria occupied the presidential chair. Thirty-eight member states constituted the General Assembly, their votes varying in number according to their size. They made decisions regarding matters of mutual concern. Even this loose form of unity was enough to prevent wars within the Confederation and to keep foreign powers from intervening in its affairs, which was what mattered. The years of peace that lay ahead brought to Germany an economic boom such as this sorely tried land had never before experienced.

Article 13, which read: "All states of the Confederation shall introduce a constitution relating to the estates of the realm," caused great problems. This was a thoroughly hollow compromise between those who really wanted to give the people a say in government through the medium of a constitution and those who merely wished, by introducing institutions related to the three estates, to give the impression that the people had a say. A more precisely worded Article 13 might have obviated many of the convulsions of 1848.

The inner strength and self-assurance of the often bizarre proceedings of the

11 *Wellington's Victory, or The Battle of Vittoria,* set to music by Ludwig van Beethoven, 1816. Historisches Museum der Stadt Wien.
This piano score once belonged to Franz Grillparzer.

12 Lovis Rados de Parma, after
J.B. Bosio the Elder: *Marie
Louise, Empress of the French,
Archduchess of Austria, Queen
of Italy,* 1810. Etching, colored,
21.7 × 45.5 cm. Historisches Museum der Stadt Wien.

Congress of Vienna can perhaps best be gaged by the fact that the final document was initialed on June 9, 1815—in other words a week before Waterloo, when it was touch and go whether Napoleon was not about to throw Europe into confusion once again, or even regain control of it.

In the meantime, however, the congress had become convinced that it was planning European affairs for a long time to come on the basis of a higher law, and not on the basis of the lightning improvisations that were all Napoleon's institutions could ever amount to. The moves of that bold genius of the battlefield simply did not count any more on the chessboard of established law, which the congress felt—with good reason—it had brought to bear.

For a long time people had been saying, " If everyone is dissatisfied, the congress has done a good job," which was absolutely true: the sober contentment of peace counts for little beside the intoxication of victory. The compromise necessary to any kind of peace is always accepted with a greater or lesser degree of reluctance; sensible people see it as salutary, but it inspires little enthusiasm.

There was one thing, however, with which no one could be dissatisfied, and that was Vienna. Vienna, the Viennese, and—inseparably bound up with them—the emperor and his court had shown the world their best side. They had communicated to their guests something of their amiable calm, something of their ironic detachment; and it can safely be assumed that they had brought an element of reconciliatory goodwill into the spirit of the debates. The world was not at all badly run for the brief moment when it revolved around Vienna. Consequently there is no event in Austrian history on which the Austrians look back with greater pleasure than on the Congress of Vienna, when their capital basked in the sun of a pacific humanity—nor is the warmth of its radiance at all diminished by our knowing, as we do today, that it was the setting sun.

Hans Urbanski

II FROM REVOLUTION TO REVOLUTION

After the Congress of Vienna

Probably one of the most brilliant theorists among the men who set themselves the task of reorganizing Europe in 1814-15 was Prince Clemens Lothar Wenzel Metternich, Austrian foreign minister since July 8, 1809, and chairman of the diplomatic conference that met in Vienna to establish a new peacetime order.[1] As Metternich saw things, an aristocratic world order based on sound common sense provided a framework for society; in it individualism, philanthropy, the leveling of society, freedom, equality and human rights, the sovereignty of the people and popular representation had no place.[2] The natural and spiritual worlds were thought to be harmoniously governed by the principles of reason and morality and by the laws of nature. In this concept, the great social body represented by mankind and the smaller, individual social bodies represented by states were the scene of the eternal struggle between the moral powers and the material forces of preservation and of destruction. Since a state of equilibrium between those powers and forces was considered absolutely necessary, rapid advances on the part of the forces of destruction called for enhanced preservation of everything legitimately in existence.

From these propositions Metternich derived the intellectual connection between the "internal" and the "external," that is to say, between social and political balance. However, the absence in Metternich's philosophy of the state of a scientifically and historically genetic idea explains why it was able to take effect as a "system of stability and reaction" and yet recognize the importance of progress, in principle. Accordingly, while concessions with regard to moral and social principles were considered inadmissible, some evolution due to the changing needs of the state and the people was nevertheless possible. In times of flux, however, all one's strength must be devoted to keeping things as they were. Only nature was capable of creating new things, not man. History and the natural conditions of life were an expression of nature, while artificially created constitutions and artificially constituted national units were to be rejected. States were obliged jointly to regulate power and to safeguard the external and the internal balance; order within individual states could be preserved only by the monarchy with legitimacy as its valuable, though not indispensable, mainstay. The authorities had an obligation to be powerful, to promote the natural bodies corporate, to take preventive measures against the instruments of destructive violence, and thus to encourage a synthesis of unity and multiplicity in a federation.

In the pursuit of this world view, all things revolutionary were inevitably equated with destruction; and the application of this conclusion to the actual life of the state led to paralysis and coercion.

Things had not, however, reached the point where restraint and pressure were palpable presences and where angry rejection of the "system" centered on the

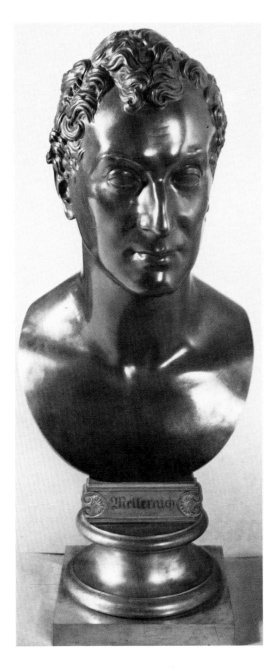

had been unmistakable signs that such recognition was on the way. How great the disappointment must have been when the hints that had been given at the great military parade and banquet held in the Prater on October 18, 1814,[4] were positively blotted out as if they had never existed, for hopes had been aroused:

"...All was life; all was gaiety, high spirits, and the blessed hope of a better future. The officers ate for the most part at the same tables as their men.... One felt in every way honored and uplifted—all were keeping watch over each one, so that those thousands of guests and spectators seemed to be one harmonious, ordered family gathered round its father to celebrate a communal feast...."[5]

With almost gullible simplicity—not even the pathos typical of the period can conceal the childlike trust—a public that the *Volkskrieg* (the "people's war") had turned into new citizens seemed to believe that political freedoms would be granted. Domestic political reality, however, was a stranger to sentiment. In the German Confederation[6] (the political solution of the German question raised by the abolition of the old Holy Roman Empire), the constitutional problems of the individual states were settled with complete disregard for the promises that had been given when it was a question of fighting Napoleon. The princes were confident that external precautions had been taken; the political map of Europe was in order. France had been pushed back within its old frontiers, and the restoration of the Bourbons was a reality. When the Final Act of the Congress of Vienna was signed, before the Battle of Waterloo, Europe had been pacified.

Metternich's chief concern, namely to restore the balance of power in Europe, was realized by a Quintuple Alliance providing for the hegemony of the five great powers: Austria, Prussia, Russia, Britain, and France. In order to guarantee the stability of Austria's empire, all the outposts that posed problems of defense had been abandoned and the monarchy turned into as compact a geographical unit as possible.[7] Reacquisition of the Austrian Netherlands[8] was never even considered, while Breisgau and the Palatinate on the

13   Josef Anton Courigier: Bust of Prince Clemens Lothar Wenzel Metternich, ca. 1810. Bronze, gilded base; H. 64 cm. Historisches Museum der Stadt Wien.
Prince Metternich, for decades the leading political figure in the Austrian Empire, gave his name to an era and to a "system." His policy of restoration in Austria became a byword.

man Metternich. It was still a question of setting up a peaceful order to which central Europe could adhere without feeling any threat, whether from the north, from the west, or from the east; balances had to be restored, and all imbalances avoided. What had become a patriotic middle class[3] in so remarkably short a space of time still hoped to receive suitable recognition of its joyous readiness to make sacrifices for monarchy and state—for there left bank of the Rhine were given up in favor of the province and city of Salzburg. The Ternopol district and the salt mines of Wieliczka were incorporated in the Austrian crown lands of Galicia and Lodomeria; and Austria, jointly with Prussia and Russia, exercised the protectorate over the neutral republic of Kraków.

This redrawing of the political map of Europe—one might even say of the political map of the world, if the colonial possessions or spheres of influence of the powers, which far exceeded their actual sovereign territories, are taken into consideration—was in a manner of speaking the real, physically tangible triumph of conservatism. The metaphysically transcendent superstructure—the religious consecration—was represented by the Holy Alliance, the league of princes erected (rather to Metternich's displeasure) on a Christian foundation by that pietistic, Romantic moralist, the czar.

Although Metternich rated the treaty as "at least unnecessary" and referred to it as a "noisy nothingness," the fact remains that it represented a last attempt to create a Christian *oikoumene* embracing all denominations: the Orthodox czar of Russia, Alexander I; the Roman Catholic emperor of Austria, Francis I; and the Protestant king of Prussia, Frederick William III; all solemnly accepted "that it is needful to found the conduct to be adopted by the powers in their mutual relations on the sublime truths taught us by the eternal religion of God... that the present Act has no other purpose than to proclaim to all the world their unshakable determination to take as their sole rule of conduct, both in the administration of their own states and in their political relations with all other governments, the commandments of that holy religion, the commandments of justice, humanity, and peace that, far from being applicable to private life alone, ought on the contrary to exert a direct influence on the decisions of princes and to guide their every step, constituting as they do the sole means of strengthening human institutions and remedying their imperfections." [9]

The Holy Alliance shared the same anachronistic quality that had characterized the outlawing of Napoleon. On both occasions it was thought possible to make religious sensibility the driving force of human behavior. On both occasions, it was felt permissible to ignore the fact that princedoms had become secularized as well as the danger of forgetting that Europe had experienced the Enlightenment and Jacobinism.

Political reality as determined in Austria by Metternich did not, of course, take its cue from these visionary concepts; yet it too was marked by the fight against revolution waged by the European powers acting in concert. For as long as the Quintuple Alliance held together politically and pacific tendencies prevailed among its peoples, this world system stood the test as a European force. Its scope became restricted as the restored political system began to break up and new ideas gained ground. It collapsed when ideals of nationalism and freedom conquered those of cosmopolitanism and social continuity, and when the reality of individual national states got the better of political universalism. [10]

The New Ideals: Nationalism and Liberalism

After a "generation of bloodshed," [11] it was not unreasonable that there should have been a longing for peace and quiet. However, the kind of peace and quiet that was imposed on the peoples of Europe was suspiciously like that found in graveyards. Peace of that kind was felt to be intolerable, and little more than two years after the congress, a student song was making the message clear:

Now let us raise a cheer
For the living and the dead,
Whom Germany, with song and sword,
Once sent out into battle.
Schill, Blücher, Oels, and Gneisenau,
Arndt, Körner, Jahn—who can recite
Every heroic name!

And in this ancient tower
Sat many a dashing lad,
Because against His Magnificence
He'd made too bold.
But if he was a merry fellow
And if he fought for freedom,
To him we shout "Hurrah!" [12]

31

14 *The Military Parade in the
Prater on October 18, 1814.* Oil
on canvas, 102 × 159 cm. Historisches Museum der Stadt Wien.
The parade commemorated the
first anniversary of the Battle of
the Nations, fought near Leipzig.
Monarchs and military—officers
and men sat down at the table
together—celebrated the victory
over Napoleon as a triumph of
their joint efforts.

Der große Wiener Friedens=Congres zur Wiederherstellung von Freiheit und Recht in Europa
1. Kaiser Franz 2. Kaiser Alexander 3. König v. Preußen 4. Wellington für England 5. König v. Denemark 6. König v. Baiern 7. König v. Würtemberg 8. Churfürst v. Heßen 9. Herzog v. Braunschweig 10. Talleyrand für Frankreich 11. Mediatisirte Fürsten und Staatsminister 12. Die Gerechtigkeit

15 J. Zutz: *Satire on a Session of the Congress of Vienna,* ca. 1815. Copperplate engraving, colored, 26 × 32.5 cm. Historisches Museum der Stadt Wien. The rulers of Europe agree on the new frontiers, with each delegate trying to get the best arrangement for himself and his country. Even the knights of the Holy Roman Empire are represented, while Justice watches over the proceedings minus her usual blindfold.

16 *Allegory on the Holy Alliance,* 1815. Watercolor over pen and ink, 13.5 × 9.4 cm. Historisches Museum der Stadt Wien. Czar Alexander I of Russia, Emperor Francis I of Austria, and King Frederick William III of Prussia committed themselves in the so-called Holy Alliance Treaty to a policy of restoration. Christian moral principles and a profession of faith in patriarchal government were the keystones of the treaty.

17   Johann Lorenz Rugendas: *The Battle of Waterloo on June 18, 1815.* Aquatint, colored, 47.4 × 59 cm. Historisches Museum der Stadt Wien.
The Battle of Waterloo sealed Napoleon's personal fate. His political fate had already been decided: the Final Act of the Congress of Vienna had been signed on June 9, 1815.

Nationalism and liberalism, as expressed in these stanzas, were in reality the themes of the occasion for which the song was written, namely the Festival on the Wartburg (a castle near Eisenach in Thuringia), organized by the *Burschenschaft*, or student fraternity, of the city of Jena on October 18–19, 1817. The ostensible pretext for the festival—to commemorate the Reformation and the Battle of the Nations fought near Leipzig in 1813—underlined the desire for national liberation. This was the first time that the colors black, red, and gold were worn as a symbol of German national unity,[13] and also the first public appearance of the German student fraternities. During the festival, books by twenty-eight authors were burned, authors whose views, in the opinion of those taking part, stood in contradiction to the mood of the general public.

A reaction on the part of the state was inevitable. The German Confederation saw the beginning of a series of "demagogue hunts," and in 1818 the signatories of the Final Act of the Congress of Vienna met again for the first time, in accordance with their declaration of solidarity against

revolution, at the Congress of Aachen. In addition to settling French affairs—the occupation of France under the Treaty of Paris of 1814 was to be lifted—the main item on the agenda was the revolutionary stirrings at the German universities and the threat they posed to the principle of conservatism. And stirrings there certainly were, culminating on March 23, 1819, when a student by the name of Karl Ludwig Sand shot the German writer and councillor of state August von Kotzebue. On August 31, a spezial conference of ministers passed the Carlsbad Decrees:[14] the *Burschenschaften* were dissolved; the universities were placed under strict supervision; a highly restrictive press law was enacted, together with rigorous censorship provisions; and a Central Committee for the Investigation of Revolutionary Activities was set up in Mainz.

The drive for freedom had not died out in the rest of Europe either. In Spain, in Portugal, but also in Naples, attempts to wrest constitutional concessions were crowned with success. Repercussions on the system of absolute monarchy inside Austria could not be ruled out; moreover, Metternich had to reckon with unrest in

18   Prince Metternich's office in the state chancellery, 1829. Gouache, 20.2 × 29.3 cm. Historisches Museum der Stadt Wien. The office placed at the disposal of Prince Metternich looked out on Vienna's Löwelstrasse.

AUGUST VON KOTZEBUE.

Geboren am 3ten Mai 1761. Meuchelmordet von C. F. Sand am 23ten März 1819.

Friede seiner Asche! Erkentniß und Reue seinem Mörder!

19 Johann Michael Siegfried Löwe: *August von Kotzebue,* 1819. Aquatint, 16.7 × 14 cm. Historisches Museum der Stadt Wien.
Of German origin, Kotzebue—a man of letters and director of Vienna's Hofburg Theater for a time—began working for the Russians in 1781; in 1813 he was made a Russian councillor of state and in 1817 was sent to Germany as a political observer. In his *Literarische Wochenblatt* ("Literary Weekly"), founded in 1818, Kotzebue mocked the liberal ideas and patriotic ideals of the *Burschenschaften,* or student fraternities. In 1819 he was stabbed to death in Mannheim by a student from Jena, Karl Ludwig Sand, who considered him an enemy of German freedom and unity.

the Hapsburg possessions in Italy. Austria—which under a treaty with Naples signed on June 12, 1815, enjoyed the right to prevent constitutional forms of government from being established in Italy—massed troops for a military intervention; furthermore, Metternich considered it necessary to involve the other great powers. Accordingly they met at the Congress of Troppau in 1820, at the Congress of Laibach (Ljubljana) in 1821, and at the Congress of Verona in 1822.

While the projected system of intervention appeared to be working at first,[15] the Verona congress in particular, at which the question of Greece was an additional preoccupation, demonstrated that Europe was far from thinking as unanimously as it had been designed to do. Only Metternich still felt that the "legitimate" sovereignty of the sultan ought not to be infringed; neither Russia nor Britain was prepared to put a stop to Romantic enthusiasm for the Greek freedom fighters, who were being rapturously feted by the German public as well. Verona spelled the end of the Holy Alliance, and by the time undisguised action by Anglo-French naval units and detachments of the Russian army had brought freedom to Greece and the Congress of London had, on Feb-

ruary 3, 1830, legalized and set its seal upon an action contravening the principle of intervention, the dream of an antirevolutionary world order lay in ruins.

The successful July Revolution in France in the same year, bringing victory to the middle-class opposition in the shape of the Orléans monarchy, fundamentally breached the system of conservative Europe. This was no peripheral violation, as in the case of Greece. The July Revolution convulsed what was supposed to be the permanent structure of the Quintuple Alliance in its most sensitive area and completely altered the situation on its northwestern flank. The buffer state of the Greater Netherlands collapsed, and the Kingdom of Belgium was created—after the Belgian people became so unexpectedly inflamed with patriotism on the occasion of the first performance in Brussels of the opera *Masaniello* by the French composer Daniel Auber.

An echo of that event was heard in Austria, too, but there the defenses of governmental authority were still strong enough to prevent any real effects. Austrian troops doused the fires flickering on the Apennine peninsula, intervening in Modena, Parma, and the Papal States. The victory of the revolution in Belgium was the signal for Polish patriots in Warsaw to rise up against the authority of the czar, but the rebellion was quelled by Russian troops. Russia abolished the Polish constitution and henceforth ruled the country as a subject province. Polish revolutionaries fled abroad and, from this point on, were to be found taking part in insurrections wherever these occurred.

In the delicately balanced political system of Europe the weights began to shift noticeably. As the liberal forces increased in strength and importance in western Europe, the conservative powers sought to draw themselves together even more closely to provide a counterpoise. This new effort to reinforce the old system was, however, to prove a failure. Events in Poland showed the extent to which individual interests, even in the case of the conservative powers, were beginning to break up the balanced structure of European unity.

How powerfully everything was now in flux could be seen from the fact that, all police measures notwithstanding, one or another trouble spot was always flaring up again. On May 27, 1832, the democratic republican movement held a rally in the ruins of Hambach Castle (above Neustadt, in Rhineland-Palatinate) at which nationalist voices were also heard. Speaker after speaker saluted France and Poland, countries that had "burst their chains," and demands were made for sovereignty of the people, for a republic, and for German unity. The reaction of the authorities was predictable: the governing body of the German Confederation, the *Bundestag*, abolished freedom of the press and of assembly, and the spokesmen of the Hambach Festival had to flee or face prison sentences.

While there were no direct repercussions on the situation inside Austria, there can be no doubt that all these events only served to harden the opposition of those who were already critical of the prevailing domestic system. An example was Karl Postl, who emigrated in 1823 and published under the pseudonym Charles Sealsfield.[16] His *Austria As It Is* (which came out in 1828) was a bitter account of Metternich's Austria, and Postl returned to the attack in 1834 with *Seufzer aus Österreich und seinen Provinzen* ("Sighs from Austria and Its Provinces").

Karl Postl's was by no means the only critical voice to be heard in spite of everything that censorship could do. Copies of *Spaziergänge eines Wiener Poeten* ("Walks of a Viennese Poet," first published in Germany in 1831) repeatedly found their way into Austria, showing very clearly that criticism of the conditions prevailing in the monarchy was being expressed even among the higher nobility (the man behind the symbolic pseudonym "Anastasius Green" was Count Anton Alexander Auersperg).[17]

Yet the machinery of government in the Hapsburg Empire continued to trundle along *ad hoc* lines almost undisturbed, leaving people with no real alternatives between a tight rein and free play, allowing them only unsuitable, im-

20   *The Naval Battle of Navarino on October 20, 1827.* Chalk lithograph, colored, 27.3 × 39.7 cm. Historisches Museum der Stadt Wien.
A peace mission with the object of concluding an armistice between the insurgent Greeks and the Turks on the Peloponnese ended with the Turkish fleet being destroyed by a joint Anglo-French-Russian squadron.

posed opportunities. And of course Metternich—who, in 1821, took the title of Chancellor, which had been in abeyance since Prince Kaunitz resigned—was the man responsible. But what made it possible for Metternich to pursue that policy was the total concurrence of Emperor Francis—indeed, it was basically the political credo of this first of the Austrian and last of the Holy Roman emperors that his loyal minister and chancellor put into practice.

Francis I, the strongwilled, tenacious, conscientious eldest son of Leopold II, was intellectually a man of far less stature than his uncle and his father, as well as decidedly inferior to his younger brothers Charles and Johann in terms of talent, imagination, and openness to new ideas.[18] Emperor Francis had survived the crises of the struggle against revolutionary France with a remarkable blend of missionary awareness and private business sense[19] and had initially shown signs of continuing his uncle's style of "enlightened despotism." Now all his faculties had congealed in a single determination: to cling rigidly to legitimacy and to uphold, as the sole dogma of public life, the rule of the bureaucracy and the police.

Without it having been obvious, it is nevertheless remarkable how well Francis I managed to keep his name and his person clear of any association with the oppressive nature of Metternich's system. In his habits of mind and in the whole way in which he conducted himself, the emperor contrived to appear to the middle classes as "one of them"; the quiet gardener—which indeed he was—fitted the Biedermeier idyll as nicely as did the irritation we know him to have expressed over the country's censorship: "Our censorhip really is silly."[20] People seem to have been very ready to believe that the emperor himself was a prisoner of the system—though it would have lain within his power to alter the way it operated. An actor at the Hofburg Theater, Karl Ludwig Costenoble, wrote in his *Diary* on September 3, 1832, that he had personally recommended a play to Francis I and given him the manuscript to look at. "I'll read it," the emperor told him, "but you'll see—I have no influ-

ence."[21] The personal eulogy in Costenoble's private diary is all of a piece with the image of *der gute Kaiser Franz;* what was almost insufferable, on the other hand, was publicly expressed adulation of the kind contained in the sentimental ballad *Die Schreckensnacht auf den 1. März 1830* ("Night of Horrors: March 1, 1830"), in which Viennese who had been swept to their deaths by a flood were assured:

...
A father watches o'er your little ones;
He is known as "Austria's Father Francis."[22]

Behind the naivety of such verses, the emperor was able to feel secure in the veneration of his people, a people who failed to see that, in reality, he held absolute sway over them, his actions and omissions alike setting the country's political course. Within the lifetime of Francis I, Metternich recognized that a state bound by such formal rigorism was doomed to failure; yet he was unable to rouse himself to make a decisive stand against tradition, to throw off his role of passive onlooker—he lacked the moral conviction. The death of Francis I on

21 Norbert Bittner: *The State Chancellery,* ca. 1830. Drawing in India ink, 14.8 × 19.4 cm. Historisches Museum der Stadt Wien.
The state chancellery, scene of negotiations during the Congress of Vienna, was the headquarters—as well as the home—of Prince Metternich.

22 Balthasar Wigand: *Empress Caroline Augusta Enters Vienna on November 10, 1816.* Gouache, 20.5 × 31.4 cm. Historisches Museum der Stadt Wien. Caroline Augusta, daughter of the King of Bavaria, Maximilian II Joseph, became the fourth wife of Emperor Francis I on November 10, 1816. To celebrate the occasion, 200,000 *Taler* were distributed among Vienna's poor.

Der 10 November 1816 in Wien.

Wigand f

March 2, 1835, put an end to any possibility of doing something constructive to reorganize Austria's internal politics.

No one was in any doubt that his successor, Ferdinand I, was incapable of taking up the reins of government: he was neither intellectually nor physically up to the task. This basically pitiable person, constantly in need of help, was sworn by Francis I to uphold the latter's own political conviction and bound to his will by means of a legacy of political guidelines that Metternich had a hand in drawing up: "...Make no change in the foundations of the structure of the state; govern and alter nothing; take your stand firmly and unshakably on the [same] principles that, through my constant observance of them, have not only brought the monarchy through the storms of difficult times but also secured for it the high station it rightfully occupies in the world.... Place in Prince Metternich, my most loyal servant and friend, the same trust as I have placed in him over so many long years. Reach no decisions regarding public matters or persons without first hearing his views...."[23] Possibly Metternich hoped that this passage of the "legacy," so carefully tailored to his requirements, would help him to gain a decisive influence over Ferdinand I. By 1836 at the latest, any ideas he may have entertained along these lines had had to be abandoned.

In December of that year the Conference of State—a sort of regency council—was set up; Metternich shared the leadership of it with Count Franz Anton Kolowrat. The Conference of State never actually worked, however, being split by the personal antagonism between these two men, paralyzed by the inflexibility of its chairman (Archduke Ludwig, the deceased emperor's brother) and hampered

23 Tommaso Benedetti, after Friedrich v. Amerling: *Emperor Francis I,* 1834. Copperplate engraving, 37.4 × 29.3 cm. Historisches Museum der Stadt Wien. Francis I, eldest son and heir of Leopold II, was the last emperor of the Holy Roman Empire (as Francis II) and the first Austrian emperor. Having survived the crises of the struggle against revolutionary France with the aid of a strong sense of mission, coupled with considerable personal shrewdness, he came to embody a rigid adherence to the principle of legitimacy and the sole supremacy of bureaucracy and police in public life.

in its operations by the open opposition the members of the imperial family showed the chancellor.

Contrary to Metternich's intentions, a centralizing state administration was retained. He had wanted a moderate federalism with the ruling dynasty as its strong center in order to prevent any disunity among the linguistically and culturally distinct parts of the whole. These ideas of Metternich's had done no more than germinate under Francis I. Now, however, Austria was in fact "feebly administered but not governed"[24] and, with undoubtedly even more fateful consequences, no proper Austrian sense of political identity was developed.

In addition, the financial position of the state was growing progressively worse, undermining the basis for urgently necessary reforms in many areas, while stirrings of nationalism and desires for greater freedom, which had been aroused

earlier, were beginning to gather strength. In Bohemia there was growing antagonism between Germans and Czechs, and clear evidence of Pan-Slavic tendencies. In Hungary the antagonism was not only between Magyars and Illyrians, but also between new social and political forces and the outmoded federalism. Poles and Ruthenians were in conflict, and the Italian subjects of the Hapsburg Empire had, as we have already remarked, no reason worth mentioning to develop a specifically Austrian political identity.

Austria was also affected by events in the German Confederation and in Prussia. The populations of the German Confederation experienced it as an enormous police institution in which despotic rule was possible. In Prussia, however, liberalism awoke after a long sleep to a new and vigorous life when Frederick William IV decided—against Metternich's advice—to convene the United Committee of the Provincial Estates in 1842 and the United Estates in 1847.

The middle class, commercially and industrially strengthened, was calling ever more audibly for a constitution; it demanded freer trade and release from bureaucratic pressure. The lower strata of society, on the other hand, were sinking ever deeper into poverty and wretchedness. A novel but already obtrusive feature of the political scene were the strident tones of the radical propaganda of Socialists and Communists; according to their ideas pauperization was not a fate to be suffered in silence, but rather a deep wrong that had to be put right.

In foreign affairs, too, deeper and deeper cracks were appearing in the system, as the conflict between the Ottoman sultan and an insubordinate vassal—Muhammad Ali, Viceroy of Egypt—escalated into an international affair over which it took some time for the great powers to reach agreement.

Austria took advantage of an aristocratic rebellion in Galicia, which was defeated by the resistance of the Polish and Ruthenian peasant farmers, to annex the free state of Kraków in 1846. Thus Metternich robbed of its existence a state that he had helped to found. Even though

26 W. Böhm: *The Bone Collector,* 1844. Copperplate engraving, 23.2 × 14.1 cm. Historisches Museum der Stadt Wien.
The bone collector occupied the bottom rung of the job-status ladder. He searched the city's trash for bones to sell to factories for processing into buttons, soap, cart grease, and such products.

his motive was the preservation of Austria's internal and external security, this demonstrated that the Final Act of the Congress of Vienna could no longer stand surety for European order. For Austria, however, there was to be no waiting to see what this precedent might lead to—time had run out.

The Outbreak of the Revolution

On February 24, 1848, the Second Republic was proclaimed in Paris. Students, workers, and the National Guard had forced the Citizen King to abdicate. The forces of destruction against which the Metternich system was erected had made a crucial breach. Although the news of the outbreak of the February Revolution was immediately suppressed by the Austrian government, the event could not be kept secret in the long run.

Eventually, on March 3, a speech given by Lajos Kossuth to the Hungarian Diet sitting in Pressburg (Bratislava), little more than 50 miles from Vienna, aroused

a tremendous response and served to trigger the collapse. Liberalism and nationalism—those ideas that Metternich had denied were apt to constitute any kind of state authority—were now presented in the first petitions to the government as the embodiment of the desire for change. More and more clear, too, was the demand for a liberal constitution for all the countries ruled by the monarchy. Metternich still had enough authority to make the government and the court adopt a fundamentally negative attitude in response. But the events of March, 1848, were to impart such incredible speed to developments as to take them beyond the range of everyone's calculations.[25]

On March 12, Vienna's students drew up a crucial petition: they demanded freedom of the press and of speech,[26] academic freedom for teachers and students, equality of citizenship for the members of all religious communities; public, oral court proceedings; a general parliament and local self-government. In so doing they not only gave expression to a very concrete program; they also made themselves the spokesmen of the coming revolution. On the following day (March 13), the court having taken no notice of their petition, the students marched to the Landhaus in the Herrengasse, where the provincial diet of Lower Austria sat. That body also constituted the political representation of the citizens of Vienna, for the city itself had long possessed only limited opportunities for political autonomy.

Vienna was situated in the archduchy of "Austria beneath the Enns"[27] and came under the governor of Lower Austria, who also appointed the city's mayor for life. The civic freedom the Viennese had once enjoyed to elect their own political representatives had been lost a long time ago.[28] It was hoped, therefore, that the provincial diet would now mediate between the petitioners and the court. Clearly under the influence of a political awakening that was intensifying daily, a huge crowd drawn from various strata of the population gathered on that day outside the Landhaus in the Herrengasse.[29] People even pushed their way into the courtyard of the building where, standing on the fountain, a young doctor by the name of

Adolf Fischhof delivered the first speech of the Viennese revoultion.[30] He reiterated the demands made in the petition of the previous day and went on to call for a solution to the national problems of the Austrian monarchy: "If we think of the Germans with their aspirations after high ideals; the tenacious, industrious, and persistent Slavs; the gallant, vivacious Magyars; and the skilful, perspicacious Italians working with combined, and consequently enhanced, strength at the joint tasks of the state, there can be no doubt in our minds but that Austria's position among the states of Europe must become a commanding one."[31]

A deputation of members of the diet did indeed call on the emperor in order to plead at court for the wishes of the people, and to recommend that they be met. At court, however, all was confusion, perplexity, and crippling indecision; the dominant emotions were consternation and fear. Clearly the usual security arrangements had failed. There was no knowing whether the court already faced an embittered or even a rampaging people. Individual members of the imperial family and representatives of the highest echelons of government were already in a mood to grant concessions, while others felt that the movement

43

could still be suppressed by force of arms without too much effort.[32] Once again, however, Metternich got his way, insisting on a categorical rejection of the demands that had been presented. The chancellor had already reacted with cool imperturbability shortly before this, when a Polish student by the name of Julias Joseph Elias Burian began addressing a crowd that had gathered outside the Chancellery in the Ballhausplatz and making violent attacks on Metternich.[33]

This time, however, the chancellor's stance was unsuccessful. More and more people began to gather; news of the first strikes came in from the factories in the suburbs, and in the early hours of the afternoon the army was ordered to clear the Herrengasse. After the troops had made several vain attempts to do this and Archduke Albrecht, the provincial commandant of Lower Austria, had been ridiculed and reviled—and possibly even assaulted with sticks and stones—Albrecht gave the

28 Franz Kollarz: *The Duchess of Orléans in the Chamber of Deputies in Paris When the French Republic Was Declared on February 24, 1848.* Chalk lithograph, colored, 46 × 65.5 cm. Historisches Museum der Stadt Wien.

29 Heinrich Gerhardt: *Lajos Kossuth,* ca. 1849. Chalk lithograph, 46 × 28.2 cm. Historisches Museum der Stadt Wien.
Kossuth was the leader of the Hungarian independence movement; his speech in the Hungarian Diet started the Austrian revolution.

30 *The Orator Burian,* 1848. Chalk lithograph, 26.1 × 27.1 cm. Historisches Museum der Stadt Wien.
In the speech he made to students on March 13, 1848, Burian called for freedom of expression and religious liberty.

31 J. Albrecht: *The First Victims of the Revolution—the Scene outside the Landhaus in Vienna on March 13, 1848.* Chalk lithograph, colored, 29 × 22.4 cm. Historisches Museum der Stadt Wien.
The use of troops to clear the Herrengasse of demonstrators led to five deaths.

order for an armed attack. An engineer battalion under the command of Colonel Frank von Seewies advanced on the crowd with bayonets and rifles. The demonstrators fled in terror, leaving five dead behind them—a woman and four men.[34]

At this point revolution broke out in earnest. Class barriers fell as, for the next several hours, proletarians, workers, students, and members of the lower and upper middle classes united in angry resistance to a government that had ordered soldiers to fire on unarmed people. The crowd demanded weapons and tried to storm the arsenals, which led to even harsher countermeasures by the army and further bloodshed. Fighting even extended to the suburbs, with furious workers attacking and destroying factories and machinery; fires raged throughout the city, and there was a complete breakdown of law and order. At long last the government was ready to make concessions, and it was felt at court that the time had come to drop the unpopular Metternich.

KOSSUTH LAJOS

32 Bachmann-Hohmann: *The Triumphal Procession with the Wounded Tailor Josef Abeck through Am Hof Square on March 13, 1848.* Pencil, 14.7 × 18 cm. Historisches Museum der Stadt Wien.
In the struggle with the military, wounded men were repeatedly paraded in triumph through the streets of Vienna on March 13.

33 A. Bettenhofer [August von Pettenkofen]: *A Cavalry Attack in Front of the Municipal Armory,* 1848. Chalk lithograph, colored, 35 × 48.8 cm. Historisches Museum der Stadt Wien.
During the course of March 13, 1848, the insurgents mounted an assault on the municipal armory, among other places, in order to arm themselves. Naturally, the army took action to thwart such attempts.

34   Franz Kaliwoda: *The Burnt-Out Ruin of the Granichstätten Cottonprinting Works in Sechshaus, March 14, 1848.* Sepia brush, pen and ink, partly watercolored, 21.3 × 29.3 cm. Historisches Museum der Stadt Wien.

When the workers in the suburbs, learning of events in the Herrengasse, decided to go to the assistance of the insurgents and found the gates of Vienna locked against them, they turned round and unleashed their anger on their employers and on the machines they blamed for their poverty.

35   Franz Kollarz: *The Fall of Metternich on the Evening of March 13, 1848.* Chalk lithograph, 45 × 61 cm. Historisches Museum der Stadt Wien.

In the space of a few hours, on March 13, 1848, a demonstration had become a revolution. As a visible sign of their willingness to change the "system," influential circles in the court called for the chancellor's dismissal. The emperor agreed.

At the suggestion of Archdukes Johann and Francis Charles—and possibly under the influence of the latter's wife Sophie—Archduke Ludwig summoned Prince Metternich to the Hofburg at half past six and informed him that the deputations wished him to resign. Since even the emperor was said to have remarked, "Tell the people I agree to everything," Prince Metternich tendered his resignation.

In his letter to that effect, addressed to the emperor and written in his own hand that same evening, the chancellor acknowledged that a new age had dawned, the onslaught of which the old world, by now impotent, was no longer capable of withstanding: "I am resigning in the face of a higher power than that of the sovereign himself."[35]

Günter Düriegl

36 Johann Christian Schoeller: *Caricature of Metternich's Flight,* 1848. Watercolor, 11.2 × 14.2 cm. Historisches Museum der Stadt Wien.
Having resigned on March 13 and had his villa destroyed on the following day, Metternich fled with his family by way of Feldsberg, Prague, Dresden, Hanover, and Holland to England, which he reached on April 20, 1848.

NOTES

1 On the subject of Metternich's earliest reactions to the revolution, see Günter Düriegl, "Der Staatsmann," in: *Die Aera Metternich* (catalog of the 90th special exhibition at the Historisches Museum der Stadt Wien), Vienna, 1984, p. 7.

2 On what follows, see Heinrich Ritter von Srbik, "Klemens Lothar Metternich," in: *Grosse Österreicher: Neue Österreichische Biographie ab 1815,* Vol. XI, Vienna, 1957, pp. 20 f.

3 In 1805 there was still a substantial amount of pro-French feeling in Vienna; in 1809 Napoleon met with cold rejection there.

4 The military parade took place on the occasion of the anniversary of the Battle of the Nations near Leipzig. The scene was the Lusthaus in the Prater, with its immediate environs, and the adjacent section of the Simmeringer Haide, separated from it by a narrow arm of the Danube. The troops were paraded before the monarchs assembled for the Congress of Vienna; afterwards there was a banquet, with the royalty dining inside the Lusthaus and the officers and men of the Viennese garrison being served on long tables set up in the open air.

5 Caroline Pichler, *Denkwürdigkeiten aus meinem Leben* (ed. by Emil Karl Bümml), Vol. 2, Munich, 1914, pp. 30 ff.

6 The German Confederation was established by the Federal Act of June 8, 1815, and further developed by the "Viennese" Final Act of May 15, 1820. Its members, in addition to the individual German states, included Denmark (for Holstein and Lauenburg), Britain (for Hanover), and the Netherlands (for Luxembourg and Limburg). Austria and Prussia, the two leading powers of the Confederation, were members only in respect of those parts of their territories that had belonged to the old Holy Roman Empire until 1806. The sole organ of the Confederation was the Federal Diet, or *Bundestag,* which met in Frankfurt; Austria occupied the chair. The Federal Act remained in force—with various modifications—until 1866.

7 See Erich Zöllner, *Geschichte Österreichs: Von den Anfängen bis zur Gegenwart,* 5th ed., Vienna, 1974, p. 347.

8 I.e. Belgium and Luxembourg.

9 *Die Heilige Allianz,* September 26, 1815, Paris; Vienna, Austrian State Archives: section Haus-, Hof- und Staatsarchiv, AUR.

10 Srbik (see above, note 2), pp. 20 f.

11 Taken from the German edition: Henry A. Kissinger, *Grossmacht Diplomatie: Von der Staatskunst Castlereaghs und Metternichs,* Düsseldorf, Vienna, 1962, p. 11.

12 *Kurze und wahrhaftige Beschreibung des grossen Burschenfestes auf der Wartburg bei*

37 Michael Neder: *The National Guard of the Suburb of Döbling in 1848.* Oil on canvas, 63 × 78 cm. Historisches Museum der Stadt Wien.

Kein Champagner! abgezogenen Johannisberger am Steinweg.

Eisenach am 18ten und 19ten des Siegesmonds 1817. (Nebst Reden und Liedern) ("A Brief and Veracious Description of the Great Students' Festival in the Wartburg near Eisenach on the 18th and 19th of [October] 1817 [Including Speeches and Songs]"), printed in that year, p. 61: "Die Burschenfahrt nach der Wartburg, am 18. Oktober 1817 (Weise: Ein freies Leben führen wir)" ("The students' procession to the Wartburg on October 18, 1817 [to the tune of "We lead a Free Life"]), verses 4 and 5.

13   The Lützow "free corps" wore black tunics with red facings and gold buttons.

14   Those involved were the ministers of Austria, Prussia, Hanover, Saxony, Mecklenburg, Baden Baden, Nassau, and Württemberg.

15   At Laibach Austria, Russia, and Prussia agreed on the principle of armed intervention: "Europe knows the reasons that brought the allied sovereigns to the decision to stifle the conspiracy and put an end to the disturbances that threatened the existence of the universal peace that it had cost so much effort and sacrifice to establish...."
Das Manifest von Laibach ("The Laibach Manifesto"), May 12, 1821, Laibach; Vienna, Austrian State Archives: section Haus-, Hof- und Staatsarchiv, Stk. Kongressakten, Kart. 22 (alt 41).

16   See *Österreich Lexikon*, Vol. 2, Vienna and Munich, 1966, p. 1055.

17   See Hanns Leo Mikoletzky, *Österreich: Das entscheidende 19. Jahrhundert*, Vienna, 1972, p. 241.

18   Zöllner (see above, note 7), pp. 329 f.

19   See the handwritten letter from Emperor Francis I to Metternich, April 12, 1814, Troyes; Vienna, Austrian State Archives: section Haus-, Hof- und Staatsarchiv, Stk. Vorträge, Kart 195, fols. 21–22.

20   Mikoletzky (see above, note 17), p. 247.

21   *Ibid.*

22   *Die Schreckensnacht auf den 1. März 1830*, by Aloys Dworzak, printed by the Mechitarist fathers, 1830.
During the exceptionally severe winter of 1829–30, the Danube froze and there was a big build-up of ice. A sudden thaw produced catastrophic results in the night between February 28 and March 1, 1830, with unprecedented flooding in the surburbs of Leopoldstadt, Jägerzeile, Rossau, Thury, Liechtenthal, and Althan, in the Alservorstadt, the Landstrasse, the Unteren Weissgerber, and also in lowlying parts of the city center such as Rotenturmstrasse, Adlergasse, the Fishmarket, and the Salzgries. An appalling number of lives were lost: twenty people drowned in Rossau alone.

23   *Politisches Vermächtnis des Kaiser Franz I. für seinen Sohn und Thronfolger Ferdinand I.* ("Political Legacy of Emperor Francis I to His Son and Heir to the Throne, Ferdinand I"), February 28, 1835, Vienna; Vienna, Austrian State Archives: section Haus-, Hof- und Staatsarchiv, Familienurkunden No. 2347B.

24   Sbrik (see above, note 2), p. 33.

25   See Peter Csendes, *Geschichte Wiens*, Vienna, 1981, p. 105.

26   "Freedom of the press" meant freedom to publish any kind of printed matter, not just newspapers.

27   I.e. the present-day province of Lower Austria.

28   The charter af Archduke Ferdinand I for Vienna (March 12, 1526, Augsburg) ended the medieval autonomy of the city, and further restrictions were imposed through the reorganization of the city council by Emperor Joseph II (August 16, 1783, Vienna).

29   Csendes (see above, note 25), p. 106.

30   Dr. Adolf Fischhof (1816–93) was a member of the Academic Legion and commander of the medical corps; he served until July 17, 1848, as president of the Comittee for Public Safety. By then he was already in charge of the public-health department at the Ministry of the Interior (July 2 to December 20, 1848). In the short-lived Austrian Imperial Diet that sat in Kremsier (Kromeriz in Czechoslovakia), Fischhof was a member of the constitutional committee. Arrested after the abolition of the Diet, he was later acquitted. He settled in Vienna to practice medicine; in 1875 he moved to Carinthia.

31   Quoted in Heinrich Reschauer, *Das Jahr 1848: Geschichte der Wiener Revolution*, Vol. 1, Vienna, 1872, p. 183.

32   See Friedrich Walter, *Wien: Die Geschichte einer deutschen Grossstadt an der Grenze*, Vol. 3, Vienna, 1944, pp. 168 f.

33   See Ernst Violand, *Die soziale Geschichte der Revolution in Österreich 1848*, (ed. by Wolfgang Häusler), Vienna, 1984, note 47: Julius Joseph Elias Burian, a law student born in Suczawa in 1823, had to leave Austria because of political offenses. Police records traced his career via Dresden and Switzerland to Paris, where he was living "in wretched circumstances" in 1852.

34   Anna Serflinger, inmate of a home for the aged, crushed to death; Peter Fürst, vinegar boiler, householder, bullet wounds; Karl Heinrich Spitzer, technical student, bullet wounds; Isidor Langer, hosier, bullet wounds; Bernhard Herschmann, journeyman weaver, broken skull.

35   *Metternich sucht um seinen Rückritt an* ("Metternich Tenders His Resignation"), March 13, 1848, Vienna; Vienna, Austrian State Archives: section Haus-, Hof- und Staatsarchiv, Minister-Kolowrat-Akten Z1. 640/1848.

III THE BIEDERMEIER MENTALITY

The City and Its Inhabitants

Reading certain contemporary descriptions of Vienna during the Biedermeier period, one has difficulty in suppressing the thought that they were written for propaganda purposes, as it were to boost the tourist industry by whetting the traveler's appetite for the city on the Danube that the congress of 1814–15 had made so famous. That had been the first time that people discovered what Vienna—the city and its inhabitants—had to offer. "The city needs to be savored like an exquisite supper—slowly, contemplatively, bit by bit; indeed, you need to have become a bit of it yourself before the full wealth of its content and the delights of its surroundings will become your personal property." The words are Adalbert Stifter's and introduce his great essay on Vienna and the Viennese *(Wien und die Wiener, in Bildern aus dem Leben)* in which, on page after magnificent page, he painted a remarkable portrait of Vienna in the 1840s, an expansive portrayal that is still today an outstanding source of information on the Vienna of the period.

The Viennese were extolled as good-natured, honest, hospitable folk with a marked propensity for good living—principally good eating and drinking. They were generally thought of as great consumers ("which had its reason in the country's abundant natural resources"), although after 1840 a change in the economic situation caused spending to decline. Yet even then a contemporary guidebook averred: "The Viennese is still

the same good-humored lover of a cheery enjoyment of life he always was, though the circumstances of the time have not been without their effect."[1]

In 1824, there were 289,598 people living in Vienna, 49,550 of them within the city walls. In accordance with its geographical location, a striking feature of Vienna—indeed it constituted a large part of its charm—was the wealth of different nationalities found in the city: Hungarians, Poles, Serbs, Croats, Greeks, Turks, and many more. Among themselves they spoke their own languages, though of course German served as the common language for general use. French and Italian were spoken in cultivated circles; however, English was coming increasingly into fashion. The emperor and the imperial princes spoke German, with the result this was also expected of foreigners who came to Vienna. Ordinary people used the Viennese dialect, elements of which also colored the language of the upper strata of society.

It would be inconceivable to paint a picture of Austria during the Biedermeier period without casting a glance at one or two of the high-ranking personages of the time. Above all, it is important to present the figure of the emperor—*der gute Kaiser Franz,* to use the label that has been attached to him by a certain superficial view of history. As always, of course, the question arises whether such a man helps to characterize an age, or whether the spirit of that age makes the man what he is seen as having been.

The critical opinion of Emperor Francis I voiced by his uncle, Joseph II, is

38 Count Carl Vasquez: *Map of the Royal Imperial Capital and Residence Vienna Together with Views of its Preeminent Commercial Establishments,* ca. 1835. Pen lithograph, colored, 57.5 × 72 cm. Historisches Museum der Stadt Wien.
Beginning in 1827, Count Carl Vasquez published a series of maps of Vienna and its suburbs. Their originality rests mainly on the many marginal *vedute,* or views, of important places of interest.

an initial obstacle to any assessment of the man as a person. It is not necessary here to examine the emperor's approach to matters political. What features particularly characterized him in the years of his reign subsequent to the Congress of Vienna and are important as regards the essence of Biedermeier? At least in respect of his later years, Francis I is rightly said to have been revered and loved by the people. And what people revere and love they also accept as a model. Convinced of his monarchical duty and, like many members of the nobility, appalled by the events of the French Revolution, he was prepared to combat—uncritically and unreservedly—any tendency that even seemed to lead in that direction. Here he acted without compunction as he had done, for example, at the beginning of his reign against the members of the so-called Jacobin Conspiracy. This was the real Francis, who—in contrast to his public image—lacked "all generosity, the grandeur of passion, even goodness and forgiveness."[2]

Nor was Emperor Francis in any way an embodiment of youthfulness: even at the Congress of Vienna (when he was only forty-seven years old), he had struck observers as old, frail, and gray. In fact, he was anything but an attractive figure, much less an elegant one. He was the homely, paternal type, so that it was above all on simpler natures that he made an impression. On the other hand, he impressed certain people precisely because of the petty-bourgeois air that he exuded. The small-mindedness to which he gave repeated expression could, of course, in many ways be extremely damaging in its effects: offenses against the state or its principles he took as personal insults, and he treated those who were guilty of them with a corresponding lack of mercy or understanding.

He was deeply and utterly convinced that legitimacy, in the shape of the monarchical state, was the only proper form of government; the French Revolution and the tendencies to which it gave birth, he saw as nothing less than the works of the devil. However much his attitude sprang from a feudal way of thinking, his conduct gave an impression of cozy middle-class respectability. All in all, "the good emperor" was indeed a "bulwark of the old powers."[3]

First and foremost he sought to preserve the external and internal peace of his country. This, he was convinced, was the best means of safeguarding the well-being of his subjects. The emperor, in other words, showed himself to be no different from his people in many respects. And the people were no different from what it was felt the emperor might be. Conservatism, middle-class respectability, a horror of everything new, delight in the family, avoidance of any kind of conspicuous elegance—all were qualities that were widely esteemed as virtues, and that people believed they could also realize in themselves.

A certain section of the nobility also behaved like the emperor, while some of his family took the French aristocracy as their model. Many of the higher civil servants were recruited from the middle ranks of the nobility. But the class that really left its mark on the age was the bourgeoisie, which was divided into various strata. (The middle stratum of the bourgeoisie produced the liberals who were later to set the political tone in Austria.)

Anyone traveling to Vienna had certain preconceptions about the Viennese. In general their character was held in high esteem; contemporary accounts mentioned repeatedly how good-natured the Viennese were. Eduard Forstmann wrote, "A basic trait of the people is their good-humoredness; consequently this is also found among the common people. Isolated outbreaks of brutality, contempt for foreigners, and hatred of the authorities are features of universal occurrence and are possibly less conspicuous here than anywhere else, for the secret police is very strict."

A convivial people, then; however, limits were set to that conviviality by the authorities. Restaurants and cafés could stay open till midnight but no later. Only at *Fasching*, or carnival time, when the great balls were held, were exceptions made. House entrances had to be closed at 10 o'clock in the evening—at 9 o'clock in the suburbs in winter. Theater performances began at 7 o'clock at the latest and

39 Rudolf von Alt: *View of Vienna from the Leopoldsberg,* 1833. Watercolor, 24.9 × 36.6 cm. Historisches Museum der Stadt Wien.
This early work by Rudolf von Alt shows the view over Vienna and its suburbs from the parvis of the church on the Leopoldsberg, looking toward the Anninger, one of the hills to the south of the city.

On the following pages:

40 Rudolf von Alt: *View of Vienna from the "Spinnerin am Kreuz,"* 1841. Watercolor and body colors, 37.3 × 59 cm. Historisches Museum der Stadt Wien. From the "Spinner at the Cross," a medieval wayside shrine high on the Wienerberg, there was a particularly fine view northward over the city of Vienna.

41 Tobias Dionys Raulino: *Heiligenstadt,* 1821. Watercolor, 35 × 50 cm. Historisches Museum der Stadt Wien. Heiligenstadt, one of the favorite winegrowing suburbs of Vienna at the foot of the Nussberg, was the goal of many an excursion from the city.

42 Franz Eybl: *Viennese Middle-Class Couple in the Studio,* 1834. Oil on panel, 36 × 29 cm. Germanisches Nationalmuseum, Nuremberg: Georg Schäfer Collection.

43 Michael Neder: *Viennese
Middle-Class Family,* 1854. Oil
on canvas, 62 × 79 cm. Historisches Museum der Stadt Wien.

44 Ferdinand Georg
Waldmüller: *Young Lady at her
Dressing Table,* 1840. Oil on
panel, 39.5 × 30.9 cm. Historisches Museum der Stadt Wien.

45 Heinrich August Mansfeld:
Nursery Tea, 1844. Oil on card,
26 × 32 cm. Historisches
Museum der Stadt Wien.
Two children play teatime with
"doll's china."

Die Wasserträger.
WIEN bey J. Bermann.

46   Joseph Lanzedelly: *The Water Carrier,* 1818. Chalk lithograph, colored, 40.7 × 50.8 cm. Historisches Museum der Stadt Wien.
Although Vienna had had water pipes since the beginning of the nineteenth century, during the summer months there were repeated water shortages. It was then that the water sellers went into action, bringing huge barrels of Danube water into the city.

usually ended at 10. From then on, life in the city gradually ground to a halt.

There were no brothels, and it was pointed out approvingly that "Vienna is possibly the only capital in which one is not importuned on the streets in the evening by the unfortunate women whose numbers are in fact supposed to be reduced by such houses."[4] All the same, in 1827, there were allegedly 20,000 women living by prostitution, though they "had no papers to that effect." If they fell ill as a result of the profession they exercised, they were taken to a specially equipped hospital where a young Jesuit preached moral sermons at their bedsides. In this way an attempt was made to reintegrate them into society, though clearly with only limited success: every second prostitute admitted to the hospital soon fell back into her old ways. It was impossible to say with any certainty which sections of the population were involved here, be-

cause some of these prostitutes were "exceptional dilettantes and celebrated women, including some countesses...."[5]

There were rogues and thieves everywhere, too—especially pickpockets, who haunted theaters, churches, masked balls, and concerts. The thieves were a cautious lot, selling their booty abroad. International links often made it difficult to trace both stolen goods and criminals—an indication that even so close-woven a police net as covered Vienna is incapable of stopping crime.

The lower strata of society were generally very badly off, and after 1830 their standard of living declined progressively as a result of changes in the economic structure. Poverty increased, and many people suddenly found themselves facing total destitution. Yet every good deed performed during this period, in an attempt to change things or to improve them, was blocked by the authorities who

Die Wasch-weiber.
Wien bey J. Bermann.

were clearly there for that purpose. Private associations were founded with the object of combating poverty. But "an elaborate chancellery decree made the establishment of practically every kind of association dependent henceforth on a detailed examination and approval procedure" with the result that such private charitable societies as existed in Vienna before 1848 were subject to constant financial supervision. Special attention was also paid to ensuring in this way that religious and moral integrity was preserved.[6]

Poverty and social distress had many consequences. One of these was a high mortality rate, the principal direct cause of which was a rampant epidemic of tuberculosis. No one at the time had any proper idea of what caused the epidemic, but of course the real reason why it was so devastating in its effects lay in poor sanitary conditions and, above all, in the wretchedly inadequate housing conditions in which a large section of the population (particularly in the suburbs) was condemned to live.

The better accommodations were behind the bastion walls in the inner city. Here dwellings were relatively spacious and included secondary rooms. But they were inhabited by prosperous members of the middle class, who set great store by physical comfort—a key feature of the Biedermeier mentality. Living one's life in the bosom of one's family and one's friends was among the most important characteristics of the Biedermeier period, and the way in which the Viennese bourgeoisie cultivated home decor represented one of its highpoints.

Property rents were determined by how close the house or apartment concerned lay to the city center. This meant, of course, that different districts acquired different "images," which they retained,

incidentally, until well into the twentieth century. The density of housing in the city (definitely on the high side since the end of the eighteenth century) changed little over the years. Certain suburbs— Liechtenthal, for example, where Franz Schubert was born—were particularly overcrowded. The usual form of domestic architecture was the *Pawlatschenhaus*, a low dwelling with open wooden galleries, which stemmed from the eighteenth century.

In the 1830s housing density did sink somewhat, though the quality of housing also declined. In the suburbs (where the population was, in the main, financially weak and where there were many workers' houses), shabby, small, low–ceilinged rooms were the rule, rooms in which the whole life of the family was acted out. Smoke billowed in from the kitchen; washing was draped everywhere; children ran about. There were at most two beds, which might be occupied during the day as well, by so-called bed-goers.

Much of the spreading evil of poor housing was caused by speculation.[7] The

smaller houses, in which apartments had been available at affordable prices, were falling into decay and being replaced by large apartment buildings in which the rents were out of all proportion to people's incomes. Speculators were clearly trying to reduce the supply of available accommodation in order to be able to charge more for it. In the 1840s this contributed toward worsening the social situation. Increasing industrialization reduced the number of jobs, incomes declined, and pauperization extended its hold over ever larger sections of the population. Most working-class households paid between a quarter and a third of their income for rent.

So there was a dark side to the Biedermeier period, although one still reads occasionally that these were "the good old days." In fact, the impression repeatedly given is that a warm golden sun hung over the whole period, and that everyone was happy. That may just possibly have been true of the period immediately following the Napoleonic Wars, when despite police pressure—particularly obtrusive in those years—people at least felt free of one burden, namely the risk of war.

"Oh Happy We Who Have the Prater!" (A. Stifter)

How did people console themselves in life's more difficult moments? What were their pleasures? What did they do in their very limited free time?

The normal place of resort for ordinary people on Sundays and holidays was the tavern. In the suburbs there were tavern gardens, which were particularly popular in the summer. The more well-to-do section of the population went for walks or undertook excursions in the countryside around the city. As a guidebook put it: "It is in the open air, amid the delights of nature, that one must look for the Viennese if one would enjoy hearty, unforced, lively, yet never boisterous jollity."[8]

Music was "the spice of public and domestic life." Here, of course, standards varied enormously according to the level of demand. The simplest form of musical

48 *A Viennese Waiter.* Copperplate engraving, colored; plate 32.5 × 22.8 cm, sheet 42.2 × 27.3 cm. Historisches Museum der Stadt Wien.

49 Johann Christian Schoeller: *The Passion for Newspapers,* 1837. Copperplate engraving, colored; plate 21.3 × 24.8 cm, sheet 23.3 × 29.6 cm. Historisches Museum der Stadt Wien. Cafés and newspapers are practically synonymous in Vienna. A "café culture" was already taking shape in the Pre-March period, though it was not until the turn of the century that the Viennese coffeehouse acquired its legendary reputation.

Die Zeitungsliebhaberey.
M. _ Ich bitt um die Allgemeine oder die Theaterzeitung.

Wien, im Bureau der Theaterzeitung, Rauhensteingasse N.º 926.

50 *The Theater an der Wien.* Copperplate engraving with watercolor, plate 16 × 21.3 cm. Published by Tranquillo Mollo. Historisches Museum der Stadt Wien.
The Theater an der Wien and the Carltheater were the principal playhouses cultivating folk theater.

51 Joseph Lanzedelly: *The Theater Lovers—a Scene from Life.* Lithograph, 28.9 × 36.6 cm. Historisches Museum der Stadt Wien.
The picture caricatures the Viennese passion for the theater, for it was not just the comedies of Raimund and Nestroy that aroused the city's interest.

52 Joseph Lanzedelly: *A Hearty Appetite,* 1820. Lithograph, colored, 27.1 × 36 cm. Historisches Museum der Stadt Wien. A picture showing that even highly placed personages are not averse to receiving handouts.

53 Matthäus Loder: *Glutton and Beggar,* 1818. Watercolor, 13.6 × 12.6 cm. Historisches Museum der Stadt Wien. Loder's watercolor points to the contrast between rich and poor, a reference—albeit a very mild one—to a social problem which people at the time believed charity could resolve.

54 Johann Matthias Ranftl: *Beggar Children on the Glacis,* 1852. Oil on panel, 47 × 37.5 cm. Historisches Museum der Stadt Wien.
Ranftl, who produced a series of paintings on socio-critical themes, particularly attacked the evils of Vienna in the 1840s.

55 Carl Geyling: *Three Workmen in an Ironworks.* Oil on panel, 44 × 55 cm. Germanisches Nationalmuseum, Nuremberg: Georg Schäfer Collection.

56 Ferdinand Georg
Waldmüller: *The Seizure,* 1847.
Oil on panel, 70.5 × 87.5 cm. Historisches Museum der Stadt
Wien.
The treatment is dramatic, not to
say melodramatic. Yet the social
distress of peasant farmers was
clearly something that preoccu-
pied the painter, as witness his
portrayal of this seizure of live-
stock.

57 Franz von Maleck: *Living Room,* 1836. Watercolor, 25.8 × 38.1 cm. Historisches Museum der Stadt Wien.
The living room depicted was in the house of the Teutonic Order and commanded a view of St. Stephen's Cathedral.

58 Joseph Schütz: *Bed-sitting-room,* ca. 1843. Watercolor, 25.3 × 36.4 cm. Historisches Museum der Stadt Wien.

68

59 *Writing Cabinet,* ca. 1840. Watercolor, 25.2 × 21.6 cm. Historisches Museum der Stadt Wien.
This study clearly belonged to a woman, since among the writing materials there is also a piece of knitting.

60 *Aristocratic Social Gathering in the Drawing Room,* ca. 1830. Gouache, 23.3 × 34.7 cm. Historisches Museum der Stadt Wien.
The picture gives an idea of what wealthy peoples' drawing rooms looked like, with comfortable furniture and a generously designed decor.

61 *Room in a Suburban House,* 1837. Pencil and watercolor, 20 × 25.3 cm. Historisches Museum der Stadt Wien.
One of the few examples of the domestic living conditions of "the poor." This would have been the home of a laborer or a craftsman and has only the most essential appointments: a bed, a stove, a shelf.

entertainment was provided by organ-grinders. In Vienna they were called *Werkelmänner,* and they plied their trade "in countless numbers from house to house, at the gates of the city, and on promenades, droning out the favorite melodies from the music hall and the opera until eventually the cobblers' boys, many of them showing great virtuosity, whistle along with the 'arias'." Itinerant harpists were still to be found, circulating with their instruments like the organ-grinders. Finally there were improvisers who performed ballads to musical accompaniment, often taking political circumstances as the object of their biting scorn.

Above all, people had begun to discover nature. Whenever they had an hour to spare, they went out into the woods and fields to enjoy the fine weather. In this way the immediate, and even the more remote, surroundings of Vienna became increasingly important to the people of the city. We see this chiefly in painting, of course, which took its subjects from the landscapes around Vienna: the forest known as the Wienerwald to the west, the Schneeberg and Rax mountains to the southwest, but also the Salzkammergut, far to the west near Salzburg. Mainly, however, it was the Prater that played a vital role—an indication of the importance that this "recreation area" had for the Viennese.

It was Emperor Joseph II who, in accordance with his philosophy of life, had opened the Augarten and the Prater (spacious lands adjoining the Danube) to the general public. Until his day, only members of the higher nobility had been permitted—at certain times—to enter this parklike hunting ground. And even they had been forbidden to leave their carriages or to dismount from their horses. The layout of the *Jägerzeile,* or "hunting row," a broad, treelined avenue leading to the Prater (today's Praterstrasse) likewise goes back to the time of Emperor Joseph II. But what did the Prater mean to Biedermeier Vienna?

62 *Scene at an Inn,* ca. 1800. Pen drawing, colored, 12.5 × 16.5 cm. Historisches Museum der Stadt Wien.

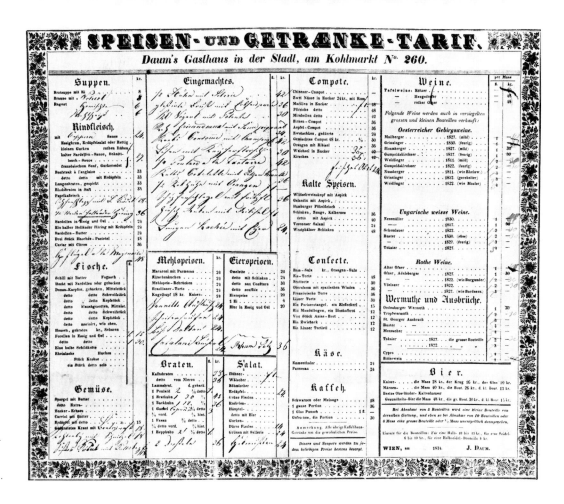

63 Menu with handwritten entries from Daum's Inn in the Kohlmarkt, at No. 206. Historisches Museum der Stadt Wien.

64 Josef Koll: *View of the First Coffeehouse on the Prater Avenue,* 1810 (?). Watercolor, 27.5 × 39.5 cm. Historisches Museum der Stadt Wien.

"Few of the world's capitals can boast such a thing as our Prater. Is it a park? 'No.' Is it a meadow? 'No.' Is it a garden? 'No.' A forest? 'No.' A pleasure resort? 'No.' What is it then? All those things together." Again our source is Adalbert Stifter's essay "Vienna and the Viennese" (*Wien und die Wiener*). The Prater was hugely popular with the Viennese. On fine days streams of people poured into it by way of the *Jägerzeile*, which began immediately beyond the bridge over the Danube Canal. The stream of people continued along the main avenue, where there were many restaurants for those of higher rank as well as others for ordinary folk. All classes were to be found in the Prater, so that, while walking there, one might even encounter Their Majesties the Emperor and Empress, as Stifter relates in his essay.

The Würstelprater was already in existence then, an area that took its name from Hanswurst, the typical figure of eighteenth-century Viennese popular comedy; it was the site of many places of entertainment, with merry-go-rounds, bowling alleys, swings, puppet theaters, and other pleasures provided for the delectation of the public. Above all, though, the Würstelprater was the site of many taverns and restaurants: in 1846 there were no less than fifty-four of them serving wine and beer. Some of the Prater taverns became particularly famous, enjoying an extraordinary degree of public affection. Among the facilities provided by the Green Parrot (*Zum grünen Paperl*), a restaurant near the center of the Würstelprater, was a veritable fried-chicken paradise, chicken-in-the-basket being already one of Vienna's favorite meals.

One of the Prater's principal entrepreneurs was Basilio Calafati, whose steam merry-go-round was soon dubbed *Zum grossen Chinesen*, after the huge figure of a Chinaman in the middle, and later became known simply as *Zum Calafati*.

The Three Coffeehouses in the main avenue of the Prater were enormously popular. They were patronized chiefly by the fashionable world. The First Coffeehouse established a regular concert platform: Joseph Lanner played there for the first time in 1819, and Johann Strauss the Elder in 1824. Another big public attraction was the Circus Gymnasticus, designed by the architect of Biedermeier Vienna himself, Josef Kornhäusel. The building, with its glass dome resting on wooden columns, was mainly used by equestrian performers. The founder of the enterprise, Christoph de Bach, liked to show off his own dueling, riding, and dressage skills there.

What the people of Vienna liked doing most was celebrating festivals, for festivals distracted them from their difficulties and allowed them to forget that they were living in a police state. Holy Week, of course, brought its round of church festivities. The Easter procession in the city center, like the one on Corpus Christi, in-

volved the participation of the emperor and the court. Every church had its Easter celebration; the whole city was astir on that day. People turned out in their smartest clothes to show reverence to this highest feastday of the Christian church. On Good Friday and Holy Saturday it was customary to walk through the city via the Kohlmarkt, the Graben, and the Stephansplatz, where the great cathedral of St. Stephen, like all the other churches, was draped with black inside. One of the side altars did duty as the Holy Sepulchre, and before it the faithful knelt in prayer.

The Easter festivities involved tremendous public participation. At 4 o'clock on Holy Saturday afternoon the crowds were at their thickest. Easter itself—the Feast of the Resurrection—was celebrated in the Burghof initially, then continued in the cathedral. After that the Viennese went shopping; the shops were open everywhere, giving people the chance to lay in a supply of food for the next day, Easter Sunday, which was considered so great a feastday that no shops were allowed to remain open for business. It was a day when everyone hoped for fine weather in order

65 Johann Adam Krafft, after Johann Nepomuk Passini: *People Enjoying Themselves in the Prater*, 1826. Etching and copperplate engraving, 15.7 × 22.6 cm. Historisches Museum der Stadt Wien.

that they might enjoy to the full, for the first time in the year, the beauties of Vienna's natural surroundings—beauties that were coming to occupy an increasingly important place in their minds and imaginations.

In fact, Easter Sunday marked the recommencement of many pleasures that people had been denied during the winter months. Particularly popular were the firework displays, held between four and six times a year in a field in the Prater specially set aside for the purpose. There was always one in May and one on July 26, the feast of St. Anne, known as *Annentag*. Each display consisted of between six and eight "fronts," let off at short intervals, one after another. The man in charge was the famous "art and aerial pyrotechnician" Anton Stuwer. When Stuwer "let off his fantasies," wrote Adalbert Stifter, the scene at the Firework Plaza in the Prater was of "a crowd standing shoulder to shoulder as if the place were paved with heads, and all looking up into the night sky that is cut through by rockets as by piercing shrieks, or in which he [Struwer] suddenly fastens a star that floats now red, now green, now blue, now golden in the dark heavens and, borne by the wind, drifts slowly sideways

and down, or the star bursts and scatters a handful of brightly colored fire-flowers through the night air—or suddenly a burning town stands before you in filigree, calmly blazing away, often presenting to the more discerning eye the most ingenious poems in flame."[9]

A favorite festival with the people of Vienna was the *Brigittenkirchtag*, the dedication day of the Church of the Brigittines, likewise celebrated in summer in the Brigittine meadow. This was "the true public festival of the Viennese." It was held on two consecutive days and invariably attracted between forty and eighty thousand visitors. Franz Grillparzer began his novella *Der arme Spielmann* (1848, "The Poor Street Musician") with a description of this festival:

"In Vienna, the Sunday after the full moon in July of each year, together with the day after, is a real public festival, if ever a festival deserved the name. The people patronize it as well as put it on themselves, and if such as are of higher rank attend it, they are able to do so only in their capacity of members of the people. Here there is no possibility of segregation; at least until a few years ago there was not.

"On that day the Brigittenau, which with the Augarten, Leopoldstadt, and the Prater forms one uninterrupted pleasure row, celebrates its dedication day. From one Brigittine dedication day to the next, the working people count the days. At last the long-awaited Saturnalian feast dawns.

"Then there is uproar in this calm, good-natured city. A surging crowd fills the streets. There is a tramping of feet and a murmur of voices, pierced through here and there by a loud cry. Class distinctions disappear; citizen and soldier are stirred as one."

Eduard Forstmann described his experiences at the festival itself: "I should need to be Jacques Callot [the early seventeenth-century French engraver of scenes from popular life] to describe all the groups of drunkards, dancers, musicians, and so on. People sit around in the open or in the shade of trees, the beer or wine barrel beside them and food in their laps or in baskets and boxes. From every

66   Georg Emanuel Opitz: *The Morning Concert in the Augarten,* ca. 1825. Watercolor and sepia, 37.5 × 25 cm. Historisches Museum der Stadt Wien. Social gatherings in the open air were a favorite pretext for musical entertainment.

67 L. Welden: *The Restaurant At the Sign of the Green Parrot in the Prater,* 1817. Watercolor, 27 × 40.3 cm. Historisches Museum der Stadt Wien.
The Prater restaurants were like places of pilgrimage to which the Viennese repaired to consume their favorite food—*Backhendl*, or cakes and pastries. The Green Parrot was one of the best-known.

68 Joseph Lanzedelly: *Free Monday at the Prater Wine Tavern,* 1818. Chalk lithograph, 28.3 × 36.5 cm. Historisches Museum der Stadt Wien.
According to an ancient practice, some craftsmen were given the whole day or half a day off on Mondays. The custom of a free Monday was not universal, however, and was later banned.

direction comes music, music, and more music in bright harmonies and clashing discords; whirling dancers sweep the grass until it is worn quite away and clouds of dust rise from the bare earth. Propriety is frequently offended in the antics of these menads—yet a wholly shameless performance is scarcely ever to be seen. The nobility of Vienna do not think it beneath them to come here and look on. And so it continues, with dancing and feasting, from morning until late in the evening; and when the provisions have all been consumed and the barrels emptied, the delighted, blissfully happy people stumble and cheer and sing and play their way back to the city."[10]

In winter, the great pleasure was *Fasching*, the carnival held in the weeks immediately preceding Lent. The Viennese loved *Fasching* because it was above all a time for dancing, and the Viennese of the period were absolutely crazy about dancing, which they regarded as their chief pleasure in life.[11]

In summer it was slowly becoming customary to move out into the country; indeed, this was a typical feature of the Biedermeier period. Consequently various places—some near, some farther away—took on something of the character of a "Little Vienna." They were served by coaches that, particularly in summer, left Vienna several times a day. The fashionable world accordingly moved out to such places as Hietzing, Penzing, Hütteldorf, and of course to the vicinity of the imperial castle at Schönbrunn. More and more villas were built in these places. The summer-holiday locations extended to the south as well, where Kalksburg, Rodaun, and Kaltenleutgeben were favorite resorts. A major center of attraction was the health resort of Baden, some 25 kilometers to the south. Baden, the "idol of the Viennese," received its architectural personality during this period.

The Watchful State

Censorship and the way in which it was practiced exhibited certain distinctive features during the Pre-March period, though it was not invented then. The

69 Norbert Bittner: *A Prater Café*, 1810 (?). Etching, plate 13 × 15cm, sheet 20.5 × 25 cm. Historisches Museum der Stadt Wien.
Many of the Prater cafés were meeting places for the fashionable world.

"censorship principle" had been invented in the time of Emperor Joseph II—with, however, quite a different object, namely to "enlighten" and educate the people. Now the authorities used it to obtain information about everything that was happening in the country with the object of preventing new, and possibly subversive, tendencies from gaining a foothold. The method adopted by the authorities during the Pre-March period needs to be understood in terms of a general incapacitation of the people. In Emperor Joseph's day, an attempt had been made to educate people toward independence of judgment and a certain willingness to make decisions for themselves. Now the opposite was the case: citizens were expected to accept instructions on what was right and what was wrong.

The determining factor in this recasting of the censorship provisions was, of course, the events of the French Revolution, which had made an impression on the whole of Europe. The *Polizeihofstelle,* or police authority, was set up in Vienna in 1793. On February 22, 1795, all previously existing censorship

70 Jakob Alt: *Panorama in the Prater with the Bach Circus,* 1815. Watercolor, 27.2 × 41 cm. Historisches Museum der Stadt Wien.

PRATER.

DER FEUERWERKSPLATZ. №32. LA PLACE DU FEU D'ARTIFICE.

A Vienne chez Tranquillo Mollo.

71 *Prater—The Firework Plaza,* ca. 1825. Copperplate engraving with watercolor, 15.5 × 21.5 cm. Published by Tranquillo Mollo. Historisches Museum der Stadt Wien.
The Prater, the favorite outing of the Viennese on fine days, was often the scene of costly firework displays drawing huge crowds.

Wien zu sehen von der Brigittenau zur zeit der Kirchweihe.

72 Balthasar Wigand: *Vienna as Seen from the Brigittenau during a Fair,* ca. 1830. Gouache, 12.5 × 19.5 cm. Historisches Museum der Stadt Wien.
A great fair was held annually on St. Bridget's day (October 8); it was tremendously popular with the Viennese and attracted countless visitors. Franz Grillparzer described it vividly in his novella *Der arme Spielmann* ("The Poor Street Musician").

73 Anton Ziegler: *A Masked Ball* (Redoute) *in the Imperial Ballroom.* Watercolor, 8 × 16 cm. Historisches Museum der Stadt Wien.

74 Michael Neder: *Five-Cross Dance,* 1829. Oil on canvas, 41 × 55 cm. Historisches Museum der Stadt Wien.

75   Georg Emanuel Opitz: *The Lemonade Stall in the Graben,* ca. 1820. Watercolor, 36.5 × 26.5 cm. Historisches Museum der Stadt Wien.

76   Anton Elfinger (pseudonym: Cajetan): *Every Day Is Ball Day.* Watercolor, 22.1 × 19.6 cm. Historisches Museum der Stadt Wien.

77   Eduard Gurk, after Johann Nepomuk Höchle: *Viennese Rack Wagon,* ca. 1830. Copperplate engraving, colored, 34.1 × 45.1 cm. Historisches Museum der Stadt Wien.

Procession de la fête Dieu à Vienne avant la demolition de la Maison, dite „Hirsch Apotheke", entre le Graben et le Kohlmarkt.

78 Balthasar Wigand: *Corpus Christi Procession in the Graben,* before 1820. Gouache, 19.2 × 31.3 cm. Historisches Museum der Stadt Wien.
The Corpus Christi procession and the Easter procession were held in old Vienna on the two most important church feastdays; even members of the imperial family and the higher nobility participated in them.

79 Copy after Anton Zampis: *Soiree in the Volksgarten,* ca. 1845. Watercolor, 36 × 50 cm. Historisches Museum der Stadt Wien.
The Volksgarten, nicknamed the "paradise garden," was one of the most popular social meeting places in Biedermeier Vienna.

provisions were brought together under one "general censorship decree," and in 1801 the new police authority was given the task of putting that decree into execution. The purpose of such censorship was not to suppress ideas aimed at the public in the form of literature so much as to couch those ideas in a form that would not harm, but rather benefit the state.

Efforts to bring about a general incapacitation of the people included, for example, the gradual restriction of self-government for Vienna—demonstrated by the reduction of the decision power exercised by the mayor. In the Pre-March period, all financial matters relating to the city of Vienna had to be decided by the provincial government of Lower Austria.[12]

People knew or told one another stories about what huge sums of money the city spent on policing. And everyone testified to the fact that the police, while they might be efficient, were a nuisance because they concerned themselves with everything. To take one example, simply traveling to Vienna was a laborious affair. Every traveler who crossed the frontiers of the monarchy had, of course, to be in possession of a passport issued by an Austrian ambassador, consul, or chargé d'affaires. At the city limits the traveler was relieved of this document and informed in writing that he must report to the Royal-Imperial Passport, Conscription, and Notification Office within twenty-four hours in order to obtain the requisite "residence card." Note that if you wished to stay in the city and find a job, you had to have your residence card first; only then was an employer prepared to consider hiring you. You might, however, be told by the police, "Residence in the city can be permitted only if a person is able to show adequate evidence regarding means of support and proper employment." You might easily, in other words, end up in the kind of unfortunate situation that Franz Kafka described in his novels less than a century later.[13] If the authorities had any difficulties with travelers or suspicions regarding applicants for residence permits, they suggested to them that they should leave

Vienna as soon as possible—certainly within a few days. Anyone arriving in Vienna immediately became involved with the authorities and possibly with the censor as well.

If you were so incautious as to travel to Vienna with books in your luggage, you were required to present these, on your arrival, at a special office set aside for this purpose. If they failed to comply with the Austrian censorship provisions, the books had to be surrendered and deposited. Only on leaving Vienna would you receive your books back.[14]

Life with the censor was complicated to the extent that one was basically at the mercy of the censorship officers. New censorship provisions had been adopted in 1803, together with general and specific guidelines for their administration, but they had never been published. At all events, any expression of opinion that offended against religion or was regarded as immoral or politically subversive stood no chance whatever of receiving the approval of the censorship officers. Far from being confined to literature, the theater, and graphic art, the censorship provisions applied to shop and business signs, and even to inscriptions on tombstones. All printed matter—not just books, but also maps, town plans, and so on—had to be submitted to the Royal-Imperial Central Book-Checking Office beforehand, that is to say, "the original or the drawing," in order to obtain permission to print. Surviving censored plates show the kind of thing that met with the disapproval of these strict civil servants. Female nudity was high on the list: "cover the breast," we read on one graphic plate where a lady's bosom can be clearly made out, or on another depicting an oriental slave-market, "non imprimatur," because female slaves with partially unclothed bodies can be seen being felt by prospective purchasers. These two examples of censorship are taken more or less at random. Censorship also extended to any kind of criticism of political conditions or of measures taken by the authorities.

Someone we know to have suffered particularly from censorship (because he complained about it a great deal in his writings, above all in his autobiography)

80 Ferdinand Georg
Waldmüller: *A Recruit's Farewell,* 1858 (?). Oil on panel,
78.5 × 95 cm. Historisches Museum der Stadt Wien.

was Franz Grillparzer. Two circumstances
were largely responsible for this: his
poem "Campo Vaccino" about the Christian cross in the Colosseum in Rome
(written in 1819) had attracted the
unfavorable attention of the censor and
aroused the displeasure of the church,
and the fact that he was a civil servant
himself meant that he was watched par-

ticularly closely. The poem had to be torn
out of every available copy of the *Aglaja*
almanac, which actually contributed to
the poet's popularity because scandals in
such connections always have a propaganda effect. Grillparzer's drama *König
Ottokars Glück und Ende* (1825, "King
Ottokar's Good Fortune and His End")
was not released by the censor for a long

time, prompting Grillparzer to express the view "that there is no place for a writer in Austria under these circumstances." The performance of his *Ein treuer Diener seines Herrn* (1828, "A Loyal Servant of His Master") led to a particularly curious episode.

The day after the successful first performance, given in the presence of Emperor Francis I, Grillparzer was summoned by the chief of police, Count Sedlnitzky, who informed him that the play had pleased His Majesty so much that he wished to acquire sole possession of it. The author was offered a substantial sum of money, the idea being to take the play out of circulation and so prevent its reaching a wider public and becoming known beyond Vienna. Grillparzer, invited to do so, proposed a specific sum, though not without noting on a page of his diary, "Whatever the end of the affair, the invisible chains rattle on hand and foot." However, the imperial proposal was not put into effect in the end; wiser counsels had prevailed and smoothed things over. Eventually the play was allowed to be performed everywhere, without let or hindrance.

What went on inside the heads of those responsible for censorship decisions remains a complete mystery. Grillparzer tells us in his autobiography, for example, that he once ran into a senior member of the censorship office who was known to him and also well-disposed toward him. The man asked him why he was writing so little. Grillparzer replied that circumstances dictated it, robbing one of all desire to write. The official admitted to having himself held up performance of Grillparzer's play *König Ottokars Glück und Ende* for two years. Grillparzer asked what, in the official's view, had been so dangerous about the play. "Nothing at all," the man replied, "but I thought to myself: you never know!"[15]

The theater was the favorite target of the censor's attentions, of course, because an author's ideas, when declaimed from the stage, had an immediate effect on the public. Nevertheless, authors too had countless ways of achieving the desired effect and possibly outwitting the censor.

Understandably the plays of the satirist Johann Nestroy were particularly at risk. While he conscientiously presented all his comedies to the censor beforehand, they were proffered in a form that could not possibly cause offense. Since he acted in his plays himself, however, he was able to improvise and in this way bring out, on the stage, whatever was preying on his mind.

All these things naturally had a great deal to do with the personal attitude of the writer concerned. A man such as Grillparzer, who took everything very seriously, saw them as his fate and felt entitled to complain about them. Other writers—Adalbert Stifter was an example—preferred to avoid any complications. From the outset they practiced a kind of self-censorship—the attitude the government liked most, because it meant that it had unobtrusively achieved its aim. Johann Nestroy, a satirist, saw it as his job to pick quarrels with authority and was aware that his audiences expected him to come out with some sharp remarks directed against the system; he took it all good-humoredly. It was worth his while

81   Carl Schuster, after J.H. Ramberg: *Oriental Slave Market,* 1839. Pen and ink, 22 × 27.8 cm. Historisches Museum der Stadt Wien.
This portrayal of naked and partially clothed women incurred the displeasure of the censor, who wrote, "Non imprimatur 1/10 39" in the corner.

82 Vinzenz Reim: *Interior of the Acidulous-Spring Bath in Baden* (with a note by the censor), 1834. Pen and ink, 21 × 29.5 cm. Historisches Museum der Stadt Wien. Bothered by the display of female nudity in this view of the baths at Baden, near Vienna, the censor would not allow the drawing to be published in this form.

to be locked up occasionally or to have to pay a fine: it increased his popularity.

In time, particularly in the 1840s, the grip of censorship began to loosen. Those affected continued to find such official intervention burdensome, of course, and there were repeated calls for its abolition. In 1842 the newspaper editors submitted a petition to that effect. In 1845 ninety-nine Austrian writers and academics addressed a memorandum to Count Franz Anton Kolowrat, minister of state, protesting against censorship. The first name on the list was that of Franz Grillparzer, for the Orientalists Joseph von Hammer-Purgstall and Stephan Endlicher, who had originally signed the memorandum, had both withdrawn. A further request for censorship to be abolished was submitted by the booksellers. None of these attempts was successful however, which makes it easier to understand why one of the principal demands at the outbreak of the Revolution of 1848 was the abolition of censorship. On the second day of the revolution that demand was met temporarily. On March 14, 1848, the crowd marched to the monument of Emperor Joseph II in order

to decorate it with flowers and wreaths and, in so doing, to show what kind of ruler and what kind of government it desired. But it took more to get rid of censorship than that. Following the brief intoxication of the revolution, censorship was reintroduced, and it continued in existence for a long time to come.

Citizens under Surveillance

A particular type of mentality presupposes that tension exists between opposites. In the life of a people, such tension springs from either social or national causes: the contention that cultural fecundity arises only under such circumstances can scarcely be refuted. In the Biedermeier period, there was tension between the forces of progress—the demands of the time, as it were—and the rigid attitude of reaction adopted by the political authorities. The Biedermeier culture evolved under this sort of tension: the state being the stronger, the Biedermeier culture promoted the private sphere and evaded the public one. The citizen was free only within his own four walls, because even when he went to the tavern the police might be looking over his shoulder: one had to weigh what one said carefully, because someone might be present whose business it was to pass on what he heard, claiming that, for reasons of state security, the police must be put in the picture. Being an informer was one of the most thriving occupations of the period. And since this was common knowledge, citizens were aware that they could find no privacy once they had taken so much as a step into the public sphere. This was why people were increasingly inclined to withdraw into the restricted sphere of nonpolitical conventicles whose attitude toward the state was one of indifference. That was exactly what the authorities wanted; such behavior was in conformity with reasons of state, since the government was not interested in a politically committed citizenry.

It is therefore important to look at the nature and mentality of the Biedermeier era in the context of the political situation then obtaining in Austria. This was the real reason for the specific attitude evinced by the inhabitants of the country.

The beginning of the Biedermeier period is placed at the time of the Congress of Vienna—rightly so, because the congress did indeed mark the start of a new era. Europe was still reeling from the effects of the wars and social upheavals that had characterized the Age of Napoleon. The European nobility had followed with particular intensity the fate of those members of the privileged classes who had come to grief during the French Revolution. From their point of view, it was only too natural that everything should be done to prevent further outbreaks of revolution and to block aspirations for social change. And, as always in such cases, the obvious instruments were unlimited use of the power of the state and deployment of police forces with their apparatus for coercion. No attempt was made—it never is—to tackle the evil at the root by improving conditions that cried out for improvement. Instead governments worked from the premise that they were already in possession of the best of all possible worlds.

Those who lived in the Biedermeier era were not aware (any more than were those who had lived in the Baroque or Gothic periods) that their age had such a label. As a name for a style, "Biedermeier" is a twentieth-century invention. Originally it stood for "the good old days" and was taken from the "Poems of the Swabian Schoolmaster Gottlieb Biedermaier," published in a Munich weekly in 1855–57 by two doggerel poets. As a historical term, Biedermeier does not mean the same as Pre-March, though the two cover the same period; the difference is that the former relates to the cultural history of the period, and the latter to its political history.

There are problems, of course, in subdividing the course of history into fixed periods. For example, it is idle to ponder over whether Viennese Biedermeier ended with the death of Emperor Francis I in 1835, or with the outbreak of revolution in March, 1848; there were typical Biedermeier features in the period before 1815 as there were in the 1860s. As an instance of this "overlapping," the one work most characteristic of the Biedermeier era was Adalbert Stifter's novel *Der Nachsommer* ("IndianSummer"). It was written between 1848 and 1857, that is to say, outside the Biedermeier limit: yet it is totally bound up with the mental attitudes of the prerevolutionary period.

Primarily, then, Biedermeier is not so much a stylistic trend as a mental attitude. We have noted where it originated, namely in the political situation: in politics people had initially been given high hopes, which had then not been fulfilled. This set a general tone that probably harmonized with a certain propensity of the Viennese toward melancholy and Weltschmerz, which was capable of rising to heights of passion or of descending to an intense weariness with life and a longing for death. In its simplest form this mentality found expression in the celebrated condition of *Tränenseligkeit* (literally "love of tears"), though this was partly a question of fashion. "People practiced renunciation and modesty; they bowed to the invisible, chased after shadow kisses and the scent of blue flowers, abstained and shed tears" (Heinrich Heine, quoted by Egon Friedell in his famous *Kulturgeschichte der Neuzeit* ["Cultural History of Modern Times"], 1927–32). But *Tränenseligkeit* can already be found in Goethe's *Die Leiden des jungen Werthers* (1774, "The Sufferings of Young Werther"), where people burst into tears at every opportunity, be they tears of joy or tears of pain.

Let us return to the documentary evidence that best and most clearly reveals the mentality of the period, namely the works of its writers and, in particular, those of Adalbert Stifter, the earliest of which—the *Studien* ("Studies")—began to appear in the 1840s. Stifter was of a retrospective cast of mind. His *veduta*-like views of the landscape—both as a painter and as a writer—and his characterizations of people offer valuable clues about the essence of Biedermeier.

The importance and effect of the ubiquitous, everwatchful eye of authority are unmistakable even in Stifter's work, as they are in the work of all the authors of the period. Above all, one's writing had to be chaste and reserved. In his novella *Das alte Siegel* ("The Old Seal"), Stifter tells the story of an adultery, though the fact of its consummation needs to be read between the lines. The author's attitude toward that adultery is clearly not one of disapproval. Both the principal figures of the story have his sympathy, and he would obviously like them to be capable of breaking through convention to achieve their happiness. Yet there can be no doubt that Stifter's work is imbued with reverence and a sense of responsibility before God and man, and hence also toward custom and the law. To see the greatness in small things, to praise quietness and simplicity, and to take moderation as his measure—such were Stifter's principal concerns. What is timeless is perfect: nature is timeless; it expresses the essence of beauty; in harmony with nature man finds his happiness. And yet the author is aware that an unfathomable fate weighs heavily upon everything; the tragic side of life breaks through everywhere, and man must either master it or submit to it.

As Stifter had shown in *Das alte Siegel,* an exaggerated sense of honor leads to a life without happiness: the man is debarred from founding a family, and the child born of the adulterous union is denied the guiding hand of a father. The elderly principal characters of *Der Nachsommer,* Gustav Riesach and Mathilde, are no less victims of a convention that they—and especially Gustav—have obeyed. Gustav allows himself to be far too deeply affected by generally accepted custom, believing that a child must obey the will of its parents, which is sacred and inviolable. Yet Mathilde reproaches Gustav most fiercely with his lack of strength to ignore what is demanded of him in order to help his own, and her, will to victory.

This same inability to surmount tradition, "custom," the looming shadow of convention forms the subject of Franz Grillparzer's novella *Der arme Spielmann.* The protagonist (a fiddler who plays at the *Brigittenkirchtag*) fails because he is unable to master the tasks that life sets him. This extremely private, retiring person remains unfulfilled in love because the spirited and capable Barbara, though she loves him in return, cannot believe that he could ever bring himself to make decisions and face up to the challenges of life. She, for her part, cannot bring herself to enter a lifelong partnership with an incompetent. Essentially the author portrays his street musician as a victim of class arrogance and faulty upbringing, which are the causes of the fear of life that prevents him from finding fulfillment. A moderately gifted young man who only wanted to learn a trade, he has been repudiated by his own father, who had placed great hopes in him. The fiddler loses his self-confidence, and in order to be able to hold his own in a world that seems to reject him, he builds himself a private world, a world that belongs to him alone, objectively of little significance but subjectively totally fulfilling. At the end of his life he does in fact accomplish something for society by saving lives in a flood disaster. Yet he himself falls ill as a result and dies. It is a matter of conjecture to what extent, in this novella, Grillparzer was seeking to portray himself as a victim of convention and faulty upbringing. As a man of his time he certainly did not ignore the experiences of his own life in shaping his characters.

Biedermeier man appears to have been a sufferer rather than a fighter; that is the keynote, so to speak, to which he is tuned. He is invariably directed toward balance and compromise, the compromise that must be found between the ideal and the actual. He never even attempts to fight for the realization of the ideal. In the foreground there is always the feeling of self-restraint, the belief that a man must tame his passions, submit to his fate, and observe moderation in all things. This gives everything the appearance of an untouched, poetically transfigured world. The Biedermeier idyll found expression mainly in the superficial literature of the period, which was aimed primarily at achieving a wide circulation among a fairly undemanding readership. It came out clearly in the predilection on the part of publishers and the broad reading public for almanacs, pocket-sized books, newspapers.

It would be wrong, however, to think that everything that led to a good end—to the realization of moderation or to harmony with oneself—was superficial or false. When Valentin, in Ferdinand Raimund's "original fairy tale in three acts" *Der Verschwender* (1834; "The Spendthrift") sings, "Fate applies the plane and planes all even," his words express a philosophical serenity with regard to life that is achieved only gradually as the fruit of maturity. Raimund's life was particularly full of bitter discoveries, and he certainly did not arrive at such a view by any easy path. His works expressed a mentality in which such virtues as loyalty, moderation, probity, discipline, and the constant attempt to overcome evil were held up as being generally crucial for life, a mentality that could lead ultimately only to good. A dramatist writing for a large audience could not allow himself to contradict such a mentality if he wished to be understood and accepted.

This is not inconsistent with a fate to which many of Raimund's contemporaries were subject; one thinks of officebound civil servants (Grillparzer was one), with a life spent in somewhat gloomy, oppressive conditions. An area of writing that got closer to true awareness revealed a different view—probably the dominant mood among many so-called intellectuals. A passage from a Schubert song, *Der Wanderer* (1821; "The Wanderer"), with words by Georg Philipp Schmidl of Lübeck, is particularly characteristic:"I stroll in silence, a stranger to merriment/And my sighs are forever asking: where?/Forever: where?/In my mind, a whispered echo:/'Where you are not, there is happiness'."

"Good at renunciation and endurance." That verdict is not only typical of the Biedermeier period, but to a certain extent can also be applied to the Viennese character generally, which experienced its true formation during the period. This had its disadvantages: people's readiness to make decisions declined. Typically, they adopted the attitude of adjusting themselves to existing situations and avoiding a clear "yes" or "no."

Finally, there was an increasingly evident readiness on the part of certain sections of the population to practice what the German language picturesquely calls *die innere Emigration*—"internal emigration," or passive resistance of one kind or another. The prevailing system, known as the "Metternich system," was accepted as a given, especially since the middle classes in particular shared the government's desire for a continuing state of political calm (for the bourgeois, too, had long had a horror of domestic unrest and upheaval). His liking was for cozy privacy, and his ambition was to retain his modest but comfortable affluence and forgo all demands of a liberal nature. Problems, he felt, were best put off; they would crop up in any case one day, but that could wait.

Trade and Industry in the Pre-March Period

The Biedermeier years saw the continuation of a development that had begun in the latter part of the eighteenth century: the changeover from craft to industrial production. The problems posed by the introduction of machinery had long been in evidence elsewhere. In the first half of the nineteenth century they became increasingly apparent in Vienna, too. It was typical of the reserved mentality of the city, with its distrust of everything new, that attempts were made at first to halt the inexorable march of progress. When the first plans for industrial settlements were launched in Vienna at the end of the eighteenth century, they failed to come to fruition because of a ban imposed by the highest authority—the emperor himself. It was feared that industry would bring into the capital the dangerous popular masses that were a familiar image of horror from the days of the French Revolution. The testimony of Count Johann P. Anton Pergen, the minister charged by the emperor with keeping the effects and manifestations of the French Revolution away from Austria, was decisive here: he warned against the "mob"—which he equated with the industrial proletariat—because he feared it as the source of social upheaval.[16]

83   Carl Kunz, after Johann Nepomuk Geiger: *The Baker,* 1838. Chalk lithograph, colored, 49.7 × 41.1 cm. Historisches Museum der Stadt Wien.
A waiter carrying a basket fetches pastries for an inn, while the baker's wife distributes bread to the poor. The drawings round the edge depict the attributes of the baker's trade.

84   F.Kühn, after Carl Joseph Geiger: *The Butcher, Meat Smoker, and Tripe Boiler,* 1839. Chalk lithograph, colored, 39.8 × 51.5 cm. Historisches Museum der Stadt Wien.
One of a series of prints depicting Men and their Trades, this picture shows people shopping at the butcher's, which was something even fashionable ladies could do. In the drawings round the edge are emblems of the related trades of meat smoking and tripe boiling.

89

The development of industrial manufacturing in Vienna may have been delayed, but it could not be put off for ever. Most of the early industrial plants were in the Viennese basin; subsequently plants were erected nearer and nearer to the city, though this tendency did not really get under way until after 1850. For a long time the old methods of manufacture lingered on, merely being practiced on larger premises, but gradually the changeover to industrial production was effected as manufacturers installed machinery and laid off redundant labor.

This process can be examined in the light of a particular example. Great fame, not least because of the wealth they managed to accumulate over the years, was acquired by the silk manufacturers of Schottenfeld—known as the "diamond ground" (*Brilliantengrund*), precisely because of the huge earnings of the silk mills. It was partly thanks to government encouragement that the silk weavers had come to Vienna to set up shop in the first place. A further decisive factor had been that silk was a luxury product requiring, on the one hand, a skilled work force, which was more likely to be found in the vicinity of the capital and, on the other hand, a particular sort of market that Vienna provided. In 1816, a Viennese industrialist by the name of Christian Georg Hornbostel had the idea of adapting the mechanical loom already employed in Britain's cotton industry and using it to weave silk fabrics. He was the first industrialist in Europe to succeed in weaving silk on mechanical looms.

Hornbostel's achievement was an early example of the switch from manufacturing to industrial production, and of the possibility of three workers doing what had previously required sixteen.[17] One could of course cite many more examples. From the late 1830s onward, more and

86 Franz Xaver Sandmann: *Workroom No. II in the Apollo Room,* ca. 1845. Lithograph, 19.1 × 24.4 cm. Historisches Museum der Stadt Wien.
The *Apollosaal,* once the scene of unforgettable carnival balls, was eventually turned into a candle factory. One of the things this print shows is the number of women involved in the production process.

more iron foundries and engineering works were set up in Vienna, so that they soon accounted for half the national total. A great many workers were employed in the cotton industry, which also increasingly installed machinery and laid off labor, the printing section of the industry being particularly badly affected in this respect. Growing unemployment led to more pauperization among large sections of the population. It was obvious that the workers were going to become rebellious and launch a *Maschinensturm*—an "on-slaught on the machines."[18] As indeed they did in 1848.

However, this latter development notwithstanding, it is not incorrect to speak of a Biedermeier mentality, though only if it is borne in mind that the period under discussion covers some forty years: life, it must be remembered, does not stand still, but is subject to an ongoing process of change.

Robert Waissenberger

NOTES

1 A.A. Schmidl, *Wien wie es ist*, Vienna, 1840, p. 20.

2 Heinrich Ritter von Srbik, *Metternich—Der Staatsmann und der Mensch*, Vol. 1, Munich, 1925, p. 446.

3 Friedrich Walter, *Wien: Die Geschichte einer deutschen Grossstadt an der Grenze*, Vol. 3, Vienna, 1943, p. 89.

4 *Wien wie es ist* (trans. from the French by Eduard Forstmann), n.p., 1827, p. 23.

5 *Ibid.*, pp. 97 f.

6 Peter Feldbauer; Hannes Stekl, "Wiens Armenwesen im Vormärz," in: *Wien im Vormärz*, Vienna, 1980, p. 191 [publ. by Verein für Geschichte der Stadt Wien].

7 Renate Banik-Schweizer; Wolfgang Pircher, "Zur Wohnsituation der Massen im Wien des Vormärz," in: *Wien im Vormärz*, Vienna, 1980, pp. 133 ff.

8 Schmidt (see above, note 1), p. 22.

9 [Adalbert Stifter], *Wien und die Wiener: in Bildern aus dem Leben*, Vienna, 1844, p. 81.

10 Forstmann (see above, note 4), pp. 120 f.

11 Reingard Witzmann, "Fasching in Wien," in: *Fasching in Wien—Der Wiener Walzer 1750– 1850* (catalog of the 58th special exhibition of the Historisches Museum der Stadt Wien, December 14, 1978 to February 25, 1979), p. 6.

12 Walter (see above, note 3), p. 78.

13 Josef Schreyvogel, "Samuel Brink's letzte Liebesgeschichte," reprinted in: Eduard Castle (ed.), *Österreich erzählt in der Grillparzer- und Stifterzeit*, Vienna, n.d., pp. 33 f.

14 *Johann Pezzls Beschreibung von Wien*, n.p., 1841, pp. 507 ff.

15 Franz Grillparzer, *Selbstbiographie*, in: Moritz Necker (ed.), *Grillparzers Sämtliche Werke*, Vol. 12, Leipzig, n.d., p. 105.

16 Wolfgang Häusler, "Von der Manufaktur zum Maschinensturm, Industrielle Dynamik und soziale Wandel im Raum von Wien," in: *Wien im Vormärz*, Vienna, 1980, p. 49.

17 Josef Ehmer, *Familienstruktur und Arbeitsorganisation im frühindustriellen Wien*, Vienna, 1980, p. 66.

18 Häusler (see above, note 16), pp. 32 ff.

IV   FROM ECSTASY TO DREAM:
SOCIAL DANCING IN THE BIEDERMEIER ERA

Dancing on a Volcano

"Drafty and poisonous is Vienna, so the saying goes, and there is many a weak chest cannot bear frequent exposure to the dust of its siliciferous soil. Inflammations of the lungs are no rarity here, though they are not particularly dangerous; but of the ten to eleven thousand people who die here each year, usually a quarter go to the grave with diseases of the chest, for which immoderate indulgence in waltzing is partly to blame."[1] Obviously nonplussed by the dance-crazy Viennese, J. Gerning wrote these lines in his diary on a visit to the city in 1802. Such remarks can be duplicated *ad infinitum,* and numerous contemporaries—many years before the advent of Joseph Lanner and Johann Strauss the Elder—saw the consequences of over-energetic waltzing as implicit in the death statistics. Clearly not all such remarks are to be taken at face value, yet they do reveal the peculiar enthusiasm—not to say manic obsession —with which the waltz was executed in Vienna.

Certain "outbursts" of social dancing raise questions for the psychologist and the sociologist. Extreme physical exertion extending to total exhaustion offers among other things access to a certain trance state. The early waltz involved a difficult, hopping step and called for fluent, skillful movements on the part of the dancers. Endless repetition of the same turn gave rise to a feeling that the body was acquiring an existence of its own: a process invariably associated with a certain degree of self-abandonment. Danc-

ing the waltz never failed to produce an effect of intoxication that allowed a couple to forget their everyday cares, while putting the grayness and limitations of their lives behind them.

This dancing ecstasy in Vienna coincided—albeit with some variations— with a period of social change and upheaval. The Viennese waltz dominated the whole of the nineteenth century, but the creative phase, in which the Viennese waltz received its characteristic choreographical and musical form as a social dance, fell between the European revolutions of the eighteenth and nineteenth centuries. The background of working conditions, everyday behavior, custom, and usage was not by any means static during this period. In parallel with socio-economic developments, social dancing too went through particular configurations.

Vienna, for example, embraced the headlong Langaus dance, a particularly wild forerunner of the classical waltz. With the choreography of this animated early waltz, the departing eighteenth century proclaimed the equality—in the ballroom—of all dancers. The crowd on the dance floor was caught up in one enormous game, for dancing may certainly be regarded as a form of social play. During the dance, class distinctions, otherwise so much a part of life, became blurred.

Historically speaking, during this period the waltz replaced the stilted, courtly minuet as the fashionable dance. Composers humored the public taste with new pieces, though these were not known as waltzes at first, but were entitled "German dance" or simply "allemande." The three "greats" of classical music—Haydn, Mozart, and Beethoven—wrote many so-called German dances as commissioned works. The "allemande" of Vienna's classical period, usually orchestral, evolved almost imperceptibly into the waltz form. The term "waltz," referring to a piece of music, came into use gradually. Joseph Lanner's dances became waltzes only with Opus 7; before that they were called German dances or *Ländler*.[2] Lanner was also the first to give the formal structure of the waltz its definitive musical character.

The study of the musical evolution of the Viennese waltz is a still-unfinished chapter in musical history. Choreographically speaking, "German dance" was a generic term for the early waltz. On the one hand, the term was meant to denote "the German manner of dancing," with all the couples forming a circle; on the other hand, "German" also meant much the same as "common, ordinary," indicating an origin among the rural, humbler strata of the population.

In his opera *Don Giovanni*, Mozart made symbolic use of the rustic German dance to indicate a social level below that of the courtly minuet in the celebrated finale of the First Act, in which the peasant girl Zerlina is seduced by Don Giovanni. The brilliant stage music allows the different beats to react against, and interact with, each other.

Although the allemande was denounced by contemporary critics and moralists as a particularly wild and socially unacceptable dance—or possibly for that very reason—it enjoyed far greater popularity than all the other social dances of the period such as the minuet, the so-called British dances (the anglaise and the ecossaise) and the various contra dances. The allemande was danced in other cities, too (Goethe gave an account of it, for example) but, as a Weimar fashion publication wrote in 1797,[3] "the Viennese waltz, on the other hand, surpasses everything in wild rapidity of movement."

The dance and ball culture peculiar to Vienna and the passion for dancing exhibited by the city's hostesses in particular supplied the basic preconditions for the emergence of the Viennese waltz—which is indeed correctly named. In the Biedermeier era, the musical development of the waltz was influenced by folk music—by the fiddlers of Linz, for example—while the great Viennese composers of the day (Johann Nepomuk Hummel, Michael Pamer, Joseph Lanner, and Johann Strauss the Elder) enormously enriched its melodic and rhythmic vocabulary. In Vienna, at the time of the Revolution of 1848, the Viennese waltz was a musically and choreographically complete work of art that, in its perfection, had found the form in which it is still executed today.

However, the dynamic tone of the waltz had undergone a change since the early days. Whereas waltz figures had involved a frenzied whirling around 1800, during the Biedermeier period the style of movement became transformed into a "gliding progress" (*Dahinschweben*). For the waltz, this was the culmination of a complex evolution. It is not only dancing styles that give us information about the past but also dance formations: whether the dance is performed in a group, in couples, or by the individual has something to tell the cultural historian. This is even more true of a period such as the Biedermeier, when words and pictures were subject to strict censorship, meaning that for the most part only a "nice," prettified, and sometimes almost sickeningly innocent account of the way things were could be handed down. But body language and the message it carried could not be censored.

The Ballroom, the New Pleasure Arena

At the origin of Vienna's "dancing mania," back in the eighteenth century, there lay a strict official ban. In the days of Empress Maria Theresa the baroque fancy-dress parades on the streets of Vienna at *Fasching*, or carnival time, had frequently been the occasion of unbridled excesses; fights and even murders, carried out behind the protective anonymity of a mask,

All through the Biedermeier period, social dancing was characterized by dynamic intensity. The originally impassioned movements of the Viennese waltz turned little by little into a gliding motion. The rather wild galop (fashionable around 1835) was simpler to perform, as well as being more spectacular than the waltz.

had virtually been the order of the day. Under threat of the severest penalties, all classes—the nobility included—were forbidden to wear masks on the street. With this ban the authorities put a stop not only to the big fancy-dress parades but to all public carnival celebrations on the streets of the capital. The intention was to safeguard the security of the city and to nip in the bud any conspiracy against the court or against leading political figures.

This marked the beginning of withdrawal from the street to the ballroom as the new arena for carnival celebrations. From now on, dancing represented to the Viennese the one major area of freedom where, in a state between hilarity and rapture, they could remove themselves from the everyday sphere into the realm of play. For the Viennese court and the nobility the festive environment was provided primarily by the magnificently appointed ballrooms of the Hofburg and the so-called Flour Pit (*Mehlgrube*) in the Neuer Markt. The rest of the population resorted to the taverns of the inner and outer suburbs, where the publican's license also covered permission for musicmaking and dancing. To meet the huge demand, many of them built dance halls, which individually evolved into major centers of attraction during the Biedermeier era, depending on whose orchestra was playing there.

Many of the dance halls still remembered today grew out of ancient inns—for example, the one at the Golden Pear (*Zur goldenen Birn*), 63 Landstrasse. It was rebuilt in 1801; the dance hall extended into the house next door and became famous as in Vienna as the *Annen-Tempel.* From 1812 to 1822, Michael Pamer led the orchestra here, drawing huge crowds. Another example was the Black Goat (*Zum schwarzen Bock*) in the Neuen Wieden, which reached its heyday in the 1820s when Joseph Lanner and Johann Strauss the Elder played there; its license dated back to January 7, 1700.

This development from simple inn or tavern to dance hall is very clearly reflected in a police ordinance of August 30, 1820: "Circumstances having changed greatly over the last forty years and the number of licensed premises having in-

Der moderne Galopp, oder Der Tanz in die Ewigkeit.

creased hugely, with the majority in the suburbs providing dance music, it no longer appears advisable to allow the music license to be regarded as a right attaching to the publican's license, because in this way dance halls, and with them opportunities for disorders and excesses to the detriment of nocturnal peace and security, will be multiplied out of all proportion."[4]

The authorities sought to control this proliferation of dance halls by introducing a "dance-hall license" that not only reformulated the holder's rights but also, among other things, regulated music, lighting, and "propriety of dress." Ball organizers now demanded fixed admission fees and engaged a band to provide the music. This enabled a lively musical scene to develop that contributed toward the supreme achievements of dance music in Vienna.

One Viennese peculiarity remains to be mentioned in this connection. The Royal Imperial Ballrooms of the Hofburg, previously accessible only to the nobility, had been thrown open to all classes by

Der Zaubermundl.
Zauberspiel von Told.
Schluß-Scene. Der Ball in Domayerschen Caffehhaus im Hietzing bey Schönbrunn.

88 Andreas Geiger, after Johann Christian Schoeller: *Depiction of a Ball on Stage,* 1832. Etching, colored; plate 22.2 × 28 cm, sheet 23.6 × 31.1 cm; extract from *Gallerie drolliger und interessanter Scenen,* published by Adolf Bäuerle, 5th year, no. 27, Historisches Museum der Stadt Wien. The earliest mention of the waltz or German dance occurs in Viennese local farces dating from the middle of the eighteenth century. The predilection for these dances in operettas and operas led initially to the hypothesis that the Viennese waltz might have been an "invention" of the theater. That theory has long since been disproved, and an interplay between stage dancing and social dancing established.

Emperor Joseph II. Anyone—without distinction of rank—could attend the Hofburg Ball: "Everyone from the highest as well as from the lowest class has the same right, and this equality will be assured by specially appointed overseers."[5]

The nobility, however, tended to dissociate itself from the mixed company that so typified the Viennese ball, meeting in premises of its own. It was chiefly for the nobility that, in 1808, on the day when Emperor Francis I married his third wife, Maria Ludovica, a dance hall on an entirely new scale was opened: the famous Apollo Room (*Apollosaal*) in the suburb of Schottenfeld.[6] This novel place of entertainment was lit by 5,000 beeswax candles. Each room had its own name and was designed and decorated in a different style. There were artificial ponds, grottoes, and waterfalls and—as a special attraction—flying eagles. The whole interior was thoroughly Romantic in style and formed a sort of pendant to the emperor's Neogothic castle in Laxenburg, just south of Vienna. The music in this "fairy palace of the diamond ground" was provided by an orchestra of sixty musicians. The heyday of the Apollo Room was between 1817 and 1830. A few years after that it was turned into a candle factory.

In the 1830s, the dance halls of the middle classes began to assume similarly extravagant dimensions and to offer their patrons access to an "enchanted realm." The best-known example was the New Elysium, established in 1840 in spacious and most luxuriously appointed underground premises in the city center.[7] Music was no longer the main attraction; the program had been extended: exhibitions, a railway, a seraglio, etc.

89 W. Schenk: *Figures of the So-Called Strassburger Dance (Allemande),* 1808. Etching, extract from *Viertes Toilettengeschenk für Damen,* Leipzig, published by Georg Voss. Historisches Museum der Stadt Wien: Fashion Collection.

It is possible to reconstruct dance forms and dance steps from old dance almanachs. The allemande was already executed with rapid steps, but its choreography also comprised distinctive arm figures. A veritable dance frenzy seized the population at carnival time (*Fasching*), war and political difficulties notwithstanding. Since it was imposssible to execute the intricate arm figures in the overcrowded dance halls, each couple began to dance individually: the Viennese waltz was born.

The largest dance hall built during the Biedermeier period was the Odeon in Leopoldstadt,[8] completed in 1845 with an alleged capacity of up to 8,000 persons. Three years later, during the October fighting in the Revolution of 1848, it was burned to the ground; it was never rebuilt. The year of its destruction gives the Odeon a certain symbolic value in the history of dancing in Vienna. The clientele of the new luxury dance halls of the later Biedermeier period no longer consisted of a mixed company drawn from all classes; no one was refused admission, but the greater part of the population of Vienna could not—or could no longer—afford such pleasures.

The changes in technology and in the organization of labor in the early decades of the nineteenth century gave rise to social upheavals of enormous consequence. A new class of industrial workers emerged, and the middle class suffered increasing impoverishment. An 1833 trade inquiry received complaints about the "abasement of merchants to mere retailers and of craftsmen to mere day laborers" and about the "undermining of the lower orders and the middle class."[9] The Biedermeier period was characterized not only by an increase in the population and by rapid industrialization but also by trends toward an increase in child labor, unemployment, and mass poverty. Between 1837 and 1841, the number of manufacturers went up by 164 percent.[10] Around 1830, certain external manifestations of these colossal changes became noticeable: the term "pauperism" made its first appearance in the literature of the period; articles of fashion began to evince a new taste for luxury. Embellishments once again began to proliferate on utensils and furniture; the wealthy woman

once again forced her body into a corset; and in the dance hall, ostentation and decoration were increasingly prized.

The Viennese waltz itself was now executed differently by the different strata of society. At parish fairs and private dances the original, more energetic, hopping style of movement remained current for many years to come. On the more fashionable dance floors, however, the smoother, gliding style had established itself.

The Choreographic Evolution of the Viennese Waltz

Many descriptions survive from the late eighteenth century to show us how physically strenuous the German dance was at that time. A travel book of 1784 paints a vivid picture: "...Nor need it be anything but a gay, innocent dance; not a dangerous, frenzied romp that fans the passions to flame as the ordinary German dance does.... To any upstanding young man it

90 Moritz von Schwind: Frontispiece for *Halts enk zsamm: Samlung original oesterreicher Ländler* ("Hold Each Other Tight: Collection of Original Austrian Ländler"), 1824. Etching, lst edition published by Sauer und Leidesdorf, Vienna. Historisches Museum der Stadt Wien.
Among the pieces of music in this collection are waltzes by Franz Schubert. Here the young illustrator Schwind showed symbolically how the rustic dance style of the couple in the middle had been adopted by urban society. A new feeling for life found expression in the newly fashionable waltz.

91 Joseph Lanner conducts the *Hans-Jörgl Polka* (Opus 194), 1842. Etching, colored, 19.8 × 12.2 cm, extract from *Hans Jörgl*, 1842, No. 9. Historisches Museum der Stadt Wien. A glovemaker's son, Lanner taught himself the violin as well as figured bass and orchestration. He joined Michael Pamer's orchestra in 1813, and in 1819 formed his own trio—two violins and guitar—with the Drahanek brothers. Johann Strauss the Elder later joined them on the viola. It was Lanner who first defined the formal structure of the waltz. His mastery of the violin made him an outstanding interpreter of his own works.

92 Joseph Schütz: *View of the Ballroom in the Hofburg during a Masked Ball,* ca. 1815. Watercolor, 30.1 × 43 cm. Historisches Museum der Stadt Wien. The Congress of Vienna brought the rulers and statesmen of many European countries, together with their retinues, to the Austrian capital. Prince de Ligne's remark on the congress's progress—*Le congrès ne marche pas, il danse*—has gone down in history. Every ball centered on the waltz, which finally supplanted the minuet.

93 Franz Wolf: *The Elysium Ballroom,* 1833. Watercolor, 30.8 × 45.5 cm. Historisches Museum der Stadt Wien. The café proprietor Daum ran his dance hall in the "Gothic taste" in the basement vaults of the Seitzerhof for only five years. In 1838 he moved to more spacious premises.

ELISIUM IN WIEN

in den unterirdischen Localitäten des Satzerhofs.

cannot be a matter of indifference in whose arms his spouse or his loved one is swaying about, if indeed he loves her. This dance arouses often inexcusable desires that people then seek the first opportunity of satisfying. In this way husbands or lovers are not infrequently waltzed out of their women's hearts."[11]

And in the same author's *Grillen- und Seufzerbuch* ("Book of Melancholy Thoughts and Sighs"), a lover who cannot "dance German" offers this humorous lament, which also contains one or two valuable choreographic clues: "When the German dancing begins, I am always an intolerable burden to my girl and one she has to shuffle off [*abwältzen* is the German pun]. All I can do is stand there and observe how another man, a brainless leaper [another pun: to the farmer, a *Springer* is a cover animal], clasps her in his arms and feasts his eyes on her bosom; how she hops and leaps about until a flush comes to her face and the veins in her neck are swollen fit to burst; how she is pushed and kicked around, and how nevertheless all these trials are preferable to her than my company. She was confessing, nay protesting, her love for me; but in mid-protest she broke off and went bounding away because some fiddler had struck up a German. Why am I denied, by nature and upbringing, the ability to leap about like a goat? What is it worth, when the German fiddling is done and she has frolicked herself into a state of exhaustion, that she then comes back and takes me, her one and only (so she says), by the arm in order to cool off, at my expense, in the refreshment room?"[12]

Taking all the Viennese accounts from the second half of the eighteenth century together, we find that the waltz as "German dance" was performed with a hopping step and initially followed a specific figure on the floor: people in those days related better than we do today to imaginary lines on the floor. For example, the minuet, projected on the floor, traced an S-shape and a Z-shape; the courante traced an oval, a rectangle, and a triangle. The circle was the characteristic spatial figure of the German dance. The dance was executed in this strict form both at

court and in the bourgeois dance hall. Karoline Pichler included in her memoirs of the 1770s a description of the German dance in what was by then the bourgeois *Redoutensaal*, where the couples danced round in "several individual circles," and there was even mention of lead dancers.[13] Soon, however, this "waltzing in a circle, often with twenty and more couples, one behind the other,"[14] who always remained "correctly on the circumference of the circle," could no longer be performed as a party game on a grand scale. The dance halls were so full that it was almost impossible in the crush to distinguish dancing couples from onlookers.

The emergence of a great many large dance halls in the early years of the nineteenth century—built to meet a need, but also for speculative reasons—led to greater and more frequent concentrations of dancing couples than ever before. There was little room—literally—in such circumstances for the execution of intricate figures, or for particular arrangements of couples on the dance floor.

The Langaus dance, a new variant of the German dance, broke up the hitherto closed formation of the dancers. Each couple now crossed the floor individually

94   Andreas Geiger, after Johann Christian Schoeller: *Johann Strauss's Grand Galop,* 1839. Etching, colored; plate 21.8 × 25.8 cm, sheet 23.6 × 29.7 cm; pictorial supplement to the *Wiener Theaterzeitung* (Viennese Scenes, No. 28). Historisches Museum der Stadt Wien.
The Viennese passion for dancing provided caricaturists and satirists with an inexhaustible fund of material. The circle was the predominant spatial form for dances at the time, with the so-called island of men in the middle.

95 Alexander von Bensa: *Ball-room of the Pear Inn in the Landstrasse,* ca. 1840. Chalk lithograph, 28.3 × 45.2 cm. Historisches Museum der Stadt Wien. The Golden Pear was one of the most popular places of refreshment in the part of the city lying outside the walls. Early in the nineteenth century, a splendid ballroom was added, which became known as the *Wiener Annentempel,* taking its name from the dances held to celebrate the name day of Vienna's "Annes" (then as now the most common girl's name in the city). The ballroom enjoyed its heyday during the Biedermeier period, when Michael Pamer, Joseph Lanner, and Johann Strauss the Elder all played here.

with large, hopping steps, walking and turning, while the others waited before following at intervals. Adolf Bäuerle recalled: "The Langaus calls for the greatest daring. This disgraceful dance sets the dancer the task of spinning with his partner in a frenzied waltz from one corner of the room to the corner directly opposite, until a lung gives out or apoplexy ensues. One tour of the room would have been quite enough! But the circle had to be described six to eight times without a pause. And there were even those who volunteered to execute the Langaus figure twelve times at a stretch."[15]

Bäuerle's "Langaus figure" was quite clearly a round of waltzes following a circular path, except that it stretched from one corner of the room to the other, and so in fact formed an oval. Karoline Pichler, on the other hand, said of the German dance that several circles were formed in the room.[16] In the Langaus, the couple "conquered" the dance floor, which broke down the old firmly established arrangement of couples; individual couples were thus given greater scope to shape their movements in freedom.

The period also saw the beginning of the development of official municipal

dancing schools. The dancing teacher was now no longer an employee of the nobility but independently provided instruction in his school to anyone who was interested. A document in the Austrian National Library records: "These schools have been known in Vienna for but a few years—here young people from parlormaids to scullery maids congregate with their suitors on Sundays and holidays and a so-called dancing master teaches them fashion, decorum, and facial expressions, the steps, the minuet, and the Langaus in just a few lessons."[17] These establishments were set up in order to teach a wider public the latest dances in the shortest possible time.

At the beginning of the nineteenth century, the Langaus dance disappeared from dance halls as a result of an official ban. However, its emphasis on the individual aspect of the dancing couple was retained; each couple continued to dance its own circles in the room without having to accommodate itself to the others, so that the entire dance floor was now at the disposal of all the dancers—and that development took place in Vienna. Count August de la Garde, writing at the time of the Congress of Vienna, reported: "The most graceful

96 *Entrance Hall of the Apollo Room,* 1808. Etching; plate 10 × 16.7 cm, sheet 10.4 × 18.1 cm. Historisches Museum der Stadt Wien.
The ostentatious character of the enormous *Apollosaal* was suggested by the very splendid entrance hall, where most of the marble pedestals were in fact ingeniously disguised stoves. Access to the ballroom and the promenades was through "three triumphal arches supported on marble columns" (*Ansichten vom Apollo-Saal* ["Views of the Apollo Room"], Vienna, 1811, p. 8).

97 Franz Wolf: *First Compartment of the New Elysium in Vienna, Depicting the Continent of Asia,* 1840. Chalk lithograph, 28.8 × 44.5 cm. Historisches Museum der Stadt Wien.
The late Biedermeier period saw an increase in the sumptuous appointments of ballrooms. Patrons were offered additional curiosities and exhibitions, and a fairytale world of fantasy came into being—a Biedermeier forerunner of today's Disneyland.

98 Balthasar Wigand: *Vienna from the Royal Imperial Brick Kiln, on the Favoriten Line,* ca. 1835. Gouache, 10.8 × 17.4 cm. Historisches Museum der Stadt Wien.
Very important in assessing the structure of the Viennese waltz is the overall figure formed by the dancers. The old figure in the Vienna region was the round, the characteristic dance of the rural population. Each person danced around an imaginary central point, unrelated to the onlookers.

Wien von dem K.K. Ziegelöfen vor der Favoriten Linie

Kininger del.   Cl. Kohl sc. Viennæ 1793.

*Einladung zu den Gesellschaftsbällen
im Konviktsaale um 6 Uhr Abends
für den 23, und 30, Jäner dann den 6, 13,
20, und 27, Hornung.*

circles form, start to move, intersect, and overtake one another."[18]

At private dances and intimate parties for family and friends, the German dance continued to be performed as a group dance. For the famous "sausage balls" *(Würstelbälle)* organized by his friend Schober, Schubert composed waltzes, but he also continued to compose German dances at a time when these had already disappeared from the public dance halls. Such private domestic functions had been customary in Vienna since the end of the eighteenth century. During the Biedermeier period private dances, held at home, increased in number. However, the reason for this retreat within one's own four walls probably had less to do with the mentality of the Viennese than with the fact that entertaining at home was easier on the pocket. It was usual for the host to charge a small admission fee to cover expenses, and guests not known to the family had to be introduced by someone who was, as a precaution against infiltration by official informers.

Members of occupational groups whose own dwellings were inadequate for such purposes used to rent premises in the suburban taverns. These "closed" events—the laundrymaids' ball, the waiters' ball, the chimneysweeps' ball, and especially the *Fiakerball* (the cabmen's ball)—became an enormously important part of social life in the second half of the nineteenth century and contributed toward the stereotyped image of what was "genuine old Vienna." In later years, when the Ringstrasse was being built, the waltz found a new vocation: it triumphed not only in the ballroom but also in the dream world of Viennese light opera.

In the space of a century, not only the outward form but also the content of the Viennese waltz had undergone a change. Toward the end of the eighteenth century, its inner animation had been tamed and molded so that it became an urban social dance. The Viennese waltz was orginally a revolutionary, impassioned dance, whose complicated choreography gave it a kind of eternal validity. The dancers, then as now, traced a double spiral like the planets of the solar system; re-

99 Anton Elfinger [pseudonym: Cajetan], *A Concert in 1846!*, 1846. Etching, colored, 29.4 × 23.1 cm (cut); pictorial supplement to the *Wiener Theaterzeitung* (Satirical Pictures, No. 58). Historisches Museum der Stadt Wien.
A caricature of Hector Berlioz, probably conducting his *Symphonie fantastique* (1830), wich was composed for a very large orchestra. From that time on, dance orchestras, too, showed a steady increase in size.

100 Clemens Kohl, after Vincenz Kininger: Invitation Card to a Ball, 1793. Etching; plate 13.8 × 9.1 cm, sheet 20.8 × 14.2 cm. Historisches Museum der Stadt Wien.
Toward the end of the eighteenth century, it began to be fashionable in middle-class circles to have artists produce one's invitations or greeting cards. The result was a flood of delightful pieces of commercial art that today serve to document the cult of friendship and love that characterized the time.

101 *Inexperienced Ball Guests,*
Etching; plate 11.5 × 15.9 cm,
sheet 13 × 20.7 cm; pictorial supplement to *Briefe eines
Eipeldauers an seinen Vetter in
Kakran,* 1814, no. 3, p. 54. Historisches Museum der Stadt
Wien.
This caricature from a famous
Viennese periodical written in
dialect illustrates a frequent occurrence in the ballroom. Caricaturists rang endless changes on a
limited number of themes: they
pilloried the passion for dancing
itself, to which people sacrificed
their health against their better
judgement; and they highlighted
the erotic element in dancing.

Weil Unfereins die gwichsten Böden nicht gwohnt ist, bin ich auf einmahl nach
aller Längs mit ihr daglegen.

102 Johann Wenzel Zinke, after
Johann Christian Schoeller: *The
Dancing Instructor as a Theatrical Role,* 1828. Etching, colored;
plate 21.6 × 27.3 cm, sheet
26 × 37 cm; extract from *Gallerie
drolliger und interessanter
Scenen,* published by Adolf
Bäuerle, 2nd year, no. 5. Historisches Museum der Stadt Wien.
The scene is from the burlesque
Der Tanzmeister Pauxel ("Dancing Master Pauxel") by
Kringsteiner, in which all dances
were parodied. The refinement
of the intricate steps of the Viennese waltz—six steps make one
whole turn—was undoubtedly
due in part to the city's dancing
instructors, who doubled as cho-
reographers for the various
theaters. It was their artistic aspirations that invested the Viennese waltz with its grace of
movement.

Tanzmeister Pauxel, oder Faschingsstreiche.
Posse von Kringsteiner.
Tanz-Scene.

Satyrisches Bild.

Die unterbrochene Lektion beim Tanzmeister.

103 Johann Wenzel Zinke, after Anton Elfinger [pseudonym: Cajetan]: *Interrupted Lesson at the Dancing Master's,* 1844. Etching, colored; plate 21.2 × 28.2 cm; sheet 24.3 × 31 cm; pictorial supplement to the *Wiener Theaterzeitung* (Satirical Pictures, no. 37). Historisches Museum der Stadt Wien.
In dance-crazy Vienna, some dancing instructors achieved fame and fortune. However, there were many less successful ones who gave cheap lessons in their own apartments.

— es war für die andern so hart dort einz'tred'n, als bei ein'n wirklich'n Picknick von nobl'n Leud'n in ein'n Hotl garni a Billed z'krieg'n —

104 *Rustic Dance at a Country Inn,* 1818. Etching; plate 12.8 × 17 cm, sheet 14.2 × 21 cm; pictorial supplement to *Briefe eines Eipeldauers an seinen Vetter in Kakran,* 1818, no. 2, p. 66. Historisches Museum der Stadt Wien.
The improvised individual dance with arm figures continued to be cultivated in rural areas. It was from dances like this in country inns that the Laundrymaids' Ball and the Cabmen's Ball later evolved to become fixtures in the city's social calendar.

volving continuously about its own axis, the couple moved round the room in a large circle at the same time.

As the eighteenth century gave way to the nineteenth, the waltz as a social dance, instead of representing a flight from reality, represented a therapeutically beneficial reevaluation and reorganization of reality. It was stimulating and provided fresh strength for the development of a new spirituality. The stylization of the turning movement neutralized its explosive force. The old feudal order of society and its attendant equilibrium were being dissolved, and a new order prepared; dance provided the link.

This feeling of a fresh departure could not be sustained for long, however; the newly emergent forces failed to establish themselves. In the Biedermeier period, the political system associated with the name of Metternich cemented the old order back in place with no regard for social and economic changes. The lively, hopping movements of the Viennese waltz became transformed during the Biedermeier years into a gliding, floating movement that called for stronger rhythmic impulses from the music. The magical sounds of Joseph Lanner and Johann Strauss the Elder lent wing to the dancing public and carried it away in a delirium of bliss. It was the beginning of Vienna's *Walzertraum*—the "waltz dream" of the later nineteenth century.

Reingard Witzmann

105 J. Albrecht: *"Fasching" Pleasure in Vienna,* 1854. Lithograph, 52 × 34 cm, pictorial supplement to the *Wiener Theaterzeitung* (Satirical Pictures, no. 40). Historisches Museum der Stadt Wien.
This print caricatures the various terpsichorean possibilities available to the Viennese at carnival (*Fasching*) time in descending order of social eminence: Redoute (the Hofburg Ballroom), Sofienbad Room, Domeyer Casino, Elysium, barracks ball, and house party.

NOTES

1 J. Gerning, *Reise durch Österreich und Italien*, Part 1, Frankfurt a. M., 1802, p. 30.

2 See Reingard Witzmann, *Der Ländler in Wien: Ein Beitrag zur Entwicklungsgeschichte des Wiener Walzers bis in die Zeit des Wiener Kongresses*, Vienna, 1976; idem., "Fasching in Wien," in: *Fasching in Wien—Der Wiener Walzer 1750 bis 1850*, (cat. of the 58th Special Exhibition of the Historisches Museum der Stadt Wien), December 14, 1978 to February 25, 1979.

3 *Journal des Luxus und der Moden*, Weimar, 1797, p. 290.

4 Quoted in Witzmann, *Der Ländler in Wien* (see above, note 2), p. 104 [decree of Aug. 30, 1820].

5 Christian Löper, *Kommerzialschema der Kaiserl.-königlichen Residenzstadt Wien*, Vienna, 1780.

6 Now Schottenfeldgasse 15, Vienna 7, though the building itself burned down on January 27, 1876.

7 Now Johannesgasse 4, Vienna 1.

8 Now Odeongasse 2a–10, Vienna 2.

9 Heinrich Reschauer, *Geschichte des Kampfes der Handwerkzünfte und der Kaufmannsgremien mit der österreichischen Bürokratie: Vom Ende des 17. Jahrhunderts bis zum Jahre 1860*, Vienna, 1882, p. 108. See also Wolfgang Häusler, *Von der Massenarmut zur Arbeiterbewegung*, Vienna–Munich, 1979; and *Die Ära Metternich* (cat. of the 90th Special Exhibition of the Historisches Museum der Stadt Wien), Vienna, 1984.

10 Ernst Viktor Zenker, *Die Wiener Revolution 1848 in ihren sozialen Voraussetzungen und Beziehungen*, Vienna-Pest-Leipzig, 1897, p. 52.

11 Arnold (pseudonym of Johann Rautenstrauch), *Schwachheiten der Wiener: Aus dem Manuskript eines Reisenden*, Vienna, Leipzig, 1784, p. 39.

12 Johann Rautenstrauch, *Grillen- und Seufzerbuch*, Vienna, 1784, p. 40.

13 Christoph Friedrich Nicolai, *Beschreibung einer Reise durch Deutschland und die Schweiz im Jahre 1781*, Vol. 3, Berlin and Stettin, 1783–96, p. 56.

14 Karoline Pichler, *Zeitbilder aus Wien 1770–1780*, reprinted in Deutsche Hausbücherei, Nos. 112–15, Vienna, 1924, p. 88.

15 Josef Bindtner, *Alt-Wiener Kulturbilder aus Adolf Bäuerle's Memoiren*, Vienna, 1926, p. 57.

16 Pichler (see above, note 14).

17 "Sammlung über Geschichte und Rechtswissenschaft," Austrian National Library: manuscript collection, cod. 13.920.

18 August de la Garde, *Gemälde des Wiener Kongresses* (Memoiren Bibliothek), Series V, Vol. 4 (ed. by Friedrich Freska), Stuttgart, n.d, p. 36.

V THE DEVELOPMENT OF TASTE IN HOME DECORATION

"Govern, and alter nothing...." This principle uttered by Emperor Francis I,[1] so oppressive in its effects on any kind of progressive spirit in the Pre-March period, counted for nothing in the fields of industry, manufacturing, and the crafts. The subsidization and promotion of crafts and industrial production, begun by Empress Maria Theresa and Emperor Joseph II in the latter part of the eighteenth century and—following a confused interruption—resumed by the state at the end of the Napoleonic Wars, led to remarkably high standards of quality and released undreamt of creative forces. The mercantilist policy of the late eighteenth century had begun to bear fruit. A brief survey of the field in which this flowering of arts and crafts can be seen at a glance—home decoration—will illustrate this development.

The Family

Emperor Francis again: "Preserve unity in the family and regard it as one of the highest goods."[2] If the emperor's reference to the family was to some extent dictated by dynastic considerations, it also echoed the spirit of the age, for the family and everything the Romantic mind associated and continues to associate with it in the way of security, happiness, contentment, while not inventions of that age (the development had also been anticipated in the second half of the eighteenth century), nevertheless reached their culmination in what we now refer to as the Biedermeier era.[3]

A well-run household, it was thought, was the framework within which it was possible to produce so positive a moral effect upon a person—by the exercise of the bourgeois virtues of thrift, diligence, and orderliness—that he would develop sufficient resources to be equipped for the struggle for existence.[4] The effect of this attitude was nowhere so clear as in the furnishing of the domestic environment. A wealth of interior scenes, not only by well-known artists, but also—and in far greater numbers—by amateurs, bear witness both to the degree of involvement with which the people of the period fashioned their personal surroundings and to their desire to document it. Surviving gouaches enable us to obtain a very vivid impression of what people's homes looked like. Paintings, knickknacks, souvenirs, and gifts were lovingly collected and ostentatiously displayed in glass cabinets or on shelves. Colorful fabrics and cosy pieces of furniture were so casually arranged as to constitute almost a visual cliché of domestic comfort.

The Interior

When and where did this discovery—seemingly so sudden—of "living for living's sake" originate? During the periods of Rococo and Classicism, a gradual subdivision of living areas took place. There was a move away from the all-purpose room. Living, cooking, eating, and sleeping were each relegated to separate rooms. Among the upper classes, this development corresponded to the distinction now drawn between reception rooms and living quarters.[5]

The Austrian imperial family provides a perfect example of this movement away from a public style of living toward a more private one. In Empress Maria Theresa's lifetime, they began to furnish small "cabinets" sumptuously but at the same time in a comfortable, homely fashion; these were rooms in which the imperial family, far from their official duties, could relax and be at their ease. This separation of public and private spheres was taken to its logical conclusion under Emperor Francis I. Another typical example is the Fries-Pallavicini Palace on the Josefsplatz in Vienna (designed by Ferdinand von Hohenberg, 1783–84), where the living quarters were located in the lower mezzanines, for the sake of intimacy, while the bel étage (literally the "beautiful story") was reserved for the staterooms. For contemporaries such a division was nothing short of an architectural sensation.

Types of Room

Drawing a distinction between the various spheres of domestic activity inevitably led to the invention of individual types of room: dining room, music room, billiards room, library, study, writing room, bedroom, reception room, drawing room or boudoir, salon, and so on.[6] In middle-class homes, where separate rooms were usually not available in such profusion, the idea of having different types of room was retained in the so-called Wohninsel, or "living island." This made it possible to perform a number of activities in one room—writing, sewing, musicmaking—each characterized by different furniture, and quite deliberately separated from the others.

At the same time as these developments in interior design and in contrast (or perhaps as a complement) to them, people began to discover nature. The veduta ("landscape view") like the interior, enjoyed a remarkable artistic flowering. Garden furniture and arbors turned the small domestic garden into an extension of the family's living space; conversely, set pieces from nature were introduced into interiors. Accordingly screens made of trellised plants, jardinieres, innumerable birdcages, and samples of genuine nature competed in living rooms with depictions of nature—and in particular of flowers—so much in evidence in textile patterns, in paintings, and on pieces of porcelain.

The gradual evolution of domesticity and the growing number of rooms with their own special significance meant that appropriate pieces of furniture also needed to be provided. Craftsmen, it would appear, were alive to this situation and supplied the requisite furniture in accordance with demand and produced further inventions as demand developed. For example, the catalog of the firm of Danhauser offered, in addition to pipe racks, nightstands, and furniture made from antlers, a portfolio of table designs with a choice of the following variants:

64 sofa tables
42 tea tables
28 tables for flowers
22 extending and drop-leaf tables
15 washstands
35 pier tables
 6 backgammon tables
38 desks.[7]

It has been said, in connection with the architecture of the period, that "with the gradual disappearance of a numerically restricted, homogeneous commissioning class, as architectural design began to have a broader effect, the element of the unique and unmistakable also disappeared."[8] That element of uniqueness that architecture henceforth seemed to lack, that element of creative imagination, was perpetuated in interior design.

At the bourgeois price level it was possible to chose individual furnishings—from a catalog, but the choice was enormous—entirely in accordance with personal criteria of taste. What were the actual criteria that characterized a typical piece of Biedermeier furniture? Were they the features that J.A. Lux praised in 1904–5 in an article in Hohe Warte as con-

106 Anonymous: My Room in Vienna 1837–42. Gouache on paper, 20 × 35.4 cm. Historisches Museum der Stadt Wien.
A simple room, with the different functional spheres defined by the furniture: writing, grooming, needlework, seating.

107 F. Barbarini, Drawing Room, Vienna, 1839. Watercolor, 26.8 × 42.2 cm. Historisches Museum der Stadt Wien.
Various flowered patterns even invaded the male province, the study.

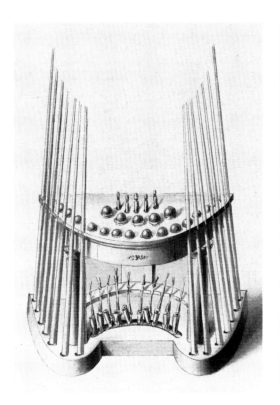

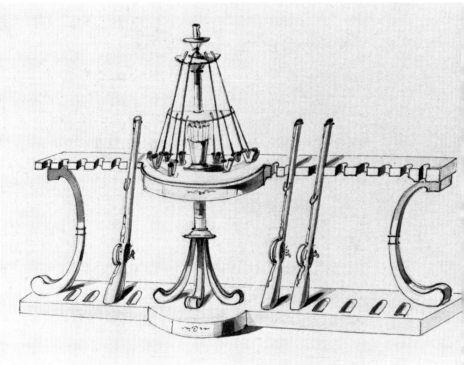

stituting the quintessence of the ideal chair?

"Biedermeier as Educator"

"The height of the seat is the first factor. It is the height that determines the depth of the seat. Crossbars between the legs are superfluous and unpractical. Inevitably people will draw their feet under the chair, in which case crossbars, particularly between the front legs, will be a great impediment. Anyone with officers at home must pay especial heed to this because spurs can easily collide with crossbars. The backs of dining-room chairs should be as low as possible in order not to impede serving. If the top of the chair back is at shoulder level, it is best straight. Then, when a person leans back, his shoulder blades will be pressed in, leaving his chest free. A chair whose back forms a curve around the shoulder blades will produce shortness of breath. If the chair back stops at the level of the small of the back or anywhere below the shoulder blades, it is best given a curve. This type is unfortunately much neglected and yet is among the healthiest and most comfortable. In the case of easy chairs with a sloping back, much trying out is called for. One's easy chair ought to be made to measure, like a jacket. The most comfortable easy chairs have an adjustable back. With easy chairs, too, great importance must be attached to ease of breathing. In the case of upholstered chairs, care should be taken that the upholstery does not force the head forward while permitting the back to sink in; the slightest discomfort in this respect will, in the course of time, cause pain."[9]

As the article's title indicates, this analysis of the function of a piece of furniture concentrated on the educational role the Biedermeier era had to play in the development of good design and good taste. It is true that all these considerations can be reconstructed in terms of Biedermeier furniture. But we gain a somewhat onesided view of the products of the period if—as is understandable in

108   Combined Billiard-Cue-and-Pipe Rack, a design from the Danhauser furniture factory, Vienna, 1815–20. Pen and wash, 21.6 × 26.7 cm. Österreichisches Museum für angewandte Kunst, Vienna.

109   Combined Rifle-and-Pipe Rack, a design from the Danhauser furniture factory, Vienna, 1815–20. Pen and wash, 21.8 × 26.9 cm. Österreichisches Museum für angewandte Kunst, Vienna.

110   Secretary, Vienna, ca. 1810–15. Fruitwood and maple, stained black; poker work, fire-gilt bronze, H. 149.8 cm, W. 91.5 cm, D. 50.6 cm. Historisches Museum der Stadt Wien.

111 Writing Case, ca. 1825.
Mother-of-pearl over wood, steel
fittings, leather, silk lining,
33.5 × 22.3 cm, H. 4.7 cm. Four
gouaches by Balthaser Wigand
under glass, ca. 13 × 9 cm and
ca. 5 × 21 cm. Historisches Museum der Stadt Wien.

112 Figured Clock, ca. 1820.
Carved wooden case with figures
(horse and rider), gilded and
lacquered black, H. 72 cm.
Uhrenmuseum der Stadt Wien.

the enthusiasm of rediscovery—we seize on functionality as the chief criterion of quality. Too much attention is still being paid today to the classical components of the products of this period, which places too great an emphasis on a single aspect.[10] Of course, in 1815, people had a solid foundation on which to build.

Antecedents of Biedermeier

Toward the end of the eighteenth century, with Classicism setting the tone all over Europe, Vienna saw the flowering of a special local variant in the Josephine style (named after Emperor Joseph II). The furnishings that the nobility and the imperial family commissioned at this time exhibited all the typical features from which the Biedermeier style was to evolve between twenty and thirty years later. The shapes of writing desks, cupboards and clothespresses, tables, and chairs were reduced to the simplest of straight profiles; geometrically speaking, only the square and the rectangle had any popularity. The Josephine style continued to present itself as courtly, its sumptuousness now confined to inlay

work (strictly centered) and to high-quality execution.

Around the turn of the century, with the new Austrian Empire, a more playful note began to creep in. In contrast to the French Empire style, which favored heavy, Classical ostentation, Viennese furniture worked itself up into a euphoria of curves and an increasing delicacy of construction that, in the end, gave an effect of fragility.[11] These exquisite, aristocratic objects were an inspiration to the craftsmen of the Biedermeier era: they stimulated delight in the experimental treatment of wood and gave rise, in conjunction with the more solid Josephine pieces, to a quite specific blend of styles.

Publications Disseminate Ideas and Fashions

All the impressions the age had to offer—principally from Britain and France—together with a substantial local tradition, were brought to the attention of anyone who was interested by a wealth of pattern books and magazines.

Stimulated by the many available publications in which cabinetmakers and artist craftsmen published their designs—Sheraton and Hope in Britain, Percier and Fontaine in Paris—Austrian craftsmen likewise offered their ideas on furniture design in the form of engravings. Manufacturers brought out portfolios in which everything from the simplest candlestick to a complete interior was available on demand. It was the first step toward the mail-order catalog that Michael Thonet perfected forty years later for his bentwood products (still unrivaled today). Even Hieronymus Löschenkohl, the worthy "pictorial reporter between Baroque and Biedermeier," was inspired by such magazines as *Meubles et Objets de Goût* and the *Journal des Luxus und der Moden* to publish, in 1803, a portfolio whose title began: "Patterns of the latest London, Parisian, and Viennese furniture...."[12] The emancipated bourgeoisie, not content with simply apeing the earlier aristocratic culture, grasped these opportunities with an extraordinary degree of creative enthusiasm and

113 Armchair. Cherry, solid and veneered, H. 95 cm, W. 57 cm. Hofmobiliendepot, Vienna.

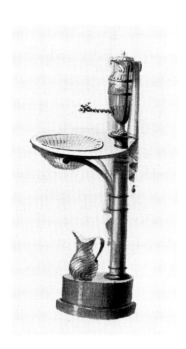

114 Washstand, a design from the Danhauser furniture factory, Vienna, 1815–20. Pen and wash, 19.4 × 23.1 cm. Österreichisches Museum für angewandte Kunst, Vienna.
Danhauser gave further proof of his inventiveness in a wide range of toilet articles.

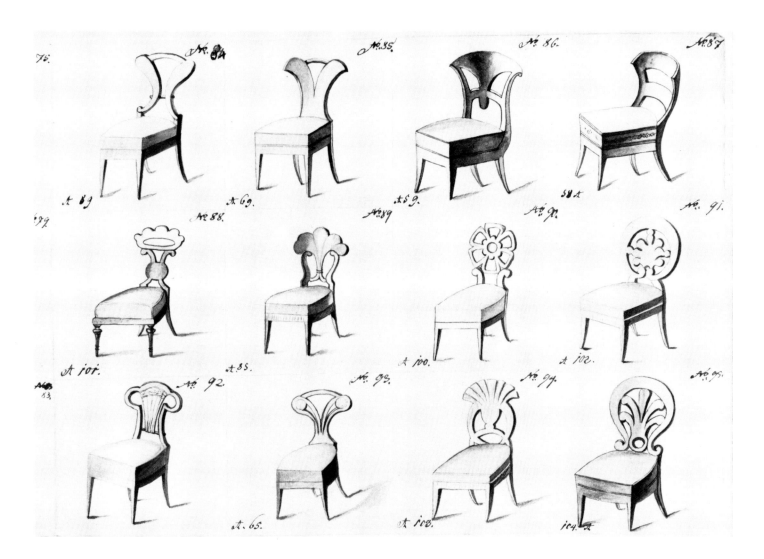

115   Chairs: designs from the Danhauser furniture factory, Vienna, 1815–20. Pen and wash, 21.5 × 27.1 cm. Österreichisches Museum für angewandte Kunst, Vienna.
A few examples of the over 150 chair designs offered in the Danhauser catalog.

began to give shape to an entirely personal style. This was the beginning of what we now refer to as interior design and decoration. The furniture alone did not account for the typical impression of the Biedermeier room; equally important were all the other furnishing items without which no interior is complete. Among the principal accessories (in the selection of which one showed one's taste and connoisseurship) were glass, porcelain, textiles, and objects of brass, bronze, and silver.

Seating Furniture

Any discussion of Biedermeier furniture is probably going to center, if not on the chest of drawers, then on seating furniture—be it in the form of chairs or settees. No previous period had produced such a wealth of different types of seating. So let us take seating as our specimen as we undertake a closer examination of the furniture of the Biedermeier era, although it might as easily have been the spittoon. (As much inventive imagination was bestowed on these small wooden objects as on every other type of furniture. The collection of the old Royal Imperial Court Furniture Depository is in the fortunate position of having a large number of these products of Biedermeier hygiene on its books.)

Functionality we have already mentioned. Was this really the prerequisite for every piece of seating design? If we look at surviving chairs, together with the designs that have fortunately been preserved in the different collections,[13] we find an astonishing wealth of variations on the basic scheme of four legs, a seat, and a back. Over the space of fifteen years, cabinetmakers worked their way up into an almost frolicsome richness of form that was without parallel until the *Jugendstil* (the German term for Art Nouveau) experiments at the end of the last century and early in this one. Yet it is a remarkable feature of all this capricious playing around that it never went so far as to deny the function of the piece of furniture entirely (though it did happen—for example, when the legs of a sofa were bent inward in an elegant curve—that the classical structural principles were called into question, not without a certain humor).

This new playfulness in form was complemented, in a way, by the advent of machine-made furniture, which was able to accomplish veritable miracles of transformation with the aid of numerous hidden features. Biedermeier craftsmen discovered to their delight that a chair could be given literally hundreds of different shapes. This in turn gave a tremendous boost to the trade of cabinetmaker. For 1827, the inland-revenue office lists show shoemakers in first place with 1,772 individuals, tailors in second place with 1,552, and cabinetmakers right up in third place with 914.[14]

The sometimes quite intricately curved backs and legs inspired Michael Thonet, who was already experimenting with curved furniture components, to invent his bentwood technique, by means of which sweeping lines and complicated curves could be manufactured more simply and at a later stage even mass-produced. The tremendous wealth of ideas and inventions inevitably led to a phase of Neoclassicism that might be termed Bourgeois Mannerism, the formal canon of Classicism being too constricting for the creative urge of the period.

The cabinetmakers were not the only craftsmen enjoying a heyday; the upholsterers were in no way their inferiors when it came to imaginative inventions in furniture and interior design. Unfortu-

nately their work can only be reconstructed from designs now. The work of the master upholsterer belongs to the ephemeral arts, and we must make do with drawings of their ideas. Pleated fabrics covered furniture, walls, ceilings, and positively rampaged in alcoves around the tester bed. For Archduke Charles, for example, the firm of Danhauser proposed a bed "for a warrior" around which draped lengths of material would be held in place by halberds and other weapons of war. How all this was managed in practice—let alone looked after and kept clean—remains something of a mystery. Studying these designs, one might well get the impression that all this represented the culmination of an anarchic desire for the completely impractical—"inscrutable Biedermeier," as one author has called it.[15]

Seen from the standpoint of "function produces form," these are subversive objects; there is no getting away from the idea that here was a kind of sublimated resistance to the regime.[16] An account by the writer and theater director Heinrich Laube, describing a dance at which Johann Strauss the Elder was playing, conveys a feeling and atmosphere that are far removed from the Biedermeier cliché of secluded domesticity:

"In the center of the garden is the orchestra, from which seductive siren sounds proceed: the new waltzes, the bane of our more erudite musicians, the new waltzes that like a tarantula's bite stir young blood into a turmoil. In the center of the garden, beside that orchestra, stands the present-day hero of Austria, Austria's Napoleon: the musical director Johann Strauss. What Napoleon's victories were to the French, Strauss's waltzes are to the Viennese.

"This man wields alarming power. He may count himself particularly fortunate that in music all thoughts are possible, that censorship does not concern itself with waltzes, and that music speaks directly to the emotions. I don't know what he can do apart from making music, but I do know that the man could cause a great deal of mischief if he fiddled ideas like Rousseau's.

116–21 Endless Variations on the Chair: never was there so much variety in seating furniture as in the Biedermeier period.

116 Three chairs (from left to right): cherry, solid and veneered, H. 89 cm, W. 42 cm; walnut, H. 92 cm, W. 46 cm; cherry, veneered, H. 91 cm, W. 47 cm. Hofmobiliendepot, Vienna.

117 Three chairs (from left to right): mahogany, veneered, H. 75 cm, Diam. 39 cm; walnut, veneered, H. 75 cm, W. 40 cm; cherry, veneered, H. 72 cm, Diam. 46 cm. Hofmobiliendepot, Vienna.

118 Three chairs (from left to right): walnut, veneered, H. 92 cm, W. 45 cm; mahogany, veneered, H. 94 cm, W. 48 cm; walnut, veneered, H. 88 cm, W. 48 cm. Hofmobiliendepot, Vienna.

119 Three chairs (from left to right): cherry, solid and veneered, H. 90 cm, W. 47 cm; ash, solid, H. 90 cm, W. 46 cm; walnut, veneered, H. 93 cm, W. 49 cm. Hofmobiliendepot, Vienna.

120 Three chairs (from left to right): walnut, veneered, H. 90 cm, W. 48 cm; walnut, veneered, H. 91 cm, W. 47 cm; birch, veneered, H. 93 cm, W. 46 cm. Hofmobiliendepot, Vienna.

121 Dressing-table chair and armchair (left): beech, stained, H. 75 cm, Diam. 60 cm, (right): walnut, solid and veneered, H. 93 cm, W. 61 cm. Hofmobiliendepot, Vienna.

119

"The Viennese would go right through the *contrat social* with him in an evening.

"It is a remarkable fact that Austrian sensuality never looks nasty. The Austrian Eve is naive and no sinner. Lust in Austria is sin before the Fall. The Tree of Knowledge has not yet made any definition necessary, any guile."[17]

But it was not only in the above-mentioned instances that Biedermeier showed an extrovert side; its choice of colors and patterns similarly evinced a liking for the most lurid contrasts that exposes what is today (with an appalling lack of imagination) offered as "Biedermeier stripe with flowers" for what it is—namely a sour imitation of mistaken pseudo-Historicist ideas.

If we look closely at the interiors painted by the artists of the period and, above all, if we study the fabrics in the Factory-Products Cabinet,[18] we discover such a variety of designs in terms of both pattern and color that there can be no question whatever of a "Biedermeier pattern." At the very most, certain types of scattered-flower designs might be described as typical. Furniture slipcovers with garish tones and edges in contrasting complementary colors made the suite the center of attention; behind it was flowered wallpaper and beneath it a machine-woven carpet in a loud check. Cashmere shawls were draped over the sofa, and curtains sought to contribute their own tones to the joyful motley.

Shopping im Biedermeier Vienna

Vienna was a popular subject in the travel literature of the period, and it is interest-

122–25 The same delight in imaginative variations on a theme went into the design and execution of spittoons.

122 Three spittoons (from left to right): cherry, veneered, H. 34 cm, Diam. 27 cm; maple, veneered, H. 42 cm, Diam. 29 cm; mahogany, veneered, H. 40 cm, Diam. 27 cm. Hofmobiliendepot, Vienna.

123 Four spittoons (from left to right): beech, veneered, H. 42 cm, Diam. 26 cm; walnut, veneered, H. 35 cm, Diam. 29 cm; walnut, veneered, H. 38 cm, W. 29 cm, D. 22 cm; walnut, veneered, H. 31 cm, Diam. 23 cm. Hofmobiliendepot, Vienna.

124 Three spittoons (from left to right): mahogany, veneered, H. 33 cm, Diam. 29 cm; cherry, veneered, H. 43 cm, Diam. 27 cm; cherry, veneered, H. 24 cm, Diam. 26 cm. Hofmobiliendepot, Vienna.

125 Three spittoons (from left to right): cherry, veneered, H. 35 cm, Diam. 27 cm; mahogany, veneered, H. 32 cm, W. 31 cm, Diam. 22 cm; walnut, veneered, H. 39 cm, Diam. 20 cm. Hofmobiliendepot, Vienna.

ing to see what foreign visitors found worthy of remark. In addition to stressing the varied social life of the city, they drew attention to the exquisite products that could be purchased as souvenirs of a visit there. The following quotations from a guidebook published in 1829 demonstrate how much importance was attached to arts and crafts.[19] Under the heading Public Collections, the author recommends the following institutions, among others:

"The National Factory-Products Cabinet at the Royal Imperial Polytechnical Institute is in Wieden, just outside the city, at no 28: the collection accepts only masterpieces that, in their execution, represent the perfection of a particular branch of manufacture. Such contributions already exceed 18,000 in number. Associated with the factory products is a collection of standard tools, comprising more than 3,000 items."[20] The Factory-Products Cabinet had been founded by Emperor Francis I in 1807 in the spirit of mercantilism. Its purpose was to provide an exemplary collection of outstanding

products, open to the public at all times. The state was able to exercise a substantial degree of stylistic influence—over the factories in its possession—and it did so in a responsible manner.

The Royal Imperial Porcelain Factory, for example, was among the finest of its kind, and a Biedermeier dwelling without its complement of painted picture-plates (known as "Viennese plates"), as well as vases, perfume pots, chocolate cups, and biscuit figures from the workshops of the factory would have been almost inconceivable:

"The Royal Imperial Porcelain Factory, just outside the city in Rossau, at no. 137, was founded in 1718 as a private business. Since 1744, however, it has been owned by the Treasury. The factory employs about 500 workers, distributed between manufacturing, fashioning the clay, illustrating, and painting. It has produced some artistic masterpieces. The porcelain made by this factory is celebrated for its long life, its strength, its whiteness and beauty of form, its painting and gilding; it also enjoys a considerable market, partic-

126 Design for a machine-made piece of furniture from a portfolio of drawings by cabinet-makers and masters. Ink and wash, 61.2 × 39.8 cm. Historisches Museum der Stadt Wien. A secretary, the chief function of which was that it could be transformed. Such pieces were often produced as masterworks by cabinetmakers and were extremely popular.

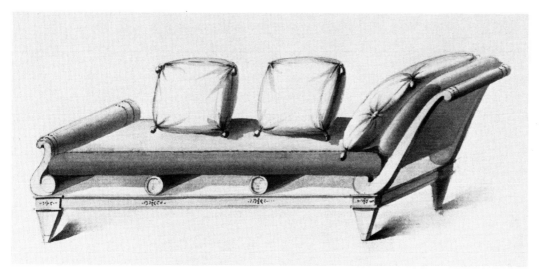

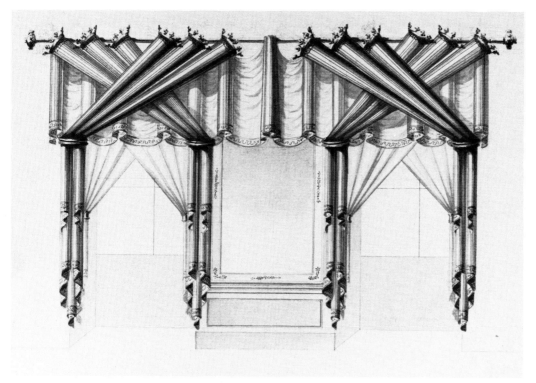

127 Design from the Danhauser furniture factory, Vienna, 1815–20. Pen and wash, 21.7 × 27.1 cm. Österreichisches Museum für angewandte Kunst, Vienna.
Pure function was not decisive in the design of such pieces.

128 Design from the Danhauser furniture factory, Vienna, 1815–20. Pen and wash, 22.1 × 26.7 cm. Österreichisches Museum für angewandte Kunst, Vienna.
One looks in vain for such intricate drapery in present-day furniture designs.

129 Design from the Danhauser furniture factory, Vienna, 1815–20. Pen and wash, 21.9 × 26.5 cm. Österreichisches Museum für angewandte Kunst, Vienna.
Guns and antlers form the framework of this settee commissioned by a Hungarian hunter.

130 Johann Stephan Decker: *Dressing Cabinet of Her Majesty Empress Caroline Augusta in the Hofburg, Vienna.* Watercolor and body color on paper, 16 × 31.5 cm. Historisches Museum der Stadt Wien.
The white muslin drapery provides an especial contrast to the colorful floor covering from the Linz carpet factory.

131 Design from the Danhauser furniture factory, Vienna, 1815–20. Pen and wash, 22.8 × 27.5 cm. Österreichisches Museum für angewandte Kunst, Vienna.
When it came to appointing the bedroom of Archduke Charles in the Albertina Palace, this splendidly martial bed was created for the victor of the Battle of Aspern, the man who had shattered Napoleon's aura of invincibility.

132 Fire Screen. Cherry and pear, dyed black, veneered, H. 140 cm, W. 95 cm, D. 57 cm. Hofmobiliendepot, Vienna.
Preserved in the covering of this screen is an original piece of contemporary wallpaper.

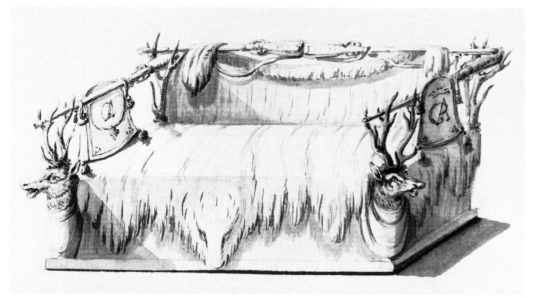

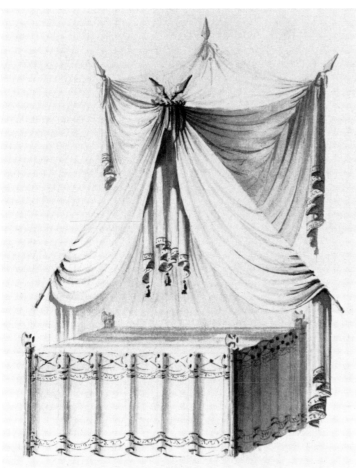

133 Sofa. Cherry, solid and ve-
neered, H. 87 cm, W. 144 cm, D.
62 cm. Hofmobiliendepot,
Vienna.
A modern fabric design (Eva
Riedl, Vienna) attempts to re-
create the colorful impact of the
Biedermeier original.

134 Design from the Dan-
hauser furniture factory, Vienna,
1815–20. Body color on paper,
22.5 × 26.9 cm. Österreichisches
Museum für angewandte Kunst,
Vienna.
Danhauser made this sofa
(Weilburg-Baden) for Archduchess Sophie, the mother of
Emperor Francis Joseph, in an
attempt to reproduce the kind of
imperial gold-mounted furniture
that was completely outmoded
in the Biedermeier period.

135 Settee. Walnut, veneered;
H. 92 cm, W. 157 cm, D. 64 cm.
Hofmobiliendepot, Vienna.
In addition to flowers, a popular
variant for furnishing fabrics was
cotton printed in cashmere patterns.

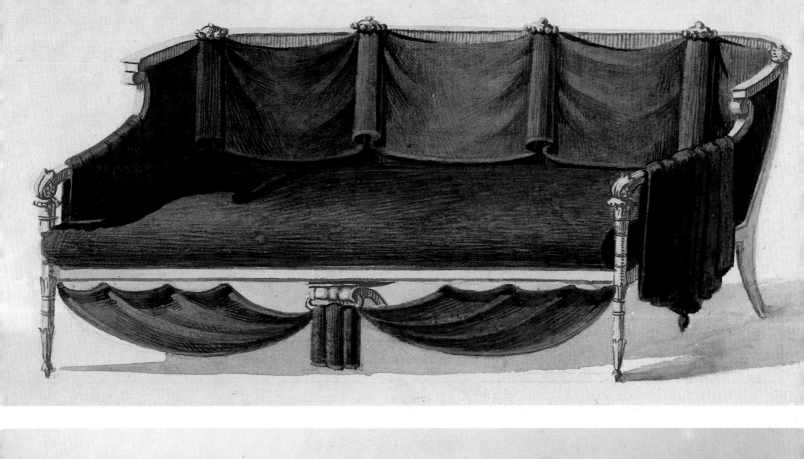

136 Three Chocolate Cups,
Vienna porcelain factory, ca.
1825. H. 7.5 cm, Diam 9 cm.
Ehemalige Hoftafel- und Silberkammer, Vienna.
The Classicist shape of these
cups was very common. Cups
were often decorated with the
same motifs as picture plates:
landscapes, genre scenes, or
copies of famous paintings.

137 Coffee Cup with Saucer, Vienna porcelain factory, 1816. Gold rims, rosettes, strawberries, foliage by Johann Wollein, Diam. 8 and 15 cm respectively. Historisches Museum der Stadt Wien.

138 Anton Kothgasser: *Ranftbecher* (a type of goblet), Vienna, ca. 1840. Clear glass, painted in bright colors and gilded, H. 12.5 cm, Diam. 9.8 cm. Historisches Museum der Stadt Wien.

139–42 The Viennese silversmiths of the Biedermeier period achieved an almost unsurpassable classical simplicity—a heritage that the Wiener Werkstätte ("Viennese Workshop") were able to take up around 1900 as if no time had intervened.

139 Josef Kern: Terrine with Lid, Vienna, ca. 1828. Silver, Diam. 16 cm. Privately owned.

ularly in the Levant, in Poland, and in Russia."[21]

In addition to porcelain, showcases also displayed painted and cut glass. The glass manufacturers of Bohemia and Silesia supplied the whole of Europe with their products. Here too there was a notable wealth of experimentation and invention in terms of cut, color, and chemical composition, so that most original creations were produced. The best-known glass manufacturers in Vienna were Gottlob Samuel Mohn and Anton Kothgasser; their *Ranftgläser* (a type of goblet that became smaller toward the base, which protruded and was often ribbed) and "friendship tumblers" were, artistically, among the most exquisite of collector's items.[22]

The silversmiths of old Vienna—the firm of St. Mayerhofer, for example—likewise produced perfectly proportioned boxes and other silverware of captivating delicacy and musicality of line. And if handmade oriental carpets were too expensive, the moderately priced alternative that, ideally, every Biedermeier interior had to have was produced by the Royal Imperial Linz Woolen Fabrics and Carpet Factory—also a state monopoly since 1754.[23] The factory's machine-made carpets, which came in various patterns (either geometrical or using scattered flowers, but all highly colorful) could be purchased by the meter and laid from wall to wall. That is one of the reasons why so few examples have survived.

"[There is] a huge selection of carpets at the sales depot of the Royal Imperial Linz Woolen Fabrics [and Carpet] Factory in the old Meat Market [Fleischmarkt], Laurence Building [Laurenzergebäude], no. 708. The following information about this establishment may be of interest to the tourist: The Royal Imperial Linz Woolen Fabrics Factory owes its foundation as well as the extension of its oriental department to a citizen of Linz named Christian Sind. The former event took place in 1672, the latter in 1722.

140 Franz Frissek: Two Coffeepots, Vienna, ca. 1818. Silver, H. 11.6 and 10 cm. Privately owned.

141 Carl Doerffer: Sauceboat, Vienna, 1821. Silver, L. 14 cm. Privately owned.

"In 1774 it was taken over by the state and became a government monopoly, as it still is today. At its busiest time (between 1780 and 1790), its yearly output was between seventy and eighty thousand items; and it was employing nearly thirty thousand people, if we include the spinners in Bohemia."[24]

It would appear that the value of products that are the pride of our museums and private collections today was fully appreciated at the time. In 1829, the attention of the visitor to Vienna was drawn to firms that are still famous names today, for example:

"*Bronze ware.* Premises of Johann Danninger in the city, on the corner of the Herrengasse, at no. 25.

"*Pianoforte.* At Conrad Graf, Vienna by Moonlight, beside the Carlskirche, at no. 102, and at Stein and Nannette Streicher, in the Landstrasse district, at Ungergasse no. 371.

"*Mathematical, optical, and physics instruments.* At Voigtländer, in Gumpendorf.

"*Porcelain ware.* Exceptionally fine paintings on cups and plates, vases, flower pieces, figurines, etc., at the Royal Imperial Porcelain Depot, Josephsplatz no. 1155.

"*Shawls.* It is well known that beautiful, fine-quality shawls are manufactured in Vienna, and that large quantities of these luxury items are dispatched annually to the Frankfurt and Leipzig trade fairs. Visitors to the city will find a large selection of moderately priced articles at Joseph Arthaber, Stephansplatz, on the corner of Goldschmiedgasse."[25]

The products of Vienna's arts-and-crafts industry exerted an influence on fashion and style far beyond the bounds of the Austro-Hungarian Empire in the years that followed the great "summit meeting" of 1815—"those months during which virtually everyone who, rightly or wrongly, for good or ill, possessed a European reputation did indeed gather in Vienna...."[26]

As a result of these external circumstances and of the policy of Prince Metternich, Vienna attained the status of a European metropolis. The quality of the city's handicrafts was clearly recognized by the visiting dignitaries: Duke Ernest I of Saxe-Coburg-Saalfeld, for example, "purchased in Vienna—as did other participants in the congress—numerous luxury articles and established contacts with artists and craftsmen who henceforth worked for the Coburg court."[27]

142 Franz Köll, Coffee Maker, Vienna, 1818. Silver, H. 20 cm. Privately owned.

143 Lady's Writing Table.
Walnut, veneered; H. 99 cm,
W. 111 cm, D. 61 cm.
Hofmobiliendepot, Vienna.
The use of double columns on
the ends of the table may be re-
garded as a Viennese speciality.

144 Music Stand. Walnut,
inlaid, H. 100 cm, W. 50 cm,
D. 50 cm. Hofmobiliendepot,
Vienna.
Domestic musicmaking, inten-
sively cultivated during the
Biedermeier period, had its own
practical multiple-purpose furniture.

131

The Change to Historicism

From the 1830s onward, furniture designers in particular resorted more and more to Gothic, Empire, and even Baroque elements. Shapes hardened and quite suddenly showed a tendency toward deliberate copying of styles. In the mid-1840s, palaces (Fries-Pallavicini, for instance) were refurnished in the Rococo style.

Where bygone styles had previously been quoted in a spirit of romanticism, academic, archeological reasons were now given for why this or that shape, whether Gothic, Renaissance, or Baroque, was taken as a pattern for a particular environment. In trying to "make a statement," immediacy went by the board. The young Emperor Francis Joseph had his apartments in the Hofburg reappointed for him by his mother, Archduchess Sophie, in pure Baroque in 1850.[28] There was a political significance in this return to the old imperial style. A further important factor, however, was each generation's natural rejection of its predecessor: in 1872, for example, we find nothing but negative comments about the period before 1820: "Polish, too, appears to have come into use in Austria around the same time, and even this

circumstance had an adverse effect, playing its part in the lapse of taste; people wanted nothing but huge surfaces that they could polish, and anything that broke them up was avoided. In the period around 1816–17, the effects of the pauperization of the middle class became apparent in this sphere as well: both the artistic and the technical aspects of furniture manufacture sank to their lowest level."[29]

It was not until the Jugendstil period, around the turn of the century, that a rehabilitation of Biedermeier began, when the generation of great Viennese architects—with Adolf Loos and Josef Hoffmann in agreement for once—saw Biedermeier as worthy of acceptance into the round of stylistic renaissances.[30]

The Court-Furniture Depository

The whole development of furniture from the second half of the eighteenth century until the end of Historicism, as outlined here, can be traced without a break in the collections of the former Royal Imperial Court-Furniture Depository.

Not only did Emperor Francis I have numerous Treasury-owned factories under his orders, he also made use of them. Indeed he demanded in decree after decree that recourse be had to the various state enterprises when furnishing apartments. Accommodating all the high-ranking delegations to the Congress of Vienna in a manner befitting their station involved hiring, and then purchasing, vast quantities of furniture from the Viennese manufacturers, principally the firms of Danhauser and Joseph Herbst. These bulk purchases mean that a comprehensive survey of the furniture of the period—from spittoons to giraffe pianos—is available to us today. Nor must we forget the complementary picture provided by the former Court Tableware and Silver Chamber, where a great quantity of porcelain with botanical designs, picture plates, and dining services from the Royal Imperial Porcelain Factory pro-

145 Wastepaper Basket. Walnut, veneered, with maple inlays; H. 68 cm, W. 64 cm, D. 40 cm. Hofmobiliendepot, Vienna.
A piece of furniture with a message: books as a rubbish container.

146 Sewing Table, Vienna porcelain factory. Maple, stained black; porcelain top, H. 81 cm, W. 67 cm, D. 49 cm. Hofmobiliendepot, Vienna.
No Biedermeier home was without its little sewing table. This example, from the imperial household, still owes much to the Empire style.

147 Stand. Cherry, H. 126 cm, W. 68 cm, D. 52 cm. Hofmobiliendepot, Vienna. Such stands and shelves served mainly to display souvenirs, miniatures, and knickknacks.

148 Flower Plate, Vienna porcelain factory, 1821. Porcelain, painted, Diam. 24.5 cm. Ehemalige Hoftafel- und Silberkammer, Vienna. The plate was decorated by the flower painter Johann Garo. Emperor Francis, one of whose interests was botany, ordered several hundred such plates.

149 Picture Plate, Vienna porcelain factory. Porcelain, painted, Diam. 24.5 cm. Ehemalige Hoftafel- und Silberkammer, Vienna. The picture is a copy by Ferdinand von Perger (1778–1841) of one of his own paintings. Perger was also a porcelain painter. It was the policy of the Vienna factory to employ well-known contemporary artists.

150 Picture Plate, Vienna porcelain factory. Porcelain, painted, Diam. 24.5 cm. Ehemalige Hoftafel- und Silberkammer, Vienna. This painting of *Iris Hovering in a Stormy Landscape* was done by Johann Ferstler (active at the Hofburg 1797–1820)

151 Picture Plate, Vienna porcelain factory. Porcelain, painted, Diam. 24.5 cm. Ehemalige Hoftafel- und Silberkammer, Vienna. The picture here is a copy by Klaudius Herr of Heinrich Füger's *Death of Dido*. Herr worked at the Vienna factory from 1791 to 1831.

vide an insight into the emperor's activites as a collector. A true child of his time, Francis I shared his people's addiction to *Blumistik* (*Blume* = flower) besides being a skilled gardener and a recognized botanist.

The pieces in these collections are no different from what would have been found in ordinary middle-class households; they were not more "imperial" or more sumptuous simply because they were purchased by the imperial family. For reasons of simple finance Emperor Francis could not afford any exaggerated ostentation. In all matters relating to furnishings he invariably asked for the most economical version.

As a result, the old court collections offer us an unusually complete view of a period that undoubtedly has more to offer the present day than is implied by its traditional image of cozy, petty-bourgeois domesticity. If that is all we see in Biedermeier—in other words, what the originally disparaging use of the term was intended to suggest—we are overlooking the fact that this was a period of outward disintegration, which led to a withdrawal into the domestic sphere and necessitated a coming to terms with one's environment. New values were revealed, as a result, and served to enrich life. This ideal possessed sufficient force to tie the objects of everyday use—both great and small—into an overall design amounting to a bourgeois synthesis of the arts.

The hope that beautiful surroundings would release positive moral forces proved illusory, yet the principal elements of Biedermeier style continue to mold our ideas of "graceful living" to this day. To our mind, the extension of the possibilites of translating colorful fantasies into reality and the way in which technical demands were met without the loss of innocence implicit in industrial mass-production constitute the enduring value, as well as the charm, of the Biedermeier period.

Peter Parenzan

NOTES

1 *Politisches Vermächtnis des Kaiser Franz I. für seinen Sohn und Thronfolger Ferdinand I.*("Political Legacy of Emperor Francis I for His Son and Heir to the Throne, Ferdinand I"), quoted in Karl Weiss, *Rückblicke auf die Gemeindeverwaltung der Stadt Wien in den Jahren 1838–48,* n.p., pp. 14 ff.

2 Weiss (see above, note 1), p. 15.

3 See Eva Schulze, "Trautes Heim—Glück allein: Über die Domestizierung der Frau im Biedermeier," in: Beiträge 4, Munich, 1980, pp. 63 ff; Phillippe Ariès, *Geschichte der Kindheit,* 4th ed., Frankfurt, 1977.

4 The fact that the reality looked rather different is beside the point; primarily it is a case of a certain portrayal of ideals becoming a driving force.

5 See Schulze (see above, note 3), and R. Goebl, "Innenraumgestaltung," in: *Klassizismus in Wien* (56th special exhibition at the Historisches Museum der Stadt Wien), June 15–October 1, 1978.

6 See Goebl (see above, note 5), and Schulze (see above, note 3), p. 64.

7 Between 1804 and 1838, Danhauser was one of the largest furniture manufacturers in Vienna. The firm left a voluminous collection of designs, now housed in the Museum für angewandte Kunst.

8 Goebl (see above, note 5), p. 41.

152 Josef Nigg: Amphora Vase with Sumptuous Flower Painting, Vienna, 1817. Porcelain, H. 60 cm. Historisches Museum der Stadt Wien.
Josef Nigg studied at the Vienna Academy under the flower painter Johann Baptist Drechsler and worked at the Vienna porcelain factory from 1800 to 1848.

9   J.A. Lux, "Biedermeier als Erzieher," quoted in: *Moderne Vergangenheit 1800–1900* (exh. cat.), Vienna, 1981, pp. 90 ff.

10   See *Moderne Vergangenheit* (see above, note 9). The exhibition compared Viennese Jugendstil articles with a selection of particularly classical pieces of furniture from the early nineteenth century.

11   F. Windisch-Graetz, "Der rätselhafte Meister P. Holl und die Wiener Kleinmöbel des frühen 19. Jahrhundert," in: *Alte und moderne Kunst,* nos. 160/161, 1978, p. 29.

12   H. Löschenkohl, *Muster der neuesten Londoner, Pariser und Wiener Meubles für Liebhaber des Geschmacks und der Bequemlichkeit, dann zum Gebrauch für Galanterie, Handelsleute, Silber und Pronce-Arbeiter, Tischler, Tapezierer, Vergolder, Uhrmacher, etc. bey Löschenkohl in Wien 1803,* Historisches Museum der Stadt Wien, inv. no. 111, 119/1–5. See also Reingard Witzmann, *H. Löschenkohl: Bildreporter zwischen Barock und Biedermeier,* Vienna, 1978.

13   Museum für angewandte Kunst, Vienna, and the Historisches Museum der Stadt Wien.

14   Wilhelm Hebenstreit, *Der Fremde in Wien und der Wiener in der Heimath: Vollständiges Auskunftsbuch für den Reisenden nach Wien etc.,* Vienna, 1829, pp. 81ff.

15   H. Pollitzer, *Grillparzer oder das abgründige Biedermeier,* Vienna, 1972.

16   Compare, in this context, the idea put forward recently by Thomas Pluch: "In the Biedermeier period—this is my assumption regarding the nature of this city—Vienna experienced its puberty. Puberty is the heyday of the unspoken, of feelings in a ferment, of whims and fancies, sweet pain, bitter disappointments, gnawing repressions, decisive complexes. If life were a map and one could enter puberty as a tract of land on it, that tract would lie in the depths of the backwoods, where the most expansive ideas have the least scope for action, where the greatest gulf exists between intention and execution, and where the finest hopes come to nothing." (Thomas Pluch, "Gibt es eine Wien-Formel?," in: *Wiener Zeitung,* May 18, 1985).

17   Heinrich Laube, "Sperl in floribus," in: *Reise durch das Biedermeier,* Hamburg, 1965, pp. 247 ff.

18   In the possession of the Museum für angewandte Kunst, Vienna.

19   Hebenstreit (see above, note 14).

20   "The institute also has a notable collection of furniture, a physics cabinet, a mathematical cabinet, a mechanical and mathematical workshop with all the auxiliary machines, an instructive collection for merchandise knowledge, and one of chemical preparations and products. Open every Saturday from April 1 to the end of October, 8 a.m. to 1 p.m." The objects, fabrics, wallpapers, and so forth form part of the inventory of the Museum für angewandte Kunst.

21   Hebenstreit (see above, note 14) further mentions examples of early industrial manufacturing methods: "Under the management of its current director, the crisis that has come upon the institute as a result of emulation by the Bohemian stoneware and porcelain factories should pass without ill effects. Of particular interest are the new arrangements inside the factory, notably the construction of the so-called Berlin kiln; the use of a 4 horsepower steam engine for crushing saggars and grinding fluorspar; and heating the finishing room on the ground floor and the painting department on the first floor by means of pipes, with the steam from the steam engine being used to provide the heat."

22   Hebenstreit (see above, note 14) directs would-be purchasers to some addresses: "Glassware: at the shop of Joseph Rohrwek, no. 571 in the Graben (particularly fine), the Görner Brothers in the Bürgerspital, no. 1099 in the city, the warehouse in the Kohlmarkt and Michaeler Hause, and Jos. Lobmayer, at the corner of Weihburggasse in Kärntnerstrasse. Fine painting and exquisite gilding on glasses is supplied by Anton Kothgasser at Währingergasse no. 275 in the suburb of Alser."

23   See Dora Heinz, *Linzer Teppiche,* Vienna, 1955.

24   Hebenstreit (see above, note 14).

25   *Ibid.*

26   Egon Friedell, *Kulturgeschichte der Neuzeit,* unabridged ed. in 1 vol., Munich, 1965, p. 975.

27   L. Seelig, "Wiener Biedermeier in Coburg," in *Alte und moderne Kunst,* nos. 178/179, 1981. Seelig's article shows in detail, with the aid of letters, invoices, and illustrations, how palaces in Koblenz came to be comprehensively furnished by Viennese firms, principally that of Josef Danhauser.

28   M. Zweig, *Zweites Rokoko,* Vienna, 1924.

29   W.F. Exner, *Beiträge zur Geschichte der Gewerbe und Erfindungen Österreichs,* 1872, p. 399; quoted in: Christian Witt-Dörring, "Schein und Sein—Form und Funktion: 1800 Das moderne Möbel 1900," in: *Moderne Vergangenheit* (see above, note 9), p. 22.

30   Both Jugendstil and the 1920s borrowed ideas that can often in fact be termed copies. It is the same today: compare the modern Italian bed design by Massimo Monozzi in: *Casa Vogue,* no. 163, 1985, p. 288, with the Danhauser drawing that happens to be reproduced on p. 188 of the same magazine.

VI ARCHITECTURE FROM 1815 TO 1848

A man is seated at a table with drawing implements before him. The furniture is Biedermeier. Musical instruments, a painting of a woman standing in a charming landscape, a cage bird, and a dog point to the man's love of music and nature; classical sculptures testify to his interest in art. The rather quaint-looking "Biedermeier" gentleman who painted this portrait of himself in 1831 was Joseph Ziegler, a middle-class architect who ran an architectural school in the suburb of Breitenfeld, submitted work to Academy exhibitions, and left a large number of architectural designs. What these were like can be seen from the self-portrait, in which they adorn the walls: they belong to Neoclassicism.

In its naive way, the painting is almost a symbol of the conceptual difficulties presented by any approach to the architecture of this period. In other spheres—for instance music, literature, furniture, or arts and crafts—the term "Biedermeier" can more readily be applied; in architecture, the problem of classification is a much more complicated one. The continuing debate about "Classicism and Historicism—epochs or attitudes?" to borrow the title of one contribution to it, in other words, about definitively choosing the terminology for the overall stylistic trends, gives an indication of the fundamental problems inherent in the architecture of the time.[1]

On top of that, the way in which "Biedermeier" has been equated with a middle-class mentality raises the question of whether the bourgeoisie evolved from within itself the specific aesthetic stance that we encounter in the architecture of the Pre-March period. In fact, the crucial impulses were prepared by an earlier age and at a higher social level. The impetus for turning Vienna into a "bourgeois" society came from above. Emperor Joseph II eschewed the residences—the Hofburg and Schönbrunn—to live in a simple *Stöckl*, or outbuilding. When a banker friend of his, Count Johann Fries, had a palace built in the Josephsplatz opposite the Hofburg in 1783–84, it was of "bourgeois" simplicity. Emperor Francis I provided a living example for his subjects of the retreat to simple ideals such as family life. These new ideals and values had certain consequences as far as the development of architecture in Vienna was concerned. In the light of a number of important examples, let us take a closer look at the way in which this branch of the arts evolved between 1815 and 1848.

Academy and Court Board of Architects

"For the cultivation, extension, and refinement of industrial diligence, the bourgeois arts, and trade—Francis the First." That was the message that the emperor had inscribed on the facade of the Polytechnical Institute, a building that was planned to meet and master the tasks of the dawning age of technology. In this way the state gave notice that it was once again attending to responsibilities that had been neglected during the Napoleonic Wars and the years of economic cri-

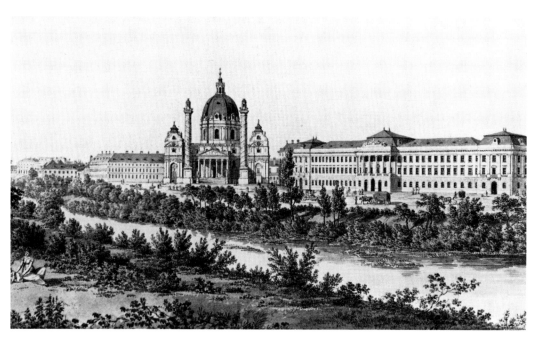

sis, specifically the training of efficient civil servants capable of supporting the internal structure of the monarchy technically, administratively, and also in terms of an appropriate deployment of artistic resources.

The Polytechnical Institute was built in the years 1816–18 from plans drawn up by the Court Board of Architects (*Hofbaurat*),[2] an institution that had been set up in 1809 to exercise state control over architectural development. Artistically the building revealed the objectives of the *Hofbaurat*. Its internal structure observed a strict economy of space; significantly, the assembly hall intended for public functions was not completed until 1842. Externally there is a clear articulation of the body of the building, matched by the animated lines of the roof. The model was Fischer von Erlach's Court Library (*Hofbibliothek*), a building belonging to Late Baroque (Early Classicism) and a product of official imperial architecture at a time when Austria had been a great power. The Polytechnical Institute, which signaled the sense of a new departure in the immediate aftermath of the Congress of Vienna, was designed by the Court Board of Architects with reference to the vernacular architecture of the eighteenth century. Its significance was

further underlined by its highly visible situation beside the Karlskirche and facing toward the glacis.

It soon transpired, however, that Emperor Francis I was of a mind to give more "modern" expression to the consolidation of his authority, particularly as far as buildings in the immediate vicinity of the Hofburg were concerned. It was a question of eradicating the memory of an act of enemy aggression: in 1809, Napoleon had blown up the *Burgbastei* (the section of the bastion beneath the Hofburg), and thus breached the old belt of fortifications around the city. In the atmosphere of reaction that followed the Congress of Vienna, it was decided to close up the wall once more and insert a new gate. (There were compensations, however: the line of the bastions was moved out, leaving room for the outer Burgplatz, the Emperor's Garden [now the Burggarten], and the People's Garden [Volksgarten] to be laid out in accordance with the plans of the court architect, Ludwig von Remy.)

Closing up the bastions and having soldiers build the Burgtor ("Castle Gate")—it was inaugurated in 1824 on the eleventh anniversary of the Battle of the Nations near Leipzig—was militarily irrelevant, but the emperor used these constructions to demonstrate a new and

strengthened national self-assurance. The fact that the Burgtor was a political monument, in the creation of which the emperor was directly involved, lends a special significance to the formal vocabulary employed. The Neoclassicism presented here in severe formal terms was a European phenomenon. It was common in the countries that had fought alongside Austria, allied against Napoleon. The strict rules of Neoclassicism made it an ideal instrument for the preservation of conservative political principles.

The man who was best at translating the emperor's ideas into architecture was Peter von Nobile. A curator of the Academy since 1811, he had been appointed the new professor of the architectural school by Metternich in 1818, at the express wish of the emperor.[3] Next to the Court Board of Architects, the Academy was the supreme artistic authority that dictated the official line in architecture. Until the Revolution of 1848, Metternich and Nobile saw to it that all ideas classed as revolutionary (Historicism) were suppressed as far as possible. Neoclassicism, with its strict formal rules and majestic motifs, remained the official artistic style until that date.

The Burgtor was not the only prestige construction designed to help cope with the historical problem of Napoleon; the Temple of Theseus in the Volksgarten (completed in 1823) likewise possessed a symbolic character—both in itself and in the piece of sculpture it housed. The group entitled *Theseus Fighting the Minotaur* (originally commissioned from Antonio Canova by Napoleon and later acquired by Emperor Francis I, who brought it to Vienna) was a monument with a double meaning, a twofold emblem of victory over hostile forces. Again built by soldiers, Nobile's creation was in fact a copy based on the Theseion in Athens. Imitation of a temple of the Doric order, the oldest and most rigorous of the Greek styles, required that the architect subordinate himself totally to his model; no scope was left for personal creative activity. With this temple, the Classicist style in Vienna achieved a purity of form, around 1820, that could not be improved upon. In the sphere of official architec-

ture, any kind of individualism was suppressed in favor of the portrayal of political ideas. In a modified form this principle continued to characterize official architecture until the Revolution of 1848.

However, the Burgtor and the Temple of Theseus were the only examples of patriotic monuments that were actually built. Two other architectural commissions that might have handed down similar ideas had to be abandoned for financial reasons: the plans for Schönbrunn drawn up by Nobile at the emperor's request in 1818, and Ludwig von Remy's proposals in 1815 for building an extension to the Hofburg, which was still an architectural torso.

A college was built, however—the Royal Imperial Institute of Veterinary Medicine. Its absolutely plain formal language made this complex a typical representative of "civil-service architecture" *(Beamtenarchitektur)*. Its strict compliance with the purely functional in the use of space and the design of the façade has always been interpreted as an expression of governmental economy and a consequence of the restrictive political system of the Metternich era. Both factors undoubtedly played an important role. However, in view of the great variety of stylistic possibilities then in use for representative purposes, the charge of lack of originality leveled against the Biedermeier era in the *Gründerzeit* (the years of rapid industrial expansion in the early 1870s) proved a somewhat superficial one. This kind of sticking to essentials, namely to function, in architecture might also be construed as expressing a modern way of thinking that had its roots in the architecture of the reign of Emperor Joseph II. One pointer in that direction is the interest in the architectural solutions of this period shown by, among others, Josef Hoffmann and Adolf Loos around 1900—at a time, in other words, when the emotional factor represented by rejection of the political conditions of the Pre-March years had lost its force.

One architect whose style was particularly influential from about 1820 was Karl von Moreau. Trained in Paris and familiar with Revolutionary Classicism, he had al-

Gurk' ad nat. del. et sc.

157 Johann Nepomuk Höchle: *Outer Castle Gate (Burgtor),* built by Peter von Nobile in 1815–24, inner side facing the parade ground in front of the Hofburg, ca. 1825. Pen and gray wash, 42.7 × 70.1 cm. Historisches Museum der Stadt Wien. After a competition to find a new design for the Outer Castle Gate, Emperor Francis I chose the project tendered by the Milan architect Luigi Cagnola, who started work in 1821. Disagreements ensued, however, and the emperor transferred the job to Nobile, whom he had appointed professor at the Academy in 1818; Nobile executed his own competition design.

Tempel d. Theseus (VIENNE) Temple d. Thésée
im Volksgarten au jardin public
Vienne *chy* Artaria et Compag.

158 *Temple of Theseus in the People's Garden,* temple built by Peter von Nobile in 1819–23, 1825. Copperplate engraving; plate 17 × 23.4 cm, sheet 24 × 32.5 cm. Published by Artaria. Historisches Museum der Stadt Wien.
A realignment of the bastion produced the People's Garden (*Volksgarten*), which became a favorite Viennese rendezvous. Nobile gave it two buildings: a café and this temple of Theseus. A scaled-down copy of the Doric original in Athens, it housed the famous marble group by Antonio Canova, *Theseus Fighting the Minotaur,* which Emperor Francis I had acquired in Rome in 1819. The purchase had a symbolic character, the group having originally been commissioned by Napoleon (it is now in the Kunsthistorisches Museum, Vienna).

144

ready been active in Vienna for some time before he built the new National Bank in the Herrengasse in 1819–21. The facade composed of flat elements and the round-arch motif, so typical of Von Moreau's work, were widely copied in subsequent years. Where round arches appeared, particularly on residential buildings, people tended to refer to them as "Biedermeier." Von Moreau's work did in fact provide an important starting point for the architect Josef Kornhäusel. But while Von Moreau built primarily for the nobility, putting forward exemplary solutions in the context of palace architecture, Kornhäusel expanded his clientele to include those members of the bourgeoisie who began increasingly to commission building work in the years after the Congress of Vienna.

Josef Kornhäusel

Literature relating to Viennese architecture in the Pre-March period associates the term "Biedermeier" primarily with the name of Josef Kornhäusel.[4] Kornhäusel is the Biedermeier architect *par excellence.*

By the time he became fully active in Vienna around 1820, Kornhäusel already had a wealth of experience as a practicing architect behind him. After completing his training at the Vienna Academy, he had worked for six years as Prince Liechtenstein's director of architecture, finding, in the prince's Bohemian possessions in particular, a varied field of activity. Leaving the prince's service in 1818, Kornhäusel applied for the job of head of the architectural school at the Academy— the job that was given to Nobile, as we have seen. Nevertheless, from the beginning of the 1820s his artistic powers were fully engaged in Vienna.

Two important commissions in which Kornhäusel was called upon to tackle traditional architectural problems came from a member of the imperial family who became a passionate builder only as a result of a change in his circumstances. This was Archduke Charles, who had both won and lost battles against Napoleon (at Aspern and Wagram respectively) in 1809. Compelled to abandon his military career, the archduke withdrew into the complete retirement of a "bourgeois" private life. Among the architects available in Vienna at that time, the archduke did not choose a representative of "official" architecture—probably quite deliberately—but opted for Kornhäusel, who turned out to be a thoroughly congenial interpreter of his patron's wishes.

In the case of the Albertina, the palace on the "bastion of the Augustinians" (*Augustinerbastei*) that Charles had inherited from Duke Albert of Saxe-Teschen,[5] the architect had to adapt the internal structure to the archduke's personal requirements, which amounted to achieving as harmonious a balance as possible between private comfort and public representation. The mandate for the Weilburg was the same except that, as a new building, it required Kornhäusel to come up with a complete spatial concept.

The very choice of setting—a picturesque location at the foot of a medieval ruin (the Raueneck) near the fashionable health resort of Baden, 25 kilometers to the south of Vienna—was symptomatic of the spirit of the age, a spirit that yearned to be close to nature, feeling a Romantic commitment to, and involvement in, it. What came into being with the Weilburg was a synthesis: a mansion (*Schloss*) using Classicist forms, yet based on bourgeois ideals of an ingeniously (and hence functionally) organized plan that met the desire for a comfortable residence. The elevated social position of the owner was thus played down in favor of bourgeois ideals.

A similar approach governed the alterations to the archduke's palace in the city. The private living quarters were deliberately separated from the rooms that were used for official functions. The suite of rooms communicating between the entrance and the banqueting hall was given a monumental character with the aid of majestic architectural and sculptural motifs. For these, Kornhäusel drew on the current formal vocabulary of Neoclassicism but gave it a more personal, more individual interpretation. The way in which the private ideals of patron and architect

affected the particular solution adopted here could be interpreted as a specifically Biedermeier force. However, the changes that now came over royal palace architecture—with mere representation taking second place to the desire for comfort—were not new to Vienna; as we have seen, they were first put into effect in the Fries Palace in 1783–84.

Almost in parallel to the work he was doing for Archduke Charles, Kornhäusel received a further representative commission: to build a synagogue for the Jewish religious community in Vienna. Here he met the requirement for monumentality by encompassing the oval interior in a colonnade and covering it with a dome. This solution struck Kornhäusel as being feasible for nonsacred interiors as well. He used very similar designs for the audi-

torium of the theater built in the suburb of Josephstadt in 1822, for the bathing room of the mineral bath at Baden in 1823, and for the library of a convent (the Schottenstift) in 1826. Freestanding columns were a feature Kornhäusel clearly preferred to use in creating interiors.

The synagogue did not constitute an independent architectural entity in the townscape. This was in accordance with one of Joseph II's decrees relating to non-Catholic sacred buildings: these were required to be concealed from the street. Therefore, the synagogue had a residential building placed in front of it, and it was to this commission that Kornhäusel applied himself with particular intensity. This is the building that established him in the mind of posterity as *the* Biedermeier architect.

159   Weilburg Mansion near Baden in Lower Austria, built by Josef Kornhäusel in 1822–23, photograph of a colored etching by Norbert Bittner, picture archives of the Österreichische Nationalbibliothek, Vienna. Kornhäusel built the Weilburg, the most important mansion (*Schloss*) of the Biedermeier era, for Archduke Charles. This summer residence beneath the Raueneck ruins achieved a successful balance between aristocratic ostentation and what was seen as an equally valid requirement—domestic intimacy. The building took its name from the archduke's wife, Henriette von Nassau-Weilburg. Contemporary descriptions of the Weilburg (now demolished) praised its 'modern technical installations, which were of great interest to the general public at the time.

The situation with regard to residential architecture in Kornhäusel's day was governed by the fact that, for centuries, Vienna had been surrounded by a belt of fortifications, which remained intact until Emperor Francis Joseph I started to remove it in 1858. This imposed strict limitations as far as expansion was concerned. The favorable political and economic circumstances of the Baroque period had seen a thoroughgoing renewal of the residential fabric of the city. Nevertheless, the Pre-March years brought a steady increase in the need for more housing. That need could be met only at the expense of the older housing, with the result that the new residential buildings contributed toward modernizing the Viennese townscape. With their rather more severe outward appearance, the residential buildings erected during this period formed a clear contrast to the older Baroque houses and the apartment houses built in

the Historicist style of the second half of the nineteenth century, which favored a more palatial design.

No part of the city underwent any systematic rebuilding at this time; it was all rather intermittent. Kornhäusel's contribution to residential architecture was very significant.[6] In the newly laid-out Seitenstettengasse near the Danube Canal, he built three large houses between 1822 and 1825. Seitenstettengasse 4 was the one in front of the synagogue. The house next door, Seitenstettengasse 2, Kornhäusel built for himself. In the rear part of the building, it included a tall, fortresslike tower containing a studio (the Kornhäuselturm); the tower remains a landmark of Vienna to this day and is largely responsible for the artist's reputation as something of an eccentric among contemporaries and posterity alike. On the other side of the street, he built a large, polygonal block for the Seitenstet-

160   Palace of Archduke Charles (the Albertina), built by Josef Kornhäusel in 1822–24: colonnade and stairs. Photograph taken from Joseph Folnesics, *Alte Innenräume österreichischer Schlösser, Paläste und Wohnhäuser,* Vol. I, plate 1, Vienna 1910–13.
In 1822 Archduke Charles inherited the palace on the "bastion of the Augustinians" together with the famous collection of graphic art that had belonged to Duke Albert of Saxe-Teschen, the son-in-law of Maria Theresa. An earlier conversion by Louis Montoyer was much altered by Kornhäusel with the object of reconciling the requirements of social display and domestic privacy.

ten Convent, the Seitenstettenhof. In 1826 Kornhäusel began building another city landmark, part of a convent, and known as the Schottenhof, between Freyung and the Schottentor. And in Rotenturmstrasse (one of the oldest and most important streets in Vienna, which was partially realigned between 1830 and 1837), Kornhäusel built a total of five residential blocks.

When Kornhäusel turned his attention to residential architecture it had already begun to acquire fresh dimensions.[7] Additional stories had increased the height of buildings, and expansion in width had brought larger facade areas and more window axes. A striking feature of Kornhäusel's apartment buildings is their emphasis on cubic shapes and volumes, and the way in which he largely forgoes breaking-up solid shapes by means of projections. Even where the site dictated an irregular ground plan he sought, in the spirit of Neoclassicism, to retain the clearest possible axial arrangement of the sequence: entrance, vestibule, staircase, courtyard. Above a ground floor enlivened with banding and an arcade, the wall of the upper part of the building remained smooth (the buildings in the Seitenstettengasse, for example). The chief optical emphasis was provided by rows of windows let into the wall without any framing. The triangular pediments or lunettes with relief decoration above them (the sculptural embellishments might also be omitted) constituted Kornhäusel's highest form of facade decoration. The upper floors had an added rectangular feature above the windows; and the topmost floors nothing at all.

All these buildings are characterized by a harmonious relationship between the individual parts, both in terms of their overall proportions and in terms of the specific balance of details. This discreet external appearance ultimately stemmed from a quite distinct attitude: Kornhäusel's (upper) middle-class patrons were giving up a degree of social display directed toward the street, since they were concentrating more on the appointment of their domicile. However, the apparently self-evident connection with modern utility architecture with its strictly functional principles did not make its first appearance during the Pre-March period. Its roots went back to the reign of Emperor Joseph II, when all branches of architecture – palace, utility, and domestic – saw a drastic reduction in the ornamentation used for facades. Probably the indigenous tradition of Baroque domestic architecture, a tradition reaching even farther back into the eighteenth century, also played an important role here.

The vocabulary of figurative and ornamental motifs, based on Classical prototypes, was already common property by Kornhäusel's day. Similar relief decoration, taken from engravings, had been used to adorn the facades of earlier buildings. These facts in no way diminish Kornhäusel's artistic achievement, particularly in the field of domestic architecture. But they do give some idea of the problems raised by uncritical use of the term "Biedermeier" in connection with this architect's work. What is certain is that Kornhäusel rounded off the Viennese version of Neoclassicism and brought it to a close.

In 1826 Kornhäusel was commissioned to carry out the architectural renovation of a religious establishment, the Schottenstift. Apart from the convent building and the library, which lay within the actual convent complex, a large apartment building was erected along the Freyung, Schottengasse, and Helferstorferstrasse frontages, incorporating older buildings. Kornhäusel's response to what—for the period—were quite exceptional dimensions was to employ a division into main and side projections, albeit shallow in depth, and to add a gable and a number of colossal pilasters. In the more intimate inner courtyard, he used the same general design as on the houses in the Seitenstettengasse. The monumentality of the facades facing the street is explained by the representative pretensions of the convent situated behind the apartment-house complex.

If Kornhäusel's Schottenhof took a decisive step in the direction of the *Zinspalast* (literally "rent palace") so typical of Vienna, that was the direction in which things were headed anyway. Even on this scale, there was no mistaking his

161 Ehrenhauss: *Interior of the Synagogue in the Seitenstettengasse,* built by Josef Kornhäusel in 1824–26. Ink, charcoal, and red chalk, 33 × 44.2 cm. Historisches Museum der Stadt Wien. The patent of toleration issued by Emperor Joseph II in 1782, while it granted the Jews certain facilities, stopped short of allowing them to found a congregation and organize public worship. Not until 1823 were they able to get Josef Kornhäusel to design a temple for them, and even then it was on condition that the building should not be visible from the street (its salvation in 1938).

162 Ludwig Schütz: *The Schottenhof,* built by Josef Kornhäusel in 1826–28: facade overlooking the Freyung, 1835. Oil on canvas, 31.5 × 39.5 cm. Historisches Museum der Stadt Wien.
The Schottenhof, an apartment-house complex fronting the old monastery, was not a new building. In redesigning it, Kornhäusel had to take account of an older contruction, to which he added stories and new facades. The prominent position of the wing overlooking the Freyung, which also contained the prelate's quarters, suggested to Kornhäusel a monumental facade design, using a colossal architectural order and triangular pediments.

163   *The Josephstadt Theater,* built by Josef Kornhäusel in 1822: the auditorium. Copperplate engraving, 15 × 20.3 cm. Historisches Museum der Stadt Wien.
From the time of Emperor Joseph II onward, a number of theaters became established in Vienna's suburbs catering for an interested audience that was now able to enjoy plays or popular light opera in the vernacular. Kornhäusel had gained considerable experience in this field: he also built theaters in Baden (Lower Austria) and the Viennese suburbs of Hietzing and Heiligenstadt.

special skill at achieving a balanced play of forces among the individual elements employed: architectural, decorative, ennobling. The residential buildings of various sizes that Kornhäusel built during the 1830s retained these qualities. However, the individual features that had appeared in his buildings in the 1820s increasingly gave way, from 1830 onward, to generalized facade structures. This phenomenon was not exclusive to Kornhäusel; it also corresponded to a contemporary trend. That trend was in the direction of the Early Historicist "rent palaces" and heralded the end of the Biedermeier phase.

The Suburbs

The changes we have been tracing in the light of inner-city examples were paralleled in the *Vorstädten,* or suburbs, between the glacis and the so-called line wall. Such land as was still available in this zone was now rapidly parceled out to keep up with the population explosion. The suburbs increasingly lost their once rural aspect. New streets were laid out in a grid pattern, which inevitably gave rise to a certain uniformity. To meet the growing demand for accommodation, additional stories were built onto the mostly single-story houses that had characterized the suburbs hitherto. The conversion of old houses and the construction of new ones was carried out by builders who took their cue from solutions already to hand. A certain schematism crept into house building, but nevertheless these suburban dwellings, most of which were erected in the decade 1820–30, developed a quite specific charm for which the Biedermeier label itself lies ready to hand.

Moreover, a particular type of house that had fallen out of use in the city itself was commonplace in the suburbs. This was the *Pawlatschenhaus* (from the Czech *pavlač,* meaning "balcony"). Access to the individual apartments was by way of an open, or possibly glazed, passage. This type of dwelling house has traditionally been regarded as being typically Biedermeier. In fact, however, the *Pawlatschenhaus,* while still common in the Pre-March period, represented an ear-

164 House belonging to the Jewish community of Vienna, built by Josef Kornhäusel in 1823: facade overlooking the Seitenstettengasse. Plan submitted to the city council of Vienna by Jakob Hainz, master builder. Pen and ink, 49.4 x 62.4 cm. Vienna, Planning Authorities (*Baupolizei*) (MA 37), EZ 1182/I.

The apartment house at No. 4 Seitenstettengasse was built in front of the synagogue to prevent the latter from being visible and from having direct access from the street. The building contained a school and a ritual bath. Together with the adjacent building and the Seitenstettenhof opposite—both also by Kornhäusel—it formed part of a homogeneous ensemble that still stands today and gives a good impression of the domestic architecture of the 1820s.

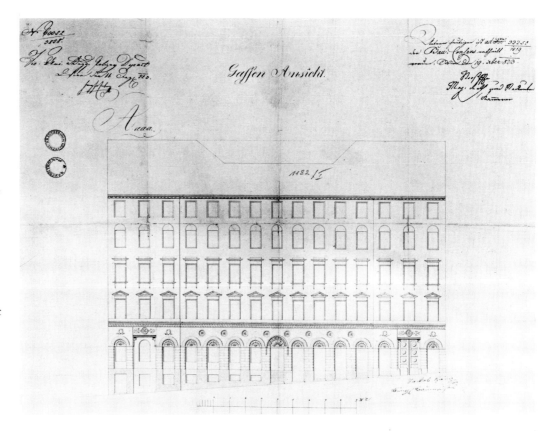

165 Apartment house belonging to the Franz Jäger and Josef Kornhäusel families, built by Josef Kornhäusel in 1825: facade overlooking the Seitenstettengasse. Plan submitted to the city council of Vienna by Jakob Hainz, master builder. Pencil and ink, with watercolor, 60.6 × 45.3 cm. Vienna, Planning Authorities (*Baupolizei*) (MA37), EZ 1180/I.

The facade elevation is typical of the domestic architecture of the period: no features extending over more than one story, no subdivision of the building mass, no central projection, economical instrumentation of the windows, somewhat richer decoration of the ground floor with a Doric portico and reliefs. Kornhäusel built the house for himself and his friends the Jägers, a family of architects and stonemasons (Theater an der Wien).

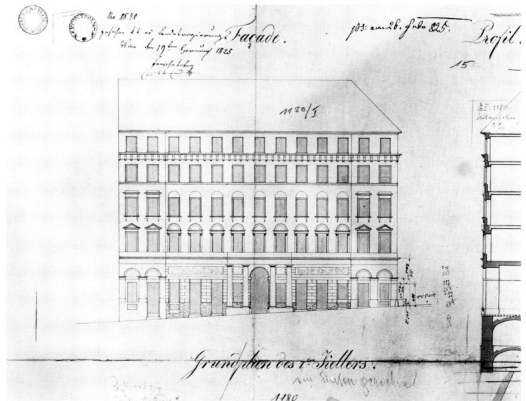

lier stage of development that had its roots in traditional village architecture. The popularization of pictures of Beethoven's house or the house where Schubert was born (Nussdorferstrasse 54 in the 9th district, built in the eighteenth century) led to this stereotyped conception.

Unfortunately we can only glimpse from isolated examples what these streets of Pre-March Vienna must have looked like. As relics of a period that had leaned toward functionality, they were soon misunderstood in their simplicity. Their facade decoration, too, soon fell short of the demands of fashion. When, in the early 1870s, the developers of the *Gründerzeit* transposed the representative pretensions of the monumental buildings and palatial apartment blocks of the Ringstrasse to the former suburbs, they did so at the expense of the architectural fabric of Pre–March Vienna. So when people's attitude to the architecture of this period underwent a change around 1900, it was too late as far as much of that legacy was concerned.

Architecture and Nature

Renunciation of a grand exterior for display purposes extended to another traditional architectural category, namely the palace. In the Baroque period this category had enjoyed tremendous popularity in Vienna. The palaces built then were still available to the nobility with the result that, in the Pre-March period, few new buildings were begun. Archduke Charles's Weilburg (in Baden near Vienna) represented an isolated peak as far as size and ambitiousness of design were concerned. Both Prince Metternich's new summer palace in the Rennweg and the summer palace of Prince Dietrichstein (Clam-Gallas) in Währingerstrasse—typical products of these years—were far inferior to the Weilburg. The Metternich palace (contemporaries usually referred to it as a "villa") was built by Peter von Nobile using Classicist forms. Again, the owner's first concern was clearly with domestic comfort, and the representative aspect

166 *The Schottenhof,* built by Josef Kornhäusel in 1826–28: view of the courtyard, ca. 1845. Lithograph, 36.5 × 43.5 cm. Historisches Museum der Stadt Wien.

Kornhäusel not only converted the apartment house; he also renovated and extended the monastery itself. The latter, which was accessible only from this courtyard, received new rooms for representative purposes and a library of monumental design. Although the sides of the courtyard are unequal in length, Kornhäusel kept his facade designs uniform, giving great homogeneity to the whole.

167 Reinhard Völkel: *Courtyard of a "Pawlatschenhaus" on the Ulrichsplatz, Vienna 7.* Watercolor, 31.6 × 22.8 cm. Historisches Museum der Stadt Wien.

As far as architecture is concerned, the terms "old Vienna" and "Biedermeier" particularly conjure up the so-called *Pawlatschenhaus.* A very common type of residential building in Vienna, it had its roots in rural village architecture. The distinguishing feature of the *Pawlatschenhaus* was that access to the individual dwellings was by way of open balconies (Czech: *pavlač),* often also glazed. It was this "neighborly" arrangement that gave rise to some of the trite ideas regarding the idyllic charm of life in the Biedermeier era.

168 Eduard Gurk: *The Villa Metternich: The East Front,* built by Peter von Nobile in 1835–37. Print from a series of views of the villa, lithograph, 36 × 55 cm. Historisches Museum der Stadt Wien.

Like so many of his contemporaries, the Austrian chancellor Prince Metternich also built a country house just outside Vienna. Whereas the buildings on his Bohemian estates tended toward the monumental, for his summer residence opposite the church of the Salesian nuns in the Rennweg (Vienna 3), he contented himself with what was outwardly a very modest building, its representative appointments being confined to the interior.

took second place. The Dietrichstein palace consisted of a simple cube with porticos of staggered columns on both sides, giving an almost forbidding appearance to the building. Both palaces were set in gardens laid out in the English manner. It is significant that contemporary guidebooks devoted more attention to Metternich's garden and to the prince's horticultural achievements than to the building. This interest in the scenic integration of architecture in nature (as represented by the garden) and this scientific preoccupation with the cultivation of plants bear witness to a shift in values. Clearly the life-style then considered desirable could be better realized in such spheres rather than through the medium of costly constructions.

The ideals of these noble palace builders and garden owners were subsequently adopted by the bourgeoisie. An outstanding example of the synthesis of architecture and organized nature was the garden that Josef Karl Rosenbaum began to lay out in the suburb of Wieden in 1816.[8] Gardens modeled on the late eighteenth-century Schwarzenberg Garden or the imperial park of Laxenburg laid out by Francis I, were now concen-

trated in a much smaller area. The principal artistic emphasis was on the garden design—a blend of the decorative and the functional based on English prototypes—into which the buildings, which included the Villa Rosenbaum, fitted harmoniously. One of the sights of Vienna, it became a favorite meeting place for bourgeois society: frequented, for example, by Kornhäusel, who was a friend of Rosenbaum.

This extension of architecture to take in the garden as well can be seen in two further examples: the Villa Arthaber (Wertheimstein) in Döbling, which still exists, and the Villa Malfatti on the Küniglberg near Hietzing, which we know only from pictures. These two are typical of the many middle-class villas built in and around Vienna during this period.

The *Sommerfrische* (a summer vacation taken in scenic surroundings for the sake of health and recreation) had been made fashionable by the emperor's annual stay at the health resort of Baden, just south of Vienna. For the duration of the summer months, Viennese society moved its domicile to Baden. Baden was not the only town that experienced an ar-

169 The Villa Arthaber (Wertheimstein), built by Anton Pichl in 1834–35. Photograph of a watercolor by Rudolf von Alt, picture archives of the Österreichische Nationalbibliothek, Vienna.

This villa—now the property of the city—is a typical example of the private summer houses of the period. The manufacturer and art collector Rudolf von Arthaber had it built by Anton Pichl, one of the busiest architects in Vienna after Kornhäusel. Situated in the middle of a spacious English-style park, with its principal facade looking toward the Leopoldsberg and Kahlenberg hills, this Late Neoclassical villa in the Döblinger Hauptstrasse (Vienna 19) presented a dignified exterior without aggressive ostentation.

170 Tobias Dionys Raulino: *Villa Malfatti near Hietzing,* ca. 1835. Lithograph, 35 × 49.6 cm. Historisches Museum der Stadt Wien.

This picture shows what was regarded at the time as the ideal domestic arrangement: a villa in a garden landscaped in the English style, merging casually with its natural surroundings and situated on a slope commanding a "picturesque view." The Viennese doctor Johann Malfatti, who became famous during the Congress of Vienna, treated some very prominent patients, and founded the Medical Society in 1837, was able to realize that ideal for himself on the Küniglberg (Vienna 13).

154

171 Norbert Bittner: *(Old) Music Society,* built by Franz Xaver Lössl in 1829–30: facade overlooking the Tuchlauben. Pen and ink, with watercolor, 13.6 × 9.7, mount 20.3 × 15.3 cm. Gesellschaft der Musikfreunde in Wien.
Between 1812, when the Society of Music Lovers in Vienna was founded, and 1870, when Theophil Hansen's new building in the Karlsplatz was completed, the society's events were held in this building. Demolished in 1885, it was the most important building erected by Lössl, who, after his training at the Academy, continued under the spell of Neoclassicism for many years to come.

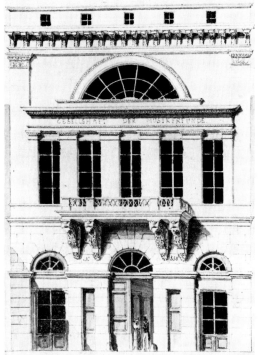

172 *The Seitzerhof Bazaar,* built in 1838–40. Mezzotint, plate 33.4 × 26.9 cm, sheet 51.7 × 36.2 cm. Published by Artaria. Historisches Museum der Stadt Wien.
A conversion of the old Seitzerhof produced this shopping passage flanked by two covered entrances. Although not roofed in, it represented an early attempt to introduce into Vienna the kind of glazed shopping bazaar already widespread in western Europe. However, both the Seitzerhof and the much more expensively appointed passage created by Heinrich von Ferstel in the bank and stock-exchange building in 1856–60 remained isolated instances.

chitectural boom around this time, with a great many new villas being built there; the picturesque hills in the more immediate vicinity of Vienna also stimulated the construction of many villas. As in the case of the palaces we have looked at, the principle behind all this private building activity—pleasure—was not illustrated in externals, despite the great wealth of those responsible for it. The portrayal of opulence turned inward once again: Arthaber, for example, had his staircase painted by Moritz von Schwind. However, like the nobility, the middle-class villa builders provided themselves with a suitable setting by laying out magnificent gardens that gave expression to the period's "romantic" feeling for nature.

The villa served exclusively to enhance private affluence: nonetheless, in Vienna there were also numerous institutions that made it possible to experience cultural activity and physical well-being collectively. In 1829, the Society of Music Lovers (*Gesellschaft der Musikfreunde*) put up its building in the Tuchlauben. Nor was balneotherapy confined to Baden; Vienna had its own facilities—the Theresienbad, for example, which was

renovated in accordance with the taste of the time in 1823. The Tivoli (built 1830) was as popular a place of entertainment as the city's many dance halls and cafés. A typical feature of the Tivoli was its superb situation with picturesque views. The café that Peter von Nobile built in the Volksgarten in 1822 served as a model here. All these buildings show how the forms of Neoclassicism were capable of being translated into popular terms: the balcony supported on columns and surrounded by a wrought-iron railing formed an almost stock motif, enabling the public to enjoy a "fine prospect."

A further, urban form of architecture for collective consumption was the glass-roofed shopping street, or bazaar. The first of these to be built in Vienna was the Seitzerhof (begun in 1838). In other countries they became very common, but in Vienna they failed to establish themselves, even at a later period.

Official Architecture From 1830 Onward

The architecture of public buildings was naturally of a more serious character then

that practiced in the private sphere. Its task, after all, was to symbolize the activities of state authorities and to exemplify the stability of the existing social order. Such were the purposes served by the only monumental building commissioned by the city council of Vienna in the Pre-March period: the Royal Imperial Municipal Criminal Courthouse (begun in 1828) achieved symbolic importance simply by virtue of its size and its eminently visible position at the edge of the glacis in the Alservorstadt. Very much in the spirit of *architecture parlante*, it was given a massive, fortresslike appearance. The artistic influence behind this deliberately intimidating effect is believed to have come from Peter von Nobile.

Another piece of architecture commissioned by the city council of Vienna around this time—the Emperor Ferdinand Waterworks—was wholly given over to a more functional approach. The scheme was begun in 1835 to improve the city's water supply, and the

powerhouse that formed part of it was executed in the variety of Neoclassicism that had its roots in the architecture of Revolutionary Classicism. That kind of predilection for a strictly stereometric repertoire of forms had been brought to Vienna by Isidor Canevale under Emperor Joseph II in the mid 1780s.

Other buildings of the 1830s also stressed the practical style—for example, the Central Mint Office designed by Paul Sprenger.[9] A pupil of Nobile, Sprenger became professor at the Academy in 1828; and from 1842 he directed the Court Board of Architects. Between 1835 and 1848, he completely dominated Viennese architecture, ensuring, for the time being, a continuation of Neoclassicism in the spirit of Nobile by his teaching at the Academy. But as soon as another professor of architecture—Carl Rösner—began teaching in 1835, the fronts started to lose some of their rigidity. The ideas of Romanticism, which Rösner professed as a result of his contacts with Roman Catho-

173   Provincial Court Building, built by Johann Fischer in 1828–39: perspective view from the Josephstadt glacis. Lithograph, 43 × 61.5 cm. Historisches Museum der Stadt Wien.
The Royal Imperial Municipal Criminal Courthouse is a late example of the assimilation of Revolutionary Classicist models in Vienna. The highly visible situation of the building, the design of which was strongly influenced by Peter von Nobile, accentuated the desired effect: "The aspect of prisons should be dreadful and at the same time proud, in order to strike fear into the hearts of those who, by their wicked deeds, have rendered themselves unworthy of human society " (quoted in Irmgard Köchert, *Peter von Nobile* [doctoral thesis], Vienna, 1951, pp. 138 ff.).

174 Central Customs Office and Provincial Revenue Administration, built by Paul Sprenger in 1840–47: facades overlooking the River Wien. Lithograph, colored, 17.1 × 22 cm. Published by L.T. Neumann. Historisches Museum der Stadt Wien.

Apart from Peter von Nobile, it was above all Paul Sprenger, as a court architect, who continued the tradition of Neoclassicism in the official sphere. In the 1840s, however, Sprenger too fell in with the contemporary trend and opted for Historicism. His clear but somewhat reserved formal language was interpreted as artistic weakness by his opponents, who resented his power in all planning matters.

lic circles close to Klemens Maria Hofbauer, began to bear fruit. That group had set itself the goal of bringing new life to ecclesiastical architecture in Vienna, which had long been in abeyance, and for this Neoclassicism could furnish no prototypes. Rösner's Church of St. John of Nepomuk (begun in 1841) in Praterstrasse, across the Danube Canal in Leopoldstadt, already showed clear evidence of a rejection of Classicist forms. The Romantic Classicism that came into effect here stood wholly in the service of a synthesis of the arts *(Gesamtkunstwerk)*, a leading idea of Historicism.

Sprenger himself entered a new phase of his development when he began using pure stylistic elements. The pluralist tendency with regard to style emerged in his building for the Provincal Revenue Administration *(Finanzlandesdirektion, 1841–47)*, in which older Classicist elements were blended with pure Renaissance forms. On the other hand, Sprenger produced a Neogothic design for the

prestige project of the day as far as ecclesiastical architecture was concerned: the Emperor Francis Memorial Church, planning of which began with the emperor's death in 1835. The facade of the *Stadthalterei* building in Herrengasse (begun in 1847) likewise revealed a departure from the principles that had governed architectural design hitherto.

The search for new forms of expression had begun to affect the Court Board of Architects even before Sprenger became its director. When Alois Pichl took over the execution of the Lower Austrian Provincial Parliament in 1833, the arguments over a suitable facade design for this monumental building had already been going on for years. Eventually it was decided to use a colossal Corinthian order extending over three stories—an unusual solution for the architecture of this period, and one that reflected older prototypes.

It was during the planning of a suburban church (the Altlerchenfelder-

Kirche) that the critical stage in the definitive supersession of Neoclassicism was reached. Sprenger's design in the "Jesuit style," the one chosen for execution, was regarded by the Romantics as sacrilegious. An outside event came to their aid —the Revolution of 1848. The events of March, 1848, destroyed the power of the Court Board of Architects and of Sprenger; Nobile, too, resigned himself to events. This left the way clear for freer development. The Arsenal commissioned in 1849 by the new emperor, Francis Joseph I, provided a monumental send-off.

The charge that the architecture produced between 1815 and 1848 was, in the main, sterile is one that scarcely stands up. The narrower framework imposed by the reactionary political circumstances of the time undoubtedly curtailed a great deal of potential. This particularly affected architecture, dependent as it is on economic factors. Moreover, architecture's reduced potential to respond to new developments affected Vienna especially, for it was the capital and the imperial residence. However, these very same restrictive circumstances gave rise to a special development in which "Biedermeier" is comprised. In the realm of architecture, this development showed itself to be primarily governed by pragmatic ideas, which thus made their own contribution to modern art, along the lines of "form follows function."

Renata Kassal-Mikula

175 Jakob Schufried: *Lower Austrian Provincial Parliament,* built by Alois Pichl in 1827–48: facade overlooking the Herrengasse. Watercolor, 18.3 × 24.5 cm. Historisches Museum der Stadt Wien. The time it took to build the Provincial Parliament gives some indication of the difficulties to be overcome in the case of official buildings. Bureaucratic inertia was partly to blame. Repeated requests for alterations by the Court Board of Architects kept holding up progress. The original architect was Kornhäusel, but his restrained formal language failed to satisfy the taste of those commissioning the building, so that planning and execution were placed in the hands of Pichl in 1833.

NOTES

1 Rupert Feuchtmüller and Wilhelm Mrazek, *Biedermeier in Österreich*, Vienna, Hanover, Bern, 1963; *Der Wiener Kongress* (exh. cat.), Vienna, 1965; *Wien 1800–1850* (cat. of the 26th special exhibition at the Historisches Museum der Stadt Wien), Vienna, 1969; Renate Wagner-Rieger, *Wiens Architektur im 19. Jahrhundert,* Vienna, 1970; idem., "Vom Klassizismus bis zur Secession," in: *Geschichte der Architektur in Wien, Geschichte der Stadt Wien,* new series, Vol. VII, no 3, Vienna, 1970; *Klassizismus in Wien—Architektur und Plastik* (cat. of the 56th special exhibition at the Historisches Museum der Stadt Wien), Vienna, 1978 [with contributions by Renate Goebl, "Einführung," pp. 6 ff., and "Architektur," pp. 32 ff.]; Géza Hajós, "Klassizismus und Historismus— Epochen oder Gesinnungen," in: *Österreichische Zeitschrift für Kunst und Denkmalpflege*, 32nd year, nos. 3/4, 1978; *Die Aera Metternich* (cat. of the 90th special exhibition at the Historisches Museum der Stadt Wien), Vienna, 1984.

2 Elisabeth Springer, "Der Hofbaurat," in: *Geschichte und Kulturleben der Wiener Ringstrasse,* Vol. II: *Die Wiener Ringstrasse—Bild einer Epoche,* Wiesbaden, 1979, pp. 21 ff.

3 Carl von Lützow, *Geschichte der kais. kön. Akademie der bildenden Künste*, Vienna, 1877, pp. 91 ff.

4 Paul Tausig, *Josef Kornhäusel—Ein vergessener österreichischer Architekt (1782-1860)*, Vienna, 1916.

5 Hedwig Herzmansky, "Die Baugeschichte der Albertina, Das Palais Erzherzog Carl," in: *Albertina-Studien*, 3rd year, No. 3, 1965, pp. 111 ff.

6 Georg W. Rizzi and Roland L. Schachel, "Die Zinshäuser im Spätwerk Josef Kornhäusels," in: *Forschungen und Beiträge zur Wiener Stadtgeschichte* (Verein für Geschichte der Stadt Wien), Vol. 4, Vienna, 1979.

7 Renate Wagner-Rieger, "Das Wiener Bürgerhaus des Barock und Klassizismus," in: *Österreichische Heimat* , Vol. 20, Vienna, 1957; GeVAG, "Wiener Fassaden des 19. Jahrhunderts—Wohnhäuser in Mariahilf," in: *Studien zu Denkmalschutz und Denkmalpflege*, Vol. X, Vienna, 1976: Eckart Vancsa, "Die künstlerische Entwicklung des Wohnbaues im 19. Jahrhundert am Beispiel der Bezirke III bis V," in: *Österreichische Kunsttopographie,* Vol.XLIV: *Die Kunstdenkmäler Wiens—Profanbauten des III., IV.und V. Bezirkes,* Vienna, 1980.

8 Hubert Kaut, "Die Wiener Gärten vom Mittelalter bis1850,"in: *Catalog of the 33rd Special Exhibition* (at the Historisches Museum der Stadt Wien), Vienna, 1974, pp. 16 ff.

9 Hans-Christoph Hoffmann, "Die Architekten Eduard von der Nüll und August Sicard von Sicardsburg," in: *Das Wiener Opernhaus: Die Wiener Ringstrasse—Bild einer Epoche*, Vol. VIII: *Die Bauten und ihre Architekten*, No. 1, Vienna, 1972, pp. 18 ff. [Central Mint Office and Provincial Revenue Administration by Sprenger].

VII AUTHENTIC BIEDERMEIER PAINTING AND GRAPHIC ART

Sculpture had been the highest form of art in the Neoclassical period, since it enabled the artist —with reference to classical antiquity —to idealize the human figure objectively. In the Biedermeier period, characterized by its preoccupation with the concrete details of everyday existence, painting took the lead, being the art form that best lent itself to narrative. Printing —and in particular the newly invented technique of lithography —made possible a far-reaching popularization of art through the medium of reproductions of paintings or popular series of original individual prints.

In comparison with the Neoclassicism that preceded it and the Romanticism that to some extent coincided with it, Biedermeier tends to be thought of as an unaffected, nonintellectual style and often attracts the label "Realism." The label is inadequate, however, in that it was usually only the choice of subject and not its treatment that was "realistic."

Even such typically Biedermeier painters as Peter Fendi and Josef Danhauser were never interested in the trite reality of everyday bourgeois life —even less so Ferdinand Georg Waldmüller, a painter whose monumental tendencies partially disqualify him from consideration in this context. In addition to its Biedermeier traits, Waldmüller's art exhibits a continued Classicist complexion, while the work of other artists of the period tends to stray into an "antibourgeois" Romanticism.

Biedermeier art is something of a problem area, not only because of these difficulties of demarcation but also because of the whole political context, which offered a point of contact eagerly seized on by later misconceptions and distortions.

The Reponse to Biedermeier Art

It is essential to trace the changing reactions that Biedermeier art has elicited in order to establish the present standpoint. As was historically consistent, it was rejected in the second half of the nineteenth century by the following generation of artists who returned to a monumental approach to art; however, Biedermeier art was able to bask in the admiration of its "grandchildren," the Secessionist generation of the turn of the century. It offered a model for that generation's attempt to combine individual arts in a "synthesis of the arts" (*Gesamtkunstwerk*), an example that would be emulated in the formal language of the day. In an essay entitled "Biedermeier as Educator," in the Viennese review *Hohe Warte*, Joseph August Lux drew attention to the comprehensive role of Biedermeier art: pictorial representations, he wrote, "help to reveal an interesting and important fact, namely that the interiors of all classes, from the emperor and the prime minister down to the petty bourgeoisie, share the same characteristic features."[1]

Without dwelling on the question of the truthfulness of these "class-reconciling" pictures, Lux proclaimed, "Today's modern art finds no such broad acceptance. It would appear that Biedermeier might be educative in this respect too." Objects of the Biedermeier era, according to Lux, "convey an engaging charm and a joyous sense of well-being." Only once did Lux mention "the miserable political conditions," saying that the sole artistic consequence of them was caricature.

Lux made extensive use of such words as "native" and "rooted," meaning to give the impression that everything had been home grown then, as it were, without any foreign influences. The reminting of Biedermeier art as a national art (*treudeutsch*) in the sense of a Germanic phenomenon was thus going on as early as 1904. Nor was this the only instance of it, as Richard Muther revealed in his *Geschichte der Malerei* ("History of Painting," 1909). Muther, too, referred to the homogeneity of Biedermeier art ("a style that genuinely and sincerely expressed the signature of the age") but went on to say: "Nevertheless it was, of course, wrong when on the occasion of the Centennial Exhibition [*Jahrhundertausstellung*] in Berlin in 1906 the view was put forward by Germanomaniac men of letters that the Biedermeier period had seen a marvelously native German national art that then had had to die out because, from 1850, it was the French who were studied." Biedermeier artists, Muther pointed out, "existed everywhere. Fendi, Danhauser and Waldmüller, Oldach and Gensler, Begas Senior, and Krüger, all had their counterparts [*Doppelgänger*] in Scotland as well as in Spain, in America as well as in Russia."[2]

Muther's straightforward view of Biedermeier art, untrammeled by any illusions, was taken up again by the "New Objectivity" (*Neue Sachlichkeit*) tendency of the interwar years, which showed an understandable interest in Biedermeier's realistic aspect. In 1930 a major exhibition of the work of Ferdinand Georg Waldmüller was held in Vienna. One of the organizers of the exhibition was Hans Tietze, whose comprehensive book on Vienna made a point of discussing artistic developments within the city in the context of their respective political and social backgrounds.[3] Consequently Tietze's survey is free of any doctoring of reality for political ends. For him, Biedermeier art was the laborious artistic legacy of the pe-

riod following the Congress of Vienna, which "invested a bygone eighteenth century with its forfeited rights."[4]

Immediately behind—or in place of—a "joyous sense of well-being," Tietze saw resignation and weariness: "The Pre-March period in Vienna was similar, in its emotional atmosphere, to a period of convalescence, the need for which is easily understandable, given the unrest that had preceded it. The system that kept Metternich in power in Austria until the Revolution of 1848 was based on the principle of leaving the status quo intact...; the Ballhausplatz in Vienna was hated

176 Peter Fendi: *Girl outside a Lottery Shop,* 1829. Oil on canvas, 63 × 50 cm. Österreichische Galerie, Vienna.
Fendi's melancholy but at the same time charming painting, which illustrates his concentration on the fate of one individual as a tiny facet of the life of the city, has been described in the literature as the first genre scene in Viennese Biedermeier painting.

and feared as the center of all reactionary movements on the Continent."[5] The author was stating quite plainly that the political oppression that weighed particularly heavily on Vienna was one of the primary causes of a specifically "domesticated" Biedermeier art—an art that "as a result of systematic interdiction was dominated by total political apathy and absolute indifference to public life."[6]

Tietze also said something about Lux's "interesting fact" of the homogeneity of interior decoration and clothing throughout the social spectrum: "The enlightened despot's claim to be the first servant of the state atrophied under Emperor Francis to a mere sense of duty as experienced by subordinate officials. His public pose of bourgeois simplicity became a pattern not only for the nobility and high society but also—since every deviation from the social norms dictated from above aroused suspicion—for the entire population. This imposition of a uniform civilian life... also applied to the things of the mind: high and low thought in bourgeois terms of well-intentioned pedantry."[7]

It was precisely this dark side, this compulsion to conform, by virtue of which the Metternich system was able to count on the consent of broad sections of the population, that made Biedermeier art such a darling of the Third Reich. The art of people under interdiction was highly suitable for people living under a fresh interdiction; the uniformity of all spheres of life in the Biedermeier era offered a precedent for the new uniformity being imposed. There was also the way in which Biedermeier subject matter suited the Nazi art dictatorship. Admittedly the subjects lacked, for the most part, any kind of militancy or aggression; but the family scenes, with their large numbers of children and excursions into the countryside, quite sufficed for the Nazis to claim them as forerunners of "blood–and–soil" art. Moreover, the "realism" of Biedermeier art could be effectively contrasted with the "degenerate" tendencies of modern art.

With corresponding emphasis, the picture was corrected again after the Second World War and freed of all distortions— unmerited as well as merited. In terms very similar to Tietze's, the German literary historian Hermann Glaser spoke of Biedermeier man as an "introvert" who "escaped inward, which either became manifest as a striving to preserve one last place of calm and of quiet happiness in the midst of a chaotic environment, or appeared as naked resignation. Deeds, passions, activity itself, all were shunned in the conviction that all were in vain. 'Escaping inward' placed one at risk of atrophying in philistine narrow-mindedness." The undeniably idealistic side of Biedermeier was "uncertain and dangerous."[8] Glaser also stressed the enduring values communicated (to this day) by Biedermeier art: "In essence, the period was genuinely introspective; it was sustained by an attitude to life that arose out of the depths of melancholy and that could be accused of political or economic incompetence but not of untruthfulness, vapid optimism, or lack of seriousness."[9]

The "Baroque" Element

Art historians have traced two genetically distinct elements in what at first sight appears to be the harmonious monolith of Biedermeier painting and drawing: a softly rounded, picturesque element that goes back to Baroque traditions and a more astringent, graphic element that is more closely associated with the preceding Neoclassicism, individual features of which it continues. This even led one researcher—Bruno Grimschitz—to represent the two elements as two separate tendencies: "Bourgeois Baroque" and "Old Viennese Realism."[10]

This kind of distinction hardly seems advisable, however, given that the two elements are mutually complementary, overlap, and—each in its own formal language—serve related intentions. For example, it is true of both currents and characterizes their adaptation of traditional forms to the requirements of bourgeois art, that they turned away from an earlier imperial and religious monumentality. As the outer dimensions of works (formats) became smaller so did their "inner" dimensions (content). In

177 Peter Fendi: *The Milkmaid,*
1830. Oil on panel, 21.5 × 29 cm.
Historisches Museum der Stadt
Wien.
For this girl "of the people," giv-
en the living conditions of the
day, the loss of her can of milk
was a particularly tragic event.
One of Fendi's services to painting lay in his choice of such subjects, which had failed to interest artists hitherto. Misfortune
and loneliness—the city with its
many people can be seen in the
far distance—are portrayed in
true Biedermeier style, with a
quiet melancholy wholly free of
pathos.

connection with the Baroque-oriented
current, Grimschitz described this new
trend toward intimacy as follows: "Bourgeois man's conception of the world
loses the dimension of universality. It
loses the spatial and temporal and tran-
scendental immensities of the Baroque,
the kind of infinity of artistic perspectives
that exceeds all the bounds of real life....
But this tremendous restriction made a
powerful urge of the challenge to grasp
and master artistically what was visible
and present in the reality of one's own
life...."[11]

The Baroque-oriented current of Biedermeier painting was gentler than the
Neoclassicist current in terms of content
as well, and the lives of its representatives
appear to have fitted more harmoniously
into the spheres of influence that surround art: the authorities, the Academy,
the critics. The works of these artists-
novel, unambiguous documents of bourgeois self-portrayal for the most part—
showed a particularly thoroughgoing

break with monumentality and pathos.
Their intellectual content, the part that
goes beyond "realism," appears to be
stated in a very discreet, almost cryptic
language that escapes the observer with
an eye purely for the objective.

It is here (principally in the painting of
Fendi) that the central subject of Biedermeier painting—the genre scene—
achieves its highest degree of intimacy.
Viennese-born Peter Fendi appears to
have led a commonplace if somewhat
brief existence that at no point came into
conflict with the authorities. After his ele-
mentary schooling at St.Anne's, he studied at the Royal Imperial Academy of
Drawing from 1810 under such typical ex-
ponents of Neoclassicism as Johann Martin Fischer, Hubert Maurer, and Johann
Baptist Lampi. In 1818 he was appointed
a draftsman and engraver at the Royal Imperial Coins and Antiques Cabinet. But it
was not the "antique" works of art he
found there that crucially influenced his
further development so much as his en-

178 Peter Fendi: *Sad News,*
1838. Oil on panel,
36.8 × 30 cm. Historisches
Museum der Stadt Wien.
The way in which Biedermeier
painting concentrated on everyday bourgeois and petty-
bourgeois family life led Fendi
to portray the darker side of that
existence as well. This young
widow being handed the officer's uniform of her fallen husband is depicted in the delicate
colors and discreet forms typical
of the Biedermeier style.

counter with works by seventeenth-century Dutch painters—Teniers, Ostade, Brouwer, Rembrandt—whose everyday subject matter and painting technique inspired his later genre scenes. Fendi found their work and became familiar with it mainly in the gallery of Count Lamberg–Sprinzenstein. The Venetians who constituted another important influence—Titian, Tintoretto, Bellini, and Veronese, among others—he saw on a business trip to Venice in 1821 in the company of the man he worked under, Anton von Steinbüchel.

The favor of the nobility brought Fendi a whole series of aristocratic and imperial commissions in the execution of which he revealed the court's and the nobles' new outward appearance (adapted to bourgeois tastes in decor and dress). The courtly aristocratic excursion into the private sphere became even more intimate in Fendi's group portraits in genre style (*Francis I and Caroline Augusta Surrounded by Their Grandchildren*, 1834; or *Morning Prayers*, 1839). His watercolor *Princess Elise Salm and Princess Fanny Arenberg with the Governess, Mlle Verneuille* (1839) derives its special charm from his loose, sketchlike painting technique, which permits a high degree of delicacy in the portrayal of people, par-

ticularly children. It was works like this that made Fendi such a popular society painter of children.

The figures portrayed in these paintings are all involved in some activity or game and are not looking at the viewer (in *Morning Prayers* they even have their backs to him). The result is self-contained scenes of gentle action, typical examples of Biedermeier genre painting.

Here Fendi's interest had spread to the (outwardly complaisant) courtly aristocratic sphere, but his main interest undoubtedly lay in the popular sphere. Researchers are agreed in describing his painting *Girl outside a Lottery Shop* (1829) as the earliest Viennese genre scene. This first example already bears witness to the honesty of an artist whose choice of subject matter did not stop short of the great poverty of large sections of the population at that time. The indigence of ordinary people was something Fendi included in his program of subtle portrayals of life and rendered visible with his delicate painting technique. A small oil painting of the previous year, *Shivering Little Boy Selling Pretzels on the Bastion* was a step in this direction; later examples were *The Milkmaid* (1830) and a painting entitled *Hard Times* (1831). The oil painting *Sad News* (1838), which shows the young widow of a fallen officer being handed the remains of her husband's uniform, is a reference to the repercussions of war in the purely private sphere.

All these subjects from the poverty-stricken milieu of—for the most part—the "lower" strata of society are executed with delicacy, sensitivity, and the kind of poetry that beautifies without ever prettifying. The way in which Fendi's pictures transcend objective reality is one indication of the inadequacy of the label "realism" as applied to this kind of painting (and to Biedermeier art in general). The idealizing tendencies in Fendi's work can also occasionally lead to delicate intimations of the religious dimension, to which Biedermeier art as a whole was largely indifferent. We are talking here, for the most part, about genre depictions of popular religious customs (baptisms, proces-

179 Peter Fendi: *Childish Devotions,* 1842. Oil on panel, 39 × 31 cm. Historisches Museum der Stadt Wien. Here the painter brings the earthly dimension—so much more important to Biedermeier man—face to face with the religious dimension, as though it were reflected in a mirror.

180 Carl Schindler: *Holdup near Terracina,* ca. 1840. Watercolor over pencil, 22.5 × 28.1 cm. Historisches Museum der Stadt Wien. Like his teacher Peter Fendi, Carl Schindler showed evidence of a dynamic readiness to experiment with color and form in his watercolors and watercolor-enhanced drawings that illustrates a vital, and as it were more Baroque, aspect of the essentially subtle Biedermeier style.

181   Carl Schindler: *Advance Detachment of German Infantry* (scene from the Wars of Liberation), 1841–42. Pencil, 18 × 25.9 cm. Historisches Museum der Stadt Wien.

sions, burials). In the painting *Childish Devotions* (1842), however, the portrayal of an "earthly" mother and child in front of a picture of the Madonna with Child sets up a most impressive mirrorlike confrontation of subject matter.

In his watercolors, Fendi took the development of a relaxed painting technique considerably further than in his oil paintings. "The elegiac casting of a spell over reality that distinguishes many of his genre pictures stems not only from the subject but above all from the colorfulness, from the ideal colors of the subjects and the characteristic, tersely suggestive way in which the paint is applied. These were Baroque traditions; Fendi made further use of them in tackling atmospheric problems and in composing his oil paintings."[12] The author of these words, Fritz Novotny, also stressed elsewhere, in connection with Fendi's watercolors, the "poetic freedom in the language of painting that is displayed here. Looking at these works, one is frequently reminded of the color harmonies of Baroque ceilings and sketches."[13]

Fendi described another native of Vienna as his most gifted pupil: Carl Schindler, whose father Johann taught drawing at the school Fendi had attended. Carl Schindler studied at the Academy under Schubert's friend, Leopold Kupelwieser, but it was from Fendi that Schindler received his decisive artistic impressions. A further influence of particular importance on Schindler's choice of what is considered his typical subject matter—the so-calledsoldier piece—was works by French military lithographers (Bellangé, Charlet, and Lami, among others). In their typically Biedermeier absorption with the private sphere, Schindler's military scenes are completely free of the stiffness of ostentation. They show the everyday aspects of army life or the areas where it overlaps with civilian life. In accordance with this subject matter, Schindler's mode of expression—Baroque-oriented like Fendi's and, again like Fendi, freer and more spontaneous in his watercolors—ranged from the idyllic to the animated. Schindler's sketches in particular not only depict the garrison

182 Friedrich Gauermann: *Grazing Cattle.* Bamboo pen and gray wash, 30.3 × 29.2 cm. Historisches Museum der Stadt Wien.

soldier but also bring out the "chivalrous and even heroic quality of soldiership in the Franciscan-Ferdinandian era."[14]

The same Baroque-oriented current in Biedermeier painting flows through the work of another Viennese-born pupil of Fendi, Friedrich Treml, whose father was head of scenery at the Hofburg Theater. After studying at the Polytechnical Institute and the Academy, young Treml became a pupil and friend of Peter Fendi, whose niece (and adopted daughter) he married in 1842. Under the influence of Carl Schindler, Treml increasingly found his subject matter in the genre-style military scene. From 1849 onward he worked mainly for the imperial court.

Among the "Baroque" representatives of Biedermeier painting in Vienna we must also—though not without reservation—include Friedrich Gauermann, who stood apart from the Fendi circle and was even more strongly influenced by seventeenth-century Dutch models. He received his first instruction from his father, the painter Jakob Gauermann, who schooled him in the traditional technique of pen-and-ink drawing (with a grey or brown wash), which he continued to use in later life. In opting for landscape painting, Gauermann was pursuing another interest of his father, who had devoted much attention to the Alps and the foothills of the Alps. Gauermann was involved in the general movement of art away from the ideal landscape and toward the natural landscape, away from the painting that was composed in the studio from plans and detail sketches and toward an artistically treated experience of nature. He captured what he had experienced and observed in rapid washed drawings of an immediacy that invites comparison with that of the watercolors of Fendi or Carl Schindler (it characterized Gauermann's oil sketches, too). His finished oil paintings, on the other hand, reveal the stronger influence of academic ideals aimed at "correcting" nature. Gauermann's own words are telling: "If only one could get it down the way one visualizes it, but painting is still a long way behind the imagination."[15]

By 1830 at the latest, when he began painting his dramatic thunderstorm scenes and animal fights, full of Neo-

baroque theatricality, Gauermann had overstepped the bounds of Biedermeier painting, for which the demands of intimacy and restraint remained valid in respect of landscape as well.

There was less conscious drama in the work of an artist influenced by (and related by marriage to) Gauermann, Josef Höger, who initially studied at the Academy under the landscape painters Josef Mössmer and Joseph Rebell. Höger was usually more subdued in his choice of subjects and in his use of chiaoscuro with the result that his landscape art remained closer to the genre manner. His generous, large-format watercolor sketches show affinities with figurative studies by Fendi, particularly since the two artists shared a preference for clear, unmixed watercolors.

Höger was also a master of lithography and, as a professor at the Academy (1849–51), published a series of courses in the technique: *Watercolor Tutor, Landscape Studies for Beginners* (1847), and *Tree Studies in Pictures* (1855). Höger's closeness to genre painting is attested to by the art historian Ludwig Hevesi: "An innocently harmonious nature, musical

through and through (he always had chamber music playing), still and in movement at the same time, full of a secret delight in appearance and in contemplation as such."[16]

Another musical artist was Thomas Ender, who paid his way through the Academy by playing the violin in a café. Like Höger, he studied under Josef Mössmer; he also studied under Franz Steinfeld. (He had a twin brother Johann who became, not a landscape painter like himself, but a historical painter and portraitist.) His studies completed, Thomas Ender went on a trip to the alpine region and Salzburg in 1812. A flower painting in watercolors by Ender that was awarded a prize by the Academy showed his aptitude for true-to-life documentary painting. It was purchased by Metternich, who suggested Ender for the retinue of Archduchess Leopoldine when she married Dom Pedro, the future emperor of Brazil. From this trip (1817–18) Ender brought back to Vienna nearly 800 watercolors and gouaches that showed "his extraordinary ability to capture the evanescent in watercolor jottings."[17] In 1819, Ender accompanied Metternich to Rome, where the artist stayed for the next four years on a scholarship; he worked for Metternich again in 1823 in the Salzkammergut; in 1829 Ender worked for Archduke Johann in Gastein. In 1837 he went on his own to southern Russia and the Orient on a study trip.

The Neoclassical Element

While the Baroque-oriented group of Biedermeier painters used a formal language derived ultimately from seventeenth-century Dutch art to communicate fresh observations of people and nature, another group of Viennese painters and draftsman stressed Biedermeier art's direct descent from the Neoclassicism that had preceded it. The mode of expression that characterized these artists appears somewhat sterner and cooler, since it is still affected by the greater severity of the Neoclassical style of drawing. At the same time, their work retains a lively sense of

183 Josef Nigg: *Flower Piece,* 1839. Oil on canvas, 79 × 63 cm. Historisches Museum der Stadt Wien.
The interest shown by Biedermeier painters in seventeenth-century Dutch painting—also a middle-class phenomenon—sometimes led to experimental imitations. Josef Nigg, for example, who worked for the Vienna porcelain factory, often based his flower pieces for the decoration of bourgeois interiors on works by Jan van Huysum and Rachel Ruysch.

184 Josef Nigg: *Flower Still Life,* ca. 1840. Watercolor, 51 × 35 cm. Historisches Museum der Stadt Wien.

185 Josef Danhauser: *The ABC,*
1843. Oil on panel,
38.5 × 35.5 cm. Historisches
Museum der Stadt Wien.
This painting, also known as
*Grandmother Teaching her
Grandson to Read,* portrays a
particularly intimate
Biedermeier family scene. The
intimacy is further enhanced by
the way in which the light is
made to fall mainly on the figures, showing the influence of
seventeenth-century Dutch
genre painting. We know from a
sketch that the figure of the
child, although a boy, was
modeled on the artist's daughter
Marie.

186 Josef Danhauser: *The Child
and His World,* 1842. Oil on
panel, 22.6 × 29 cm. Historisches
Museum der Stadt Wien.
Until around 1840 social scenes
with a moral and composed of a
number of figures had played an
important part in Danhauser's
work. It was only after that date
that he turned to quieter pictures in smaller formats, often
with a child in the domestic
context as the new subject matter. Danhauser took his own domestic circle as his starting point
and used his own children as
models.

the ethical demands of Neoclassicism, in particular the demand for "truth." Adherence to this postulate and its application to fresh artistic aspirations inevitably led to conflicts of a fiercer kind than those that affected the more neutral, less tendentious Fendi group. Danhauser and Waldmüller, for example, fell out with the critics and the Academy, while Ranftl went so far as to reject the whole regime and eventually espoused the revolutionary cause.

For the most part, the Neoclassical group of Biedermeier painters was not based on any retrospective "Dutchification," but rather on a direct line of succession. Most of the group can be traced back to two progressive Neoclassical teachers: in figure painting, Johann Peter Krafft (who had studied in Paris under Jacques-Louis David) and in landscape painting, Joseph Rebell. It was in the work of Krafft that the crucial change from classical to "national" historical painting took place as a positive reaction to the general patriotic attitude during and after the Napoleonic Wars and as a reaction to the demand—aimed particularly at art—for contemporary subject matter, a demand made principally by Joseph von Hormayr in his *Archive for Geography, History, Statesmanship, and Military Art*.[18]

"Krafft broke new ground at the Vienna Academy by pointing students toward visible reality and not toward the art of classical antiquity or the Middle Ages, and by holding them to the study of nature. 'One should see pure nature without preconceived opinions'." The words, attributed to Krafft by a later student (Danhauser[19]) constitute a rejection of Neoclassicism that did not stop at its subject matter but extended to its idealism as well. The contradiction already implicit here was to give rise to inner conflicts; for while Krafft and his school can certainly be said to have effected the requisite thematic change of direction toward Biedermeier, the abandonment of "preconceived opinions" was less easily accomplished. Here the persistence of certain Neoclassical traits led to tensions that went far beyond the bounds of the Biedermeier idyll (particularly in the work of Waldmüller).

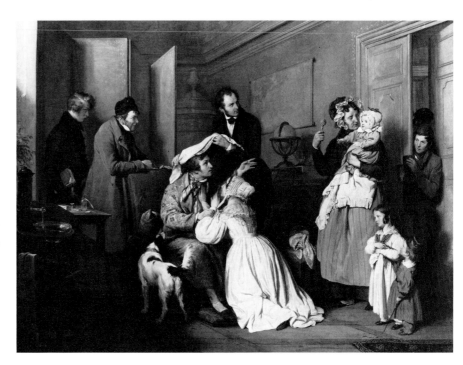

The first "national" historical picture documenting the change to contemporary subject matter was the oil painting *Archduke Charles with the Flag of the Zach Regiment at the Battle of Aspern* (painted in 1812, three years after the event). We can already recognize the transition to a "more realistic style of representation";[20] a year later, in *The Militiaman's Farewell*, we find a further decision in favor of a patriotic but at the same time thoroughly "popular" family scene.

The shift in subject matter from a general to a militiaman, from the stage of history to the domestic context, was decisive as far as the painters who came after Krafft were concerned, particularly since, with the war over, the propagandist function of painting became superfluous, leaving the way free for genre painting. The new absorption in the domestic sphere that began with Krafft and the enlistment of children as subjects (first seen in The *Militiaman's Farewell* and other works) for the purpose of "underlining the importance of the event and arousing emotions."[21] led to an even more direct portrayal of family life as a subject in itself in the work of Krafft's pupil Danhauser.

187   Josef Danhauser: *The Oculist*, 1837. Oil on canvas, 94 × 125 cm. Historisches Museum der Stadt Wien. The typically Biedermeier preference for the private sphere as the locale for detailed narrative paintings led to this scene—a patient being healed by the oculist Dr. Friedrich Jäger—being set in the living room of a middle-class house.

Josef Danhauser, son of the furniture designer and manufacturer of the same name, was born in Vienna and studied at the Academy from 1820 to 1826, mainly under Krafft. In 1826 he accepted an invitation from his patron Ladislaus Pyrker, at that time patriarch of Venice; there Danhauser studied mainly the work of Titian and Veronese. In 1838, he was appointed *Korrektor* ("correcter") for historical painting at the Vienna Academy. Promoted to professor in 1841, he resigned his chair in the following year. The very existence of a chair of historical painting in an age when there was virtually no demand any more for either secular or religious "histories" indicated the outmoded position of an institution with which Danhauser felt himself less and less in sympathy. On the other hand, his early social scenes—legitimate successors of historical painting—clearly still show much of the latter's influence in terms of format and dramatic content.

The oil painting *Abraham Dismisses Hagar* (1836)—executed in agreement with the Academy and awarded an Academy prize—was a historical painting in the traditional sense, while a pair of pictures painted very shortly afterward—*The Rake* (1836) and *The Convent's Soup Kitchen* (1838)—express the demands of religious and secular ethics in social scenes drawn from contemporary life. Here, Danhauser coupled Krafft's refusal to employ academic transcriptions of the past with the influence of the British painter David Wilkie, prompting Ludwig Hevesi to describe Danhauser as the "Viennese Englishman of olden days."[22]

In terms of subject matter, both in Wilkie's work and in that of Danhauser, the old Dutch masters once again form the background; the execution, however —in contrast to that of the Baroque-oriented Fendi circle or of Gauermann— remains more firmly committed to the graphic quality that dominated Neo-

188   Josef Danhauser: *Die Hundekomödie* ("The Dogs' Comedy" as in a dog's life), 1841. Pencil and watercolor, 21.7 × 27.5 cm. Historisches Museum der Stadt Wien.
The sketch is a study for an oil painting. The Academy refused to exhibit the painting because of the resemblance between two of the dogs and the critics Moritz Gottlieb Saphir (the dog on the table) and Baron Joseph von Zedlitz (bottom right), whereupon Danhauser quit his teaching post at that institution. The study bears the (positive) remark by the censor: "*Excudatur,* but only with the caption: 'A Careless Slip'—10./ 12. 841 Moshamer." Danhauser had suggested a second title— "The Need for Muzzles"—that clearly did not please the consorship authorities.

Lithographie von Warnuth in Wien.

Eigenthum und Verlag von
Pietro Mechetti qm. Carlo in Wien
k.u.k. königl Hof-Kunst-und Musikalienhandlung

classicism. The emergence of small-format genre pictures (intimate enough to put them close to similar works of Fendi's) came relatively late in Danhauser's case, superseding his theatrical, rather upper middle-class social scenes. This change of scale, completely in accord in both format and expression with the Biedermeier idea of restraint, occurred at the same time as Danhauser's turning toward his own family life. A step in this direction was the painting *Motherly Love* (1839), which became enormously popular. It showed Danhauser's wife, Josephine Klara (née Streit) with their newborn son Josef. The formal language is already calmer, and the painting also forgoes the pathos that had characterized Danhauser's work until then. Danhauser went on to paint a number of exceptionally unaffected pictures of children—often in several versions—using his own children, Josef and Marie, as models. They included *The Little Virtuosi, The ABC* (or *Grandmother Teaching Her Grandson to Read*), and a painting with the programmatic title *The Child and His World,* showing the private sphere of childhood with toys and pet dog, and no adults pre-sent. Adults are also liable to suffer mischief, as in *The Painter Asleep* —surely another autobiographical picture—where the children are "finishing" a painting.

The painter is also asleep in Danhauser's *Hundekomödie* (1841, literally "Dog Comedy," but with untranslatable overtones of bitterness and resignation), while dogs tear his works to pieces. Superficially this looks like another "mischief picture," but contemporaries noticed the resemblance of two of the dogs to the critics Saphir and Zedlitz. Saphir, in particular, was widely disliked in artistic and literary circles because of his slavish devotion to the regime and his venality. "Artists were beginning to pluck up courage," wrote Hevesi. "In 1836 Bauernfeld even wrote recognizable portraits of Saphir and Bäuerle, the two bugbears of all creative people, into his comedy *The Literary Salon,* which was of course promptly banned. And the hired flunkey Unruh in *Bourgeois and Romantic* is a caricature of Saphir."[23] Because of the resemblances in *Hundekomödie,* the Academy did not dare exhibit the picture, whereupon Danhauser resigned his professorship. But even before that date he

had complained in a letter about the Academy's "inadequately implemented syllabus, poor-quality students, and superiors totally lacking in understanding."[24]

Johann Mathias Ranftl was another artist who, like Danhauser, studied mainly under Johann Peter Krafft and continued Krafft's switch to contemporary subject matter with an increasingly Biedermeier absorption in the private sphere. In 1826 Ranftl traveled to Moscow and St. Petersburg, where he worked as a portraitist and illustrator; in 1838 he was in London, where he drew for the humorous weekly *Punch,* among other publications, and after that he visited Paris. The dogs that feature so frequently in his genre scenes earned Ranftl the nickname *Hunde-Raffael*—"the canine Raphael."

Politically speaking, Ranftl was even more critical of the Metternich system than Danhauser. When revolution broke out in March, 1848, he promptly espoused it and offered his services to Eduard von Bauernfeld as illustrator for Bauernfeld's book *Die Republik der Tiere* ("The Animal Republic"). In it, the principal parts in recent events were assigned to animals. For example, Count Sedl-

nitzky, Metternich's hated chief of police, appears as Police Superintendant Bullock. Illustrating the book, Ranftl was able to draw on both his gift for humor and his skill as an animal painter.

Another pupil of Krafft's who won recognition was Franz Eybl. He devoted his attention primarily to genre-style Biedermeier portraiture (over 400 of his lithographs survive) and to landscape painting. Genre painting led him from the family idyll to the matter-of -fact observation of ordinary occupations. His oil painting *Forge* (1847), for example, has been called one of the "few pictures purely of working life from the first half of the nineteenth century" in Austria.[25]

The emergence of a characteristically Biedermeier style of landscape painting is mainly due to Franz Steinfeld. He was born in Vienna as the son of the sculptor of the same name (who had worked on the program of figures for the park of Schönbrunn Palace). Trained initially by his father, Steinfeld entered the Academy in 1802 to study under Laurenz Janscha—one of the artists involved in the famous series of *vedute,* or landscape views, published by the Viennese firm of Artaria. In

1805 Steinfeld visited the Netherlands, where he made a particular study of Ruisdael's landscape painting. In 1815 he was appointed painter to Archduke Johann. From 1837 to 1859, he taught at the Vienna Academy's school of landscape; there he trained "a modern generation that called him Father Steinfeld." When he and his pupils "went on study trips in real nature, the people of the Salzkammergut or of Carinthia used to say: 'Here comes the hen with her chicks'."[26]

Steinfeld, whose art was based on the graphic precision of the *veduta* and at the same time on a study of Dutch painting, freed landscape depiction from the tyranny of the traditional academic approach, in which the studio composition took precedence over the study from nature. What Steinfeld did with his pure observation of nature, however, was to assemble them into something even his contemporaries called *Stimmungslandschaft* ("atmospheric" or "mood landscape"). Here again—as with Biedermeier figure painting—stock labels such as "realism" or

"naturalism" prove inadequate, since Steinfeld, like Fendi or the later Danhauser, gently idealized what he saw. In his fully developed Biedermeier landscapes such as *The Lake of Hallstatt with the Dachstein* (1832),[27] there is a kind of unassuming moderation: color and light contrasts are slightly subdued and jagged shapes smoothed out with the result that the "inhospitableness" of nature is somehow appeased and —as a side effect of the home-loving aspect of Biedermeier— domesticated.

The writers of the day were drawing the attention of the public to the beauties of the landscape around Vienna, but Viennese landscape painters preferred other parts of Austria, particularly the Salzkammergut. Consequently Friedrich Loos, a painter and printmaker from Graz who lived and worked in Vienna, received a special accolade from the press when he painted a panorama from the top of the Kahlenberg, a hill to the north of the city (executed as a series of six lithographs in 1842). "For a number of years now, the complaint has been heard that our land-

scape painting is afflicted with a certain wearisome monotony as a result of endlessly recurring views of Ischl and Hallstatt and suchlike places, and that the blind pull of fashion has led to a highly regrettable competitive striving for unnatural effects. This well-founded complaint is invariably accompanied by the wish that our national artists would also consider the magnificent environs of Vienna worthy of their attention. It is hoped that the next art exhibition will make a welcome start toward fulfilling that wish. The powerful landscape painter Friedrich Loos, who manfully refuses to be the slave of a flirtatious whim of fashion and who, with true enthusiasm for art, strives to achieve a classical quality and distinction, has completed a panoramic painting of the entire view from the church tower on the Kahlenberg...."[28]

The most famous Austrian painter of the period, Ferdinand Georg Waldmüller, is often referred to as the greatest and most "genuine" exponent of Viennese Biedermeier also. The claim, though almost a commonplace of art history, is nevertheless open to question, since only a part of Waldmüller's work can in fact be classified as Biedermeier. Certain of his early portraits fit into that category—*Archduke Francis Joseph as a Child* (1832), for example, or *Girl in a White Satin Dress* (1838)—as do his small-format, restful Salzkammergut landscapes such as *The Lake of St. Wolfgang* (1835) or *View of the Dachstein with the Lake of Hallstatt from the Hütteneck Alpine Meadow* (1838) and—though with reservations—certain genre scenes painted in the 1840s such as *Wedding in Perchtoldsdorf* (1843) or *The Veneration of St. John* (1844).

Whenever Waldmüller no longer felt bound by the ideals of restraint and tranquility, however, he reached beyond the narrow limits of Biedermeier. This was true particularly of the dramatic tendencies in many of his genre scenes. "As a painter he concentrated increasingly, during the 1840s, on the genre piece. Whereas previously he had very largely succeeded in realizing artistic 'truth' as he saw it, he appears to have broken faith with himself in his genre painting. Here

the moralizing tendencies—a legacy from Neoclassicism—are unmistakable."[29] Waldmüller's predilection for having the figures in his genre pieces act in a manner that is full of pathos (*The Seizure* [of goods], 1847) was coupled with a further "legacy of Neoclassicism": sharp contrasts of light and shade. These are also evident in his landscape painting, where they reinforce the three-dimensional forms of nature in a manner that echoes the Neoclassicist ideal for statuary.

We must view Waldmüller's vigorous struggle against the obsolete teaching methods of the Academy as a purely private campaign and not as any kind of championing of Biedermeier. That struggle led to his compulsory retirement; his complaint was "that one had to attend the Academy so that by studying prints, paintings, and sculptures, one came to know nature as she is not; subsequently, when one actually studied her in reality, one was ashamed to learn, because of having been so blind as to seek her by so pitifully circuitous a route."[30]

Waldmüller's work shows that his "coming to know nature" was not accomplished without a quantity of ideal concepts that can no longer be reconciled with the postulates of Biedermeier. In these transgressions—"through which Waldmüller kept on reaching fresh creative peaks"[31]—he can be compared with such celebrated contemporaries as Schubert, Beethoven, Franz Grillparzer, and Adalbert Stifter, for all of whom a classification as Biedermeier composers or writers would be too narrow. Important lines of development in Waldmüller's work—spanning the Biedermeier interlude—lead directly from Neoclassicism to the art of the second half of the century, which reached its zenith in the so-called Ringstrasse period. Much the same is true of such portraitists as Friedrich von Amerling, Josef Kriehuber, and Johann Baptist Reiter: their leaning toward ostentation frequently clashed with what Biedermeier art saw as the virtues of simplicity and unpretentiousness.

Nor is the cool objectivity emanating from the work of Rudolf von Alt, his "sceptically religious love of the reality of

195 Franz Alt: *Game of Forfeits in the Garden of Moor's Head House in the Alservorstadt,* ca. 1840. Oil on canvas, 37 × 42.2 cm. Historisches Museum der Stadt Wien. Franz Alt's father Jacob intended him to become a portraitist and genre painter, thus avoiding any competition with his brother Rudolf, who painted landscapes and townscapes. In the few years during which Franz Alt bowed to his father's wishes, he painted poetic genre scenes taken from real life, like this (autobiographical) *Game of Forfeits.*

196 Leopold Fertbauer: *Emperor Francis and Family,* 1826. Oil on canvas, 63 × 78.5 cm. Historisches Museum der Stadt Wien. In the center of the picture is Napoleon's son, with the imperial family grouped around him. On the left is Francis I, with his wife Caroline Augusta; on the right are Marie Louise, Napoleon's widow, and the two archdukes, Leopold and Francis Charles. The latter and his wife Sophie—also portrayed—were the parents of the future Emperor Francis Joseph I.

existence,"[32] easily reconciled with the Biedermeier love of the private domestic sphere. Early works by Alt's brother Franz, on the other hand, particularly the autobiographical *Game of Forfeits in the Garden of Moor's Head House in the Alservorstadt* (ca. 1840), are authentic documents of Biedermeier painting. In the case of Franz Alt, this was a product of his having studied at the Academy under —among others—Josef Danhauser.

Between Biedermeier and Romanticism

Franz Alt had also studied under Leopold Kupelwieser. The predominantly religious pictures of this Romantic artist— and friend of Franz Schubert—show a departure from the pathos of historical painting in favor of the quiet, subtle "devotional picture." Such approaches to Biedermeier within the context of Romanticism were even more apparent in Kupelwieser's secular work, especially in the two watercolors *The Schubertians' Excursion from Atzenbrugg to Aumühl* (1820) and *The Schubertians Playing Party Games at Atzenbrugg* (1821). The poetic transfiguration of these true episodes from the lives of a group of friends already contains a hint of the later—and more "worldly"—delicacy of Biedermeier genre scenes, as does the portrait of Schubert by Wilhelm August Rieder (1825). Here, as in the work of another friend of Schubert, Moritz von Schwind— whose art "belongs more to the fairy tale than to religion"[33]—the closeness to reality which characterized Viennese Romanticism redounded to the advantage of

Ich wünsche Dir das schönste Glücke,
Der Unschuld Bild mit sanften Blicke;
Du selbst die schönste Rose finden,
Und Freündschaft soll den Kranz Dir winden

198 a,b Greeting Card (with moving parts). Etching, colored, 11.1 × 8.6 cm. Historisches Museum der Stadt Wien.
The caption reads: "I wish you the handsomest luck, /A mild-eyed picture of innocence;/May you find the loveliest rose,/And friendship bind your wreath." In the transition to the Biedermeier period, the Classicist, abstract idea of friendship received a concrete, domestic connotation.

Biedermeier art. (In German painting of this period, the relationship was almost the other way round: there the predominance of the speculative element led to Biedermeier art being frequently overlaid with Romanticism.)

In Vienna the renunciation of monumentality and drama that, for all their differences, characterized both tendencies led subsequently to some interesting interpenetrations of Romanticism and Biedermeier, remarkably like fairy tales and full of trivial domesticity. An example of this is the group portrait *Emperor Francis and Family* (1826) by Leopold Fertbauer, which shows the sovereign's family in everyday Biedermeier dress, grouped in an arbor that is like a stage set, its decorative vegetation pointing in the direction of mythology.

The beauty and luxuriance of the plant kingdom offered particular possibilities

for Romantic expression in the greeting cards that were so popular at the time and which embodied people's wishes in terms of a modest, domestic happiness. The fairy-tale magic of flowers—which also dominated family albums—was underlined by appropriate words: "May we always bring you – [in garlands of flowers:] Luck, Joy, Health, and Happiness." Surprise tricks such as sections of the card that unfolded or pulled out made it possible to give picture and text an even more personal quality. (These possibilities were also exploited by pornography, which here and elsewhere—Fendi was one example—flourished in secret as the reverse side of the bourgeois righteousness so loudly proclaimed in public.) Greeting cards and family albums offered the well-developed Biedermeier collector's trade a great many possibilities in a wide variety of techniques, during a peri-

DIE WEINLESE.

199 Greeting Card, 1820–30. Etching, colored, picture 6 × 7.6 cm, with (metal-foil) frame 6.8 × 8.5 cm. Historisches Museum der Stadt Wien.
The caption here reads: "Life, amid gaiety and flirtation, pursues its happy course,/ Friendship warms the heart, and pleasure cheers the senses." Another edition of this print, which glorifies the bourgeois contentment of the Viennese at the foot of the Kahlenberg and the Leopoldsberg, bears the monogram "I.E." (Johann Endletsberger).

200 *The Vintage*, 1837–43. Pen lithographs, published by Trentsensky. Historisches Museum der Stadt Wien.
The Vienna publishing house of the brothers Matthäus and Joseph Trentsensky produced colored or uncolored sets of motifs printed on paper and designed to be cut out. Known as *Mandelbögen*, or "manikin sheets," they also included figures and stage sets for toy theatricals.

201 Franz Scheyerer: *The Jägerzeile* ("Hunters' Row," today's Praterstrasse), 1825. Oil on canvas, 57.3 × 88 cm. Historisches Museum der Stadt Wien.
The small building on the left in the foreground is the Leopoldstadt Theater, founded in 1781, and a famous showcase of Viennese folk comedy until 1847, thanks to the efforts of Ferdinand Raimund, Therese Krones, and Johann Nestroy. The church of St. John of Nepomuk is visible in the background.

202 Michael Neder: *In the Pub,* 1847. Oil on canvas, 42 × 53.5 cm. Historisches Museum der Stadt Wien. Michael Neder was the son of a shoemaker. He followed his father in the trade and at the same time studied at the Vienna Academy, afterwards practicing both professions. Untouched by the influences of seventeenth-century Dutch painting and the Viennese genre painting of his own day, Neder developed an unmistakable mode of artistic expression in which he reproduced subjects from his own sphere of life in the suburbs of the city and the villages round about. His straightforward, wholly unpretentious style was dismissed as dilettantism until the twentieth century brought an awakening of interest in his "naive" painting.

od that was also the heyday of home musicmaking and home theatricals. Characters and sets printed on paper and designed to be cut out for toy theater performances at home could be purchased from the Viennese lithographic printing office of the brothers Matthäus and Joseph Trentsensky, as could party games, sheets of pictures, and other series of cutouts (the Viennese called them *Mandlbögen,* "manikin sheets").

For the design of these recreational yet at same time educational series, the publishers sometimes went to well-known artists such as Moritz von Schwind, for example, whose *Tournament* (ca. 1824) provides a further instance of retrospective Romantic overtones in what is otherwise a predominantly contemporary piece of publishing.

As a playful piece of borrowing from Romanticism, Ferdinand Raimund incorporated fairy-tale characters, settings, and "magic" (traps, quick-change scenery, and even flying machines) in his plays, as imaginative embellishments of his Biedermeier theory of education. For the purposes of that theory Raimund not only adapted the gods of Olympus but also dreamed up new fairies, witches, and wizards. With their aid, he demonstrated clearly in *The Weatherglass Maker on the Enchanted Island* (1823), for instance, that avarice cannot lead to happiness and that wealth brings only unhappiness, the same theme as in *The Girl from the Fairy World, or The Millionaire Peasant,* a "Romantic [!], original, magical fairy tale with songs" that was first performed in 1826.

Closely associated with Raimund and with the Viennese popular theater of the Biedermeier years was the illustrator and caricaturist Johann Christian Schoeller, who achieved fame mainly through his work for Adolf Bäuerle's theater journal, *Wiener Allgemeine Theaterzeitung.* Schoeller's watercolors and drawings (most of which were engraved by Andreas Geiger) do full artistic and satiri-

203 Johann Christian Schoeller: *The Total Eclipse of the Sun on July 8, 1842.* Watercolor, 11 × 13.8 cm. Historisches Museum der Stadt Wien. This event was also recorded by other artists (Jacob Alt and Rudolf von Alt, for instance). Adalbert Stifter gave a description of the solar eclipse in the *Wiener Zeitschrift für Kunst, Theater, Literatur und Mode* ("Viennese Review of Art, the Theater, Literature, and Fashion," 3rd quarter, 1842): "Colors such as the eye had never seen roamed across the sky; the moon sat in the middle of the sun, no longer a black disk but as if semitransparent, as if overlaid with a delicate steely gleam...the loveliest luminous effect that I have ever seen...." In the right foreground, Schoeller portrayed Johann Nestroy in the role of "Knieriem."

Die totale Sonnenfinsterniß vom 8 July 1842 um 6. 55 M. früh
in Wien auf der Biberbastey von O.Otts Caffehaus. S. 1842

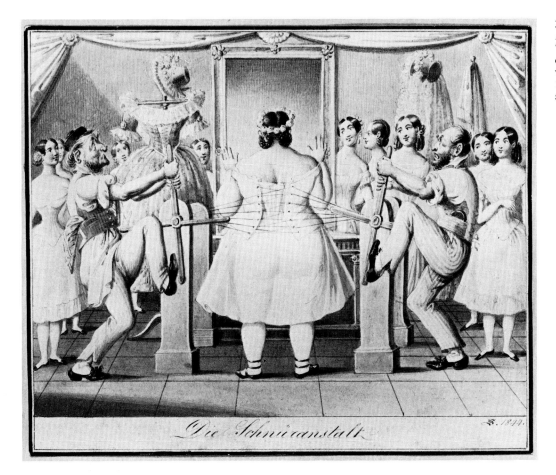

Die Schnüranstalt

204 Johann Christian Schoeller: _Die Schnüranstalt_ (perhaps "The House of Correction" best conveys the German play on words), 1844. Watercolor, 11 × 13.7 cm. Historisches Museum der Stadt Wien.

cal justice to the sets and costumes of the plays of Raimund and Nestroy; moreover, they also provide a richly informative source of social criticism for the period.

But where Schoeller as a caricaturist inevitably came into contact with the politics of the day, his limitations became apparent in the shape of the moderation and restraint that were so typical of Biedermeier art as a whole. The events of the revolution were treated with the same cheerful neutrality that had characterized his everyday scenes in the coffeehouse (_Alles Raucht_, or "Everyone Smokes/Everything's Smoking") or in the beauty salon _(Die Schnüranstalt),_ where a woman is being forced into a dress ("The House of Correction" conveys something of the German play on words here). This amused, wait-and-see attitude toward the revolution—there were exceptions, of course, such as Ranftl—revealed the passive side of a culture that, in turning its back on an unpopular government, had demonstrated a very impressive kind of artistic introspection. The regime was, so to speak, the negative prerequisite for this introspection; it is impossible to imagine the Biedermeier culture without the regime. Consequently when the Metternich era came to an end in 1848, the Biedermeier era ended with it.

Hans Bisanz

NOTES

1 J. A. Lux, "Biedermeier als Erzieher," in *Hohe Warte,* n.p., 1904–5, pp. 145 ff.

2 R. Muther, *Geschichte der Malerei,* Vol. III, Leipzig, 1909, p. 145.

3 H. Tietze, *Wien,* Vienna, Leipzig, 1931.

4 *Ibid.,* p. 311.

5 *Ibid.*

6 *Ibid.,* p. 313.

7 *Ibid.,* p. 320.

8 H. Glaser, *Spiesser-Ideologie, Von der Zerstörung des deutschen Geistes im 19. und 20. Jahrhundert,* Freiburg-im-Breisgau, 1964, pp. 66. f.

9 *Ibid.,* p. 67.

10 B. Grimschitz, *Die österreichische Zeichnung im 19. Jahrhundert,* Zurich, Vienna, Leipzig, 1928.

11 *Ibid.,* pp. 33 f.

12 F. Novotny, in: *Unvergängliches Österreich: Ferdinand Georg Waldmüller und seine Zeit,* (exh. cat.) Essen: Villa Hügel, 1960, p. 45.

13 F. Novotny, in *Peter Fendi* (exh. cat.) Vienna: Österreichische Galerie, 1963, p.4.

14 Quoted by Novotny (see above, note 12), p. 71.

15 Quoted in: *Biedermeier-Ausstellung: Friedrich Gauermann und seine Zeit* (exh.cat.), Gutenstein, 1962, p. 81.

16 L. Hevesi, *Österreichische Kunst im 19. Jahrhundert,* Vol. I, Leipzig, 1903, p. 96.

17 Novotny (see above, note 12), p. 40.

18 See the exh. cat. *Wien 1800–1850: Empire und Biedermeier,* Vienna: Historisches Museum der Stadt Wien, 1969, p. 22.

19 M. Frodl-Schneemann, *Johann Peter Krafft,* Vienna, Munich, 1984, p. 66.

20 *Ibid.,* p. 30.

21 *Ibid.,* p. 38.

22 Hevesi (see above, note 16), p. 64.

23 *Ibid.,* p. 65.

24 Quoted by V. Birke in: *Josef Danhauser* (exh. cat.), Vienna: Graphische Sammlung Albertina, 1983, p. 15.

25 Novotny (see above, note 12), p. 43.

26 Hevesi (see above, note 16), p. 91.

27 P. Poetschner, *Genesis der Wiener Biedermeierlandschaft,* Vienna, 1964, p. 128.

28 Quoted in: *Der Wienerwald* (exh. cat.), Vienna: Historisches Museum der Stadt Wien, in der Hermesvilla, 1978, p. 13.

29 M. Buchsbaum, *Ferdinand Georg Waldmüller, 1793–1865,* Salzburg, 1976, p. 132.

30 Quoted in *ibid.,* pp. 163 f.

31 *Ibid.,* p. 204.

32 Novotny (see above, note 12), p. 29.

33 Muther (see above, note 2), p. 410.

VIII SCULPTURE DURING THE BIEDERMEIER YEARS

National and Religious Content in Classicist Form

Few aspects of nineteenth-century art illustrate better than the sculpture of the first half of the century the dubious worth of using traditional stylistic labels on a par with, and in conjunction with, particular periods of political history. And when the label, like "Biedermeier," has emerged from the literary sphere and its application to the visual arts is already questionable, applying it to the specific area of sculpture is, in terms of stylistic criticism, a doubly uncertain proceeding. No one has yet succeeded in identifying any stylistic features that effectively define the term Biedermeier.

As any study of the literature concerning Biedermeier art will soon reveal, in the field of sculpture, this has never even been attempted; sculpture is usually not even mentioned. Even if the far more established terms Neoclassicism and Romanticism are examined for specific formal characteristics, it is not easy to lay down clearly definable distinctions applicable to sculpture.

For the general historian, too, Biedermeier can only be regarded as one aspect of a particular period of history. The multilayered quality of all history and the problems to which this gives rise are becoming axiomatic today; the unilaterally linear view of evolution taken by the nineteenth century is being abandoned. There are structures that operate alongside events and remain influential beyond them. In sculpture, which was an official art, particularly in the nineteenth century, we find the expression of thoughts and ideas that can be traced in an unbroken line from the time of Johann Joachim Winckelmann (1717–68) through the French Revolution, the Napoleonic Wars, and the events of 1848 into the period of Neoabsolutism. As late as 1846, echoing Herder and Goethe, Baron Ernst von Feuchtersleben wrote, "Nothing is more suited than sculpture to represent worthily the human person as a whole. As far as I am concerned, it is still the truly monumental art." The same thought was shared by representatives of the Enlightenment, rulers, and members of the liberal bourgeoisie. So it looks as if a Biedermeier sculptural style will be very hard to pinpoint.[1]

As early as 1847, Rudolf von Eitelberger, one of the principal figures in Viennese artistic politics in the second half of the nineteenth century, said: "The canker of our art is fashion." How did fashion evolve in the sculpture of the first half of the century?

Starting in the years of the Napoleonic occupation and continuing after it had been overthrown, Baron Joseph von Hormayr, a member of the patriotic circle around Archduke Johann, had sought in word and deed to give fresh stimuli to the visual arts, particularly with the *Archive for History, Statistics, Literature, and Art* that he began publishing in 1810. Hormayr was primarily interested in large-scale historical painting and sculpture, which he sought to inspire by proposing fresh subjects. In an 1825 *Archive* article about the "nationality of art," he stated that great art must above all be religious and national, and he linked it with the concepts of fatherland and dynasty.

DANZATRICE

To the most noble Georgiana Duchess of Bedford

A. Canova

205 Antonio Canova: *Dancer*. Copperplate engraving, 45 × 33 cm. Graphische Sammlung Albertina, Vienna. The plaster model of the statue is dated 1806. Canova's interest in dancers as subjects dates from around that time, as many drawings show. The finished work was for Joséphine de Beauharnais and today is in the Hermitage Museum, Leningrad; another copy went into a British private collection. Joseph Klieber used this print as the model for his *Terpsichore* in the banqueting hall of the present Albertina.

Hormayr's demands were more or less in line with the program put forward by the Nazarenes in Rome, the group of artists who had introduced what Goethe dubbed a "modern German, religious-patriotic art." Stylistically the Nazarenes went back mainly to Dürer, Raphael, and the art of the Italian Quattrocento.

However, for a long time after the Congress of Vienna, the fashion trend generally prevalent in the visual arts—particularly in sculpture—was a style whose "internationality" was based on its reference to classical antiquity: a style that in fact continued to embody the old Europe of the Enlightenment before it was torn apart by the Napoleonic Wars and by the rise of radical nationalist political ideas.

In Austria, Neoclassicism continued to prevail until the 1820s, chiefly in the form given to it by Antonio Canova.[2] The figures that Joseph Klieber made for the banqueting hall of the Albertina and for the Weilburg Mansion—both jobs commissioned by Archduke Charles—constitute outstanding examples of the style. Yet Klieber himself had never been in Rome with Canova.

This situation changed only when Johann Nepomuk Schaller returned to Vienna from Rome in 1823. Schaller, who, though he had worked in Canova's studio, had also become a member of the League of Nazarenes, at least made an attempt, by his personal example and through his work as head of the sculpture class at the Academy, to win acceptance for the new artistic ideals, addressing himself to painters as much as to sculptors.[3]

One of the young sculptors attending the Academy at that time was the Tirolese Joseph Dialer, whose best-known work is probably the bust of Schubert (1829) on the composer's grave in Währing Cemetery. The group *Duke Frederick with an Empty Pouch, Recognized and Being Paid Homage by Two Subjects* also dates from 1829, and two years later Dialer produced *The Spirit of 1809,* a classically conceived figure with a shield at its feet bearing the Tirolese eagle, a carbine, a club, and a hat.[4] Modern, patriotic subjects were also executed with the repertoire of forms derived from classical antiquity. In the sculpture of this period, stylistic quotations were not made for the purpose of expressing new kinds of content; only the accessories were changed.

Some time before Dialer another artist from the Tirol, the painter Johann Martin Schärmer, had submitted a design for the Andreas Hofer Monument planned for Innsbruck, and his entry had been among the finalists. Joseph Klieber had made the sculptural model for Schärmer, who had the backing of Archduke Johann. The archduke possessed a copy of Schärmer's design: a spirit, shown leaning on a shield that bears the Tirolese eagle, is crowning the freedom fighter with a laurel wreath. Hofer, wearing the folk costume of his homeland, has his gun in one hand and his hat in the other. As a result of the intervention of Metternich (who was a curator at the Academy) the commission was eventually given to Schaller (in 1827), who had modified Schärmer's design in accordance with Metternich's wishes. The spirit has been left out, the rifle is slung from Hofer's shoulder, the hat is on the floor, and the Tirolese eagle is half hidden under a bush beside the figure.

Only the addition of a flag in Hofer's hand conveys anything of the original pathetic impression of the national hero. In other words, simply changing a few attributes was enough to make a statement that was more in line with the prevailing political view. The artistic effect—surely unintentional as far as Metternich was concerned—produced a monument that, in formal terms, was quite advanced for its time. Not only was the argument about

206 Joseph Klieber: *Flora with Zephyr and Putto,* from the staircase of the Weilburg Mansion near Baden, 1820–23. Sandstone, H. 200 cm. Kongresshaus, Baden.
The Weilburg Mansion (see Pl. 159) was built by Josef Kornhäusel, who worked closely with Klieber. Klieber was heavily influenced by the style of Canova during these years, as this figure shows.

the admissibility of contemporary dress still going on; in the case of the Hofer monument, the dress that was reproduced was a national costume.

The Nazarenes would have treated this kind of subject differently, as we know from a design made by Schaller himself when he was in Rome: a Florentine wall tomb of the Quattrocento. Systematically it embodies the balance between the idea of the fatherland guided by God and the historical person who serves as His instrument.

Hormayr, bitter about the impossibility of getting his ideas implemented, had left for Munich in 1828; Schaller had also resigned himself to conforming to the prevailing trend: another monument to an Austrian hero of the Wars of Liberation, Field Marshal Schwarzenberg, which was to have been executed by Bertel Thorvaldsen, failed to materialize at this time.

This brought to an end the chapter in sculpture which had made a vain attempt to give artistic expression to impulses active since the Wars of Liberation. That failure was undoubtedly due, above all, to the prevailing political climate in which every kind of nationalist endeavor—not only on the part of the Czechs and Hungarians but also on the part of the monarchy's German–speaking subjects—was regarded with suspicion. There was another reason also: the poor economic situation after 1815, which did not begin to improve, slowly, until the 1820s. Only then did the postwar period of inflation come to an end.

The "court commissions," the only major work put out by the state, all went to fellowshipholders living in Rome. Even here, subjects were ultimately dictated by Vienna. *Jason and Medea* (1829) by Joseph Kähsmann (Schaller's successor in Rome) takes its stylistic cue entirely from the works of the man who, after the death of Canova in 1822, was the leading sculptor in Rome: Bertel Thorvaldsen. He was closely associated with the German artist colony and with the Nazarenes and was accepted by them. Kähsmann returned to Vienna in 1830 and became a professor at the Academy; following the death of Schaller in 1846, he headed the sculpture class until his re-

207 Joseph Dialer: *The Spirit of 1809,* ca. 1830. Plaster, H. 37 cm. Tiroler Landesmuseum Ferdinandeum, Innsbruck.
The winged spirit was a favorite subject in the Neoclassical period and was used in a variety of ways. Here the spirit takes the place of Clio, the muse of history, among whose attributes is the tablet on which the events of history are recorded.

208 Johann Nepomuk Schaller: *Monument for Andreas Hofer,* 1827–33. Tirolese marble; socle relief by Joseph Klieber, Carrara marble, H. (excluding socle) 295 cm. Hofkirche, Innsbruck. The combination of classical modeling with realistic details that possess symbolic significance is reminiscent of Dialer's work. The oak and ivy framing the Tirolese eagle stand for strength and loyalty, the blackcock feather in Hofer's hat for a bold fighting spirit. The posture of the figure follows Canova's life-size statue of Napoleon now in the Wellington Museum in Apsley House, London.

209 Bertel Thorvaldsen: *Amor Triumphans*, 1819–22. Carrara marble, H. 137 cm. , monogrammed "AT" on the tree stump. Ceremonial staircase 1, Rathaus, Vienna.
This figure, which exists in several versions, was probably commissioned by Prince Nikolaus Esterházy, who possessed another work by the artist. The larger works commissioned from Thorvaldsen during his stay in Vienna in 1819—the Schwarzenberg Monument and a monument to Count Franz Kinsky—were never executed. Moreover, Thorvaldsen's much-cited influence on indigenous sculptors turns out, on closer examination, to have been less important than that of Canova.

210 Joseph Kähsmann: *Madonna and Child,* 1836. Plaster, painted; life-size. Left transept altar, Schottenfeld church, Vienna 7.
This Madonna, with the Christ Child standing on the globe, is strongly reminiscent of a late work by Canova in its strictly frontal pose and also in key elements of the composition—the position of the right arm with its upraised hand, the drapery—namely Canova's *Religion* (1814–15). Kähsmann also decorated another altar for the same church with *Christ Crucified* and *Mary Magdalen.*

tirement in 1851. In Kähsmann's later, Viennese works, the Thorvaldsen style hardened progressively into a cold academicism. This is exemplified in the *Madonna with Child* and the *Crucifix* in Schottenfeld church (1836), where something of the Viennese Canova tradition does assert itself once again, particularly in the figure of the Madonna.

No line led from Kähsmann to the younger generation of artists, nor do his works exude anything of what we so like to refer to as "Biedermeier feeling." However, as a person, Kähsmann appears to have been very much what people fondly imagine as the typical Viennese petty bourgeois of the period. He comes down to us in a series of anecdotes as a somewhat coarse, cranky man with no higher education and with a very crude wit.[5]

Another fellowshipholder who received a court commission was Franz Bauer. His *Pietà* (1841) illustrates a change that had begun to make its appearance in the 1830s. Here neither classical art nor the contemporary Roman art of the Nazarenes and Thorvaldsen was any longer adhered to strictly. (The grand old man of sculpture had returned to Rome in 1841, after a stay in his native Denmark, and in October, 1842, he left Rome again to return home for good.) Johann Overbeck, the leader of the Nazarenes, had grown old and intolerant in his condemnation of all the art of the modern era, including that of Michelangelo. Bauer's work is a free paraphrase of Michelangelo's *Pietà* in St. Peter's, Rome, which is an early work by the Renaissance master and lacks the intensity and almost Baroque agitation of his later sculpture. Bauer has transformed his model along Romantic lines into a group that is full of feeling and spiritual expression.

Back in the 1830s, before Bauer's stay

211 Franz Bauer: *Pietà,* 1841.
Carrara marble, H. 171.5 cm.
Kunsthistorisches Museum,
Vienna: sculpture and arts and
crafts collection.
As a subject, the Pietà reappeared rather more frequently
in the first half of the nineteenth
century after a period in which it
had been relatively little used. A
rather earlier example than this
is Joseph Klieber's group (1823)
in the Perchtoldsdorf Cemetery.

in Rome, religious sculpture had already
been endowed with a number of works
conceived in the Romantic spirit. Once
again it was Johann Nepomuk Schaller
who led the way with his *Black Madonna*
in the Schottenstift in Vienna and the figure of *St. Margaret* for the fountain of the
same name, both of which are based—
Nazarene-style—on Raphael.

In architecture, on the other hand, the
Romantic tendency referred to the German Middle Ages and to Gothic art as the
national style, thus making a political as
well as an artistic statement. Sculpture
usually did not conform to this style, although one example (Johann Gottfried
Schadow's *Luther Monument* [1821] in
Wittenberg) stands beneath a Gothic baldachin by Karl Friedrich Schinkel. As regards the statue itself, the dress in the
style of Luther's day and the realistic details such as the open bible—which the
reformer seems almost to be expounding
to the viewer—constitute the progressive
element in the design. Contrary to the architecture, the statue shows no stylistic

212 Johann Nepomuk Schaller: *St. Margaret,* 1836. Lead, H. 205 cm. Margaretenbrunnen ("St. Margaret's Fountain"), Vienna 5. The suburbs often suffered from water shortages in the summer, and the local authority erected this fountain in gratitude to Emperor Francis I for allowing them, from 1829 onward, to make use of the court's water supply.

quotation. That kind of thing happened very rarely—in fact, only when the sculpture concerned was not making the statement but formed part of a "synthesis of the arts" (*Gesamtkunstwerk*) in the Gothic style.

An example of this is the Franzensburg at Laxenburg, just south of Vienna. There, around 1800, in the grounds of the old imperial summer residence, work began on a Gothic island castle to which a tiltyard was attached, decorated along one side with figures of knights. When Archduke Johann had the dining hall of his Brandhof decorated (completed around 1825), it looked like a simplified version of certain rooms in the Franzensburg.

Among the artists involved in work on the dining hall was a sculptor named Joseph Daniel Böhm, who came from the Zips, a German–speaking part of Slovakia. Böhm, who later worked mainly as a coin engraver, was an art collector and the center of a group of art lovers that included Rudolf von Eitelberger, a great admirer of his. In Rome in 1822, Böhm had become a convert to Catholicism. He decorated Archduke Johann's dining hall with statues of the Hapsburg ancestors. These stand on pedestals beneath Gothic baldachins held by shield–bearing angels with coats of arms and narrative reliefs. Some of the subjects are taken from the repertoire of Hormayr—for example, the story of Rudolf I of Hapsburg with the priest (from Schiller's ballad) and Emperor Maximilian I on the Martinswand (a rock wall with a grotto in the Tirol). The program undoubtedly stemmed from the man commissioning the work; the choice of the Gothic style for the sculpture as well, and the related link with the Franzensburg—in this case particularly with the series of figures in the so–called spinning room—constitutes a quite deliberate statement about the claim of the House of Hapsburg to a position of preeminence in Europe that could be traced back to the Middle Ages, when the Christian West had been united under the Holy Roman Emperor. The main group needs to be seen from the same point of view: in the center, Emperor Leopold II, blessing his son Francis I, who is flanked by his own sons, Ferdinand and Francis Charles.

Romantic Currents at the Beginning of Bourgeois Realism

In 1820 the Redemptorists, a religious order less than a hundred years old, received premises in Vienna by command of Emperor Francis I. They were given the Gothic church of Maria am Gestade ("St. Mary on the Bank," so–called because at one time the Danube flowed beneath its walls), which had sustained heavy damage during the French occupation of 1809. The building was in urgent need of restoration. It was restored throughout in a manner consistent with the church's Gothic style. Forty years earlier, when Johann Ferdinand von Hohenberg had made alterations to the Minorite church, the architect had concentrated mainly on removing a Baroque decor then considered undesirable—a task dictated by the austere requirements of Josephinism rather than a genuine piece of Gothicization. Unlike those alterations, the restoration of Maria am Gestade represented the first attempt in Vienna to work within the formal vocabulary of the Gothic style. It is significant that we have sketches for the pulpit and the high altar signed by Franz Jäger the Younger, who had already decorated the Franzensburg chapel, though here in Vienna he had recourse to spoils from various periods from the thirteenth to the early sixteenth centuries.

His designs were not used, however; the ones chosen were by Thomas Mařik, a lay brother from Bohemia who began studying architecture and painting at the Vienna Academy in 1832. At that time, the Kingdom of Bohemia was the part of the monarchy in which the Gothic style was most especially cultivated as the "national style." The baldachin altar executed in 1845–46 appears to hark back in form to the old Baroque high altar depicted in a watercolor by Rudolf von Alt. Despite all efforts to achieve authenticity, the Gothic style was still being interpreted in a very free manner in terms of architectural and decorative details. Only ten years later,

213 Joseph Daniel Böhm: *Emperor Leopold II as Protector of His Son Francis I and the Latter's Sons Ferdinand and Francis Charles,* ca. 1822. Plaster, painted; smaller than life-size. Brandhof, near Mariazell (Styria).

Archduke Johann purchased the Brandhof in 1818 and initiated a major conversion of the former farmhouse in 1822. The dining hall unifies and simplifies the program of the Hapsburg and Lotharingian Hall in the Franzensburg. Key figures from the early and more recent history of the dynasty are portrayed. The actual founder of the house of Hapsburg-Lorraine (Joseph II) having died without surviving issue, his brother Leopold II was considered the real progenitor. At the same time, he was also the father of Archduke Johann, whose life is portrayed in the windows. The group shown here constitutes the artistic focal point of the room.

the high altar in the Augustinian church (Augustinerkirche) was treated with much greater archeological precision.

The statues (by Franz Bauer) have a quite different stylistic provenance. The figures have a still–life quality reminiscent of the paintings of Josef von Führich who, with Leopold Kupelwieser, was among the leading representatives of the Catholic-oriented Romantic movement; at that time, Vienna was one of the movement's principal centers.

A record from 1847 in the archives of the Capuchin Friary shows that Führich's influence extended to another Viennese sculptor, for it says that he did the preliminary drawing for a statue of St. Francis by Joseph Hirschhäuter. Führich drew and painted the saint many times and gave him great prominence in his book *Von der Kunst* ("Concerning Art," published in Vienna in 1866). Anchoring art in religion was entirely typical of the Viennese Late Nazarene tendency to which Führich adhered. Hirschhäuter was another member of this group. He had spent the years 1823–26 studying under Johann Nepomuk Schaller at the Academy and belonged to the inner circle of pupils who, after Schaller's return from Rome, had fallen in with the new artistic ideas of the Nazarenes as propagated by Schaller. Only a few works by Hirschhäuter are known, most of them portraits. The 1851 relief with the head of the poet Nikolaus Lenau (who had died the year before) shows that the new approach to art had come into play in the field of secular art as well. The realistic details are subordinated to the large ideal form.

The official imperial style, exemplified by the numerous monuments to Emperor Francis I erected throughout the length and breadth of the country after his death in 1835, presented a completely different appearance. This is probably best–illustrated by the case of the *Emperor Francis Monument* in Vienna, for which the first invitation was issued—presumably for reasons of state—only five days after the emperor's demise on March 2. The commission was eventually given to the Milanese sculptor Pompeo Marchesi and not to one of the competing artists; Marchesi had already executed the *Emperor Francis Monument* in Graz in 1837.

The Vienna monument (completed in 1846) shows the emperor as a classical toga–clad figure in the pose of a Roman *imperator.*[6] The conservatism of this representative of the Milanese school is relieved only by the realistic treatment of detail on the octagonal socle. Such concessions to modern currents in matters of detail occur frequently in the work of Marchesi. Other works of his owned by the imperial court were a *Praying Angel* for Empress Caroline Augusta and a group—which never in fact reached Vienna—entitled *Buona Madre nel Venerdì Santo.* This stood in the church of San Carlo in Milan and consisted of nine figures gathered around a Pietà beneath the Cross. In 1839, in an article for the *Deutsche Kunstblatt* on the occasion of the erection of the plaster model, the artist wrote that he had sought to create a work capable of accommodating the noble in art and meant to diffuse and sustain feelings of religious devotion. Negotiations for the purchase of the group (conducted by the Vienna Academy) went back as far as 1833; thus it is possible to deduce that even Emperor Francis I accepted the conservative artistic current and pietistical content advocated by Marchesi. In the opinion of some authors—Günter Buser is an example — these might already fall into the category of religious *Trivialkunst* ("trivial" or "insignificant art").[7]

Artists from Lombardy were very deliberately encouraged for reasons other than the purely aesthetic; there were also practical considerations—Milan possessed an excellent bronze foundry—and of course political reasons as well: it was hoped that such encouragement would make the artistic community more Austria–conscious. In 1838, Emperor Ferdinand I, for example, awarded a number of commissions to Milanese sculptors when he spent some time in Milan on the occasion of his coronation—an event of supreme political importance. He purchased a *Venus and Cupid* from Marchesi, executed very much in the style of Canova. In fact, in the last decade and a half before the Revolution of 1848, the Austrian imperial court owned a greater number of works by artists from the part of northern Italy under Austrian rule than it granted commissions to fellowshipholders from the Vienna Academy between Franz Zauner's *Clio* (1779) and Franz Bauer's *Pietà* (1841). Even in 1851 most of the Austrian artists featured at the Great Exhibition in London were in fact Milanese.

Of course, state commissions were granted to Austrian artists, too. Examples are the standing figure of *Emperor Francis I* by Joseph Klieber in the dining hall of the Technical University in Vienna (1837–42), which depicts him as a Roman *imperator;* and Johann Nepomuk Schaller's *Francis I Monument* for the town of Stanislawow in Galicia (now Stanislav in the U.S.S.R.), showing the emperor in his Austrian imperial robes (1837). Compared with the work of Marchesi, Klieber's figure offers a far more familiar interpretation, laurel wreath and posture notwithstanding, while Schaller's work,

214 Joseph Hirschhäuter: *Portrait of Nikolaus Lenau,* 1851. Plaster, 46.5 × 38 cm. Historisches Museum der Stadt Wien.
This is the model for the round bronze relief on the poet's tomb in the cemetery of Weidling in Lower Austria. Hirschhäuter had already made a statuette of Lenau from a daguerrotype during the poet's lifetime. What that looked like we do not know, but the relief is an ideal portrait that bears no relation to the last descriptions of Lenau before he died insane.

(despite the fact that it used virtually the same posture) was an even more "modern" treatment for the period.

The reason lay partly in the drapery, which was regarded at the time as "contemporary," and above all in a combination of realistic details with a congruence of content and form arising out of the meaningful interpretation of attitude and gesture. The ruler (identified as representative of his time) invokes, as it were, the blessing of heaven upon the peoples whom God has entrusted to him and is thereby invested with a timeless significance. This increasing realism in detail should be seen as expressing the "here

and now" of the person portrayed in the monument; it is certainly not the expression of any "Biedermeier mentality."

A pupil of Schaller's named Adam Ramelmayr received high praise for his talent in his own lifetime. One indication of this was his appointment as a member of the Academy of Fine Arts in Vienna even before he had completed his fellowship in Rome. According to a list of works drawn up by the artist's son (and in the present writer's possession), it was in 1835 that Ramelmayr made the alabaster statuette of Archduke Charles now in the Heeresgeschichtliches Museum in Vienna. The archduke is shown relaxing in an armchair with his right hand concealed in the open coat of his uniform. For Austrian circumstances it was an outrageously modern composition. (Incidentally this statuette, which is undated, is usually attributed in the literature to 1842-43.) The hand gesture is reminiscent of the statue of Napoleon on top of the column in the Place Vendôme in Paris, a work by Charles Emile Marie Seurre (1833) that was known through lithographs.

A statue of Emperor Francis I that has come down to us through a lithograph by Joseph Kriehuber bears an even greater resemblance to Seurre's work. Here the emperor is shown standing in coat and boots with his left hand concealed in his coat. The print bears the legend "From the statue by Ramelmayr," so the figure was presumably executed. According to his son's list of his works, the artist had made a statue of the emperor in 1842, during his stay in Rome. A. Frankl's *Sonntagsblätter* (Frankl was a friend of Ramelmayr) mention a seated figure; and the *Deutsche Kunstblatt* even speaks of a colossal seated figure commissioned by the emperor's younger son, Archduke Francis Charles. Despite these somewhat contradictory references, which refer only to the form of execution, we can probably take the date given in the list of works as being correct. Here, in other words, in a work executed in the year after the ceremonial laying of the foundation stone of Vienna's Emperor Francis Monument, we are dealing with a piece that went far beyond any of the modern statues of rulers in the German–speaking world.

In another way, too, Adam Ramelmayr showed himself to be an artist with the courage to innovate. His teacher, Johann Nepomuk Schaller, had, in his final years, fallen in with the contemporary fashion for statues of artists by executing a statuette of the actor–playwright Ferdinand Raimund, but Schaller had never done a public monument. In 1842, when he was in Rome, and with Metternich's backing, Ramelmayr tried to persuade the council of the Academy to agree to a musicians' monument featuring Mozart, Gluck, and Beethoven. He was unsuccessful, although the group was not intended for a public location but for St. Charles's church (the Karlskirche) and was to have received a religious significance by placing the figure of St. Cecilia in the center. Ramelmayr received no court commis-sions after that—in fact, no more were granted.

The Transitional Period of the Mid-Nineteenth Century

The first monument to an artist erected in Austria was erected in Salzburg, not in Vienna. It was commissioned in 1839–42 by the Salzburg Mozart Society from the Munich sculptor Ludwig Schwanthaler, whose design they preferred to that of the Italian Lorenzo Bartolini.

This illustrates two trends. The center of gravity in the art world had finally shifted from Rome to Germany (princi-pally to Munich at this time), and the commissions in this modern trend with

215 Pompeo Marchesi: *Venus and Cupid,* 1838. Carrara marble, 85 × 184 cm. Kunsthistorisches Museum, Vienna: sculpture and arts and crafts collection.
The figure is based on Canova's famous *Victoria Victrix* (Paolina Borghese) in the Borghese Col-lection in Rome. The consum-mate handling of the marble is also reminiscent of Canova. It was doubtless Marchesi's sub-jects and technical mastery that made his work so popular at the Austrian imperial court.

its new kinds of subject matter came from the bourgeoisie and not from official state bodies. Thus there was little justification for Eitelberger's critical remark, made during these very years, to the effect that art was now created only for the home and the family. The remark was addressed to precisely that section of the population which, in fact, was promoting artistic initiatives and which only conventional opinion considers to have lived in pure Biedermeier self-restraint.

In 1844 the mayor of Vienna, Ignaz Czapka, commissioned the *Austria Fountain* from Schwanthaler. As in the eighteeth century, fountains presented one of the few opportunities for the local authority (*Gemeinde*) to make a public mark with a work of art. Both the *Austria Fountain* and Ramelmayr's *Rebecca Fountain* (also ordered by Czapka) were commissioned in connection with the completion of Emperor Ferdinand's new waterworks. The *Austria Fountain* is a typical product of the Munich School in arrangement (with the river gods standing and not reclining as hitherto) and in content (with the figure of Austria at the top and the inscriptions in German). As such it not only introduced fresh elements—Gothic reminiscences, realistic details—but also reintroduced elements of content that had been out of use since the 1820s (see, for example, the patriotic fountains made in 1812 by Johann Martin Fischer for the Am Hof Square, Vienna, and today in the Historisches Museum der Stadt Wien: *The Loyalty of the Austrian Nation* and *Agriculture*). This combination of reorientation and retrospection in content, coupled with a modern, realistic manner of representation, was to govern Viennese sculpture for some years to come.

Czapka, one of the most important mayors of Vienna in the nineteenth century, was not the only one to commission sculpture from Schwanthaler, as the catalog of the artist's work shows.[8] The movement that led to Rome being superseded by Munich—a city alive with artistic activity under King Louis I—began around 1830. Here again Johann Nepomuk Schaller appears to have played a crucial role: on his return from

Rome in 1823, he was invited by the king of Bavaria to enter his service, and Schaller visited Munich a number of times as a result.

In 1828 his nephew Ludwig Schaller moved to Munich permanently, armed with a recommendation from his uncle and accompanied by the painter Moritz von Schwind. There Ludwig worked partly under Schwanthaler and partly on his own account on the ambitious building schemes of King Louis I. Ludwig Schaller's most important work is the statue in Weimar of the philosopher and poet Johann Gottfried von Herder, for which he received the commission in 1846. Delayed by the upheavals of 1848, the work was not cast until 1850, when it was highly praised in a review in the *Deutsche Kunstblatt.* In a letter to A. Frankl dated February 7, 1846 (preserved in the manuscript collection of Vienna's Municipal and State Library), Ludwig Schaller states that the Herder statue would be the first monument outside Austria commissioned from an Austrian sculptor. The statue's form lies somewhere between the simple realism of the Berlin School and the more animated and more stylized tendency represented by the Munich School.

Another Viennese sculptor who moved to Munich in 1830 was Fidelius Schönlaub. The son of a Viennese sculptor, Schönlaub had begun studying at the Academy in 1819. He did a number of jobs in Upper Austria after 1853, mainly for the abbey of Kremsmünster and for the city of Linz. One of his most important works is the high altar in the parish church at Steyr (1855–57), which served as a prototype for subsequent developments.[9]

Probably the most important sculptor to leave the Vienna Academy (in 1842) to familiarize himself with the modern currents in Munich was the Carinthian Hanns Gasser. Whether Rudolf von Eitelberger was right in stating that Gasser actually preferred to go to Munich rather than to Rome is not certain, for Eitelberger also claimed that, once there, Gasser steered clear of Schwanthaler, which we know to be false: according to a manuscript catalog of works (in the print room of the Academy of Fine Arts in Vienna), Gasser

216 Ludwig Schwanthaler: *The Austria Fountain,* 1844–46. Figures: bronze, basin: granite, larger than life-size. Freyung, Vienna 1.

The program of Georg Raphael Donner's fountain in Vienna's Neuer Markt, which predates Schwanthaler's work by some hundred years, remained confined to Vienna and the two provinces of Upper and Lower Austria, with the Ybbs, Morava, Traun, and Enns rivers ranged around the figure of Providentia, representing the wise government of the city. Here the principal rivers of the entire monarchy—Danube, Po, Vistula, and Elbe—surround the figure of Austria in a programmatic foretaste of the future development of Vienna, which was to become one of the world's great cities.

217 Adam Ramelmayr: *The Rebecca Fountain.* Zinc casting, H. 176 cm. Franziskanerplatz No. 1, Vienna 1.

The subject is taken from the Old Testament: Rebecca comes to the well with her water jar; there Abraham's servant chooses her as Isaac's wife. Scene and arrangement are both in the tradition of the Viennese wall-niche fountain, a good example of which is Franz Xaver Messerschmidt's fountain with the widow of Sarepta (Johannesgasse No. 15, Vienna 1).

made the socle (1844) at least of the Goethe monument that Schwanthaler created for Frankfurt am Main in 1841–44.[10]

Another work that Gasser executed in Munich—in 1843—is a group composed of the three daughters of the painter Julius Schnorr von Carolsfeld, today in the Österreichische Galerie in Vienna. In the literature this group is usually referred to erroneously as *Herzeleide* ("Heartbreak"). The group represents two girls saying farewell to their dead sister, whereas the actual *Herzeleide* group shows two young girls with a dead bird in their laps and was executed in Vienna some five years later (1848). Such genre-style idylls, revealing a penchant for intimacy of treatment, are typical of Gasser's output, particularly at this time. The stimuli may well have come from the artist's painter friends such as Schnorr von Carolsfeld himself.

Given their subject matter and, above all, given their execution, are these works by Gasser examples of what might be called "Biedermeier sculpture"? The ideas for their conception came from the Romantics, and their basic atmospheric content is also Romantic. This comes out very strongly in the bust of the singer Jenny Lind in Klagenfurt. (Gasser probably met her in the house of the painter Wilhelm von Kaulbach, which both of them frequented.) Even Schwanthaler's Romantic tendencies became more marked in the 1840s. His *Nymph* for Anif Mansion, near Salzburg, for example, certainly invites comparison with Gasser's bust. Both artists worked on a *Tancred and Clorinda* group around this time. Schwanthaler's influence appears to be most powerful in Gasser's monument designs, particularly as regards the pretension to monumentality, even on a small scale.

After Gasser returned to Vienna in 1847, he went on working in the style of his Munich years with no apparent break through 1848 and beyond, employing that style for the patriotic subjects then considered modern in Austria. A deeply religious man, in 1856 Gasser conceived the idea of portraying Empress Elizabeth (who had just given birth to her second

218 Ludwig Schaller: *The Herder Monument*, 1846–50. Bronze, larger than life-size. Weimar.
Almost all this artist's work was done in Germany, where he was involved in the figurative program for the Alte Pinakothek Museum in Munich, for example. There are very few pieces by him in Austria. The Anif Cemetery in Salzburg has the tomb of a district official named Stollberg-Stollberg (dating from 1843) with a *Madonna and Child*. A *Mary in Glory* in the parish church of New St. Margaret, Vienna 12, was destroyed in the Second World War.

daughter, Gisela) as St. Elizabeth. The statue was to go in St. Stephen's. "...I saw it as a personification of the fatherland,.. but here it had to be something religious, and since love and veneration are qualities so divine I thought of St. Elizabeth, the loveliest prefiguration of our beloved empress," Gasser wrote in 1856 in a sketch book that is preserved today in the manuscript collection of Vienna's Municipal and State Library. A model in the Kärtner Landesmuseum shows this stage of the composition, with the crowned saint wearing a cape and carrying a basket of flowers. A clay model in the possession of the Historisches Museum der Stadt Wien reveals a further stage: a portrait statuette of the empress, her left hand clasping a medallion at her breast that contains an effigy of the emperor. The statuette conveys the same basic feeling as the first version, however. The change to the official, more stately monument style of the Ringstrasse period was not completed until 1860, when the figure was executed in marble for the hall of what is now Vienna's West Station (then called Empress Elizabeth Station).

By the 1840s, the new subject areas which the modern era of industrialization had opened up for the fine arts began to be addressed for the first time in sculpture. Franz Bauer decorated the portal of the Provincial Revenue Administration (*Finanzlandesdirektion*) in Vienna, the building erected by Paul Sprenger in 1841–46, with allegories of transport, industry, manufacturing, and commerce. Here the conservatism that clung to sculpture throughout most of the nineteenth century—mainly because it was assigned the role of preserving what was transitory and unique—became glaringly apparent in an age that saw itself as being in permanent transition and making rapid progress. All that was new in the portal figures was a number of attributes symbolic of the new industrial era; the types of figure—and particularly their attitudes—can be traced back to classical antiquity.

The same applies to Hanns Gasser's statues for the Creditanstalt (1859), a bank in Vienna, two of which are based on corresponding figures by Bauer: *In-*

219 Fidelius Schönlaub: *St. Margaret,* 1859. Wood, mounted, life-size. Presbytery, Sipbachzell (Upper Austria).
Schönlaub worked in Upper Austria, mainly for the abbey of Kremsmünster, to which the parish of Sipbachzell belonged. Until 1964 this figure stood at the high altar, which had the form of a Gothic monstrance and gave St. Margaret an architectural setting. The style of the work—its rejection of the monumental form embodied in Johann Nepomuk Schaller's *St. Margaret*, for example (see Pl. 212)—the emphasis on profound piety, and the intimate character reminiscent of children's picture books all mark a change that heralds the Neogothic religious art of the second half of the century.

dustry and *Commerce* (the models are in the Historisches Museum der Stadt Wien, and in Klagenfurt respectively). It must be admitted that *Commerce* has most unclassically become a female figure, but she still holds the caduceus in her hand. These figures prove that Gasser not only brought elements of the Munich style to Vienna but also that he had thoroughly absorbed the indigenous tradition into his work. In terms of his life-style, which was both generous and Bohemian, with the physically diminutive artist as the focus of a Neogothic studio stuffed with works of art, Gasser almost appears to us as a precursor of Hans Makart. Writing to the wife of Wilhelm von Kaulbach in 1845, the singer Jenny Lind said of the young artist: "You may not be able to read my handwriting...but Gasser, who knows so much about everything that's wild—no, not mild, wild—will be so good as to assist you with it."[11]

Gasser's friends included the young German sculptor Anton Dominik Fernkorn, who had come to Vienna early, in 1840. Fernkorn took some figures created by Gasser in 1847 for the Carl Theater (no longer extant) as models for the figures of *Dance* and *Music* that he made for Prince Auersperg's Auersperg Palace in Vienna in 1852. Thus with reference to this period, we can no longer speak of the German School as enjoying overall preeminence in Vienna.

The 1840s brought an increase in the number of small bronzes. A few series of soldiers and mythological characters have survived, and written sources cite many more. Are these figures (some of which are endowed with a wealth of accessories) what one might regard as typical of the Biedermeier period? That would mean that the small version that Ludwig Schaller made of his Herder statue was a Biedermeier work—but the monument itself was not. Furthermore, these series do not begin until quite late and continue well beyond the middle of the century. In Eitelberger's view, the heyday of the small bronze did not begin until the School of Arts and Crafts was founded at the Österreichisches Museum für Kunst und Industrie.

The increase in the number of bronzes from the 1840s onward probably had more to do with the improved casting techniques that reached Vienna around that time than with any preference for the intimate on the part of "Biedermeier man."

One of the best of the small-format sculptors was Franz Högler, whose working life extended into the second half of the century. He must have been a man of highly conservative views, because his busts and statuettes which have survived not only include such celebrated theologians of the Pre-March period as Sebastian Brunner (1848) and the cathedral preacher J.E. Veith (1849), but also Field Marshal Windischgrätz (1850), Prince Metternich (1854)—all these are in the Historisches Museum der Stadt Wien—and field marshals Radetzky and Haynau (1851), both in the Heeresgeschichtliches Museum. In terms of form, however, Högler's works are somewhat unusual for the period, with their smooth, often angular surfaces and their relatively sparing use of accessories. An Academy pupil, Högler spent the years 1836–38 in Paris, where a number of his works remain to this day. Possibly his highly distinctive and, in fact, rather unViennese style derives from that stay.

Karl Alexy, who attended the sculpture class at the Vienna Academy from 1836–39, and worked on his own account from 1841, was the author of the series of fifteen bronze statuettes of Austrian military commanders (1844–45), now in the possession of the Heeresgeschichtliches Museum. Alexy's figures (historically accurate down to the smallest detail) and his narrative, almost literary manner of representation place him much more firmly than Högler in the context of contemporary Viennese small-format bronze sculpture.

A major name in that context was Johann Preleuthner, stepson of Johann Nepomuk Schaller, for whom Fernkorn did a great deal of casting and chasing, not just in the early years when he lived and worked with Preleuthner but also later on. An early example of the collaboration of the two artists is the so-called *Guardian Angel Fountain* that Preleuthner created for the Wiedner

It has been claimed several times that these figures are Joseph Klieber's and that Bauer simply worked from models made by his former teacher. This is surely wrong, as the iconography (modern for the time) and the stylistic links with other works by Bauer confirm. Klieber was an old and very sick man by then.

Hauptstrasse in Vienna in 1843–46. The tall, narrow, octagonal socle was designed by Eduard van der Null and Sicard von Sicardsburg; the casting and chasing were done by Fernkorn. Since, according to Eitelberger, Preleuthner's group was based on a drawing by the painter Heinrich Schwemminger and since apart from the knight that adorns the staircase of Grafenegg Mansion we know of very little of Preleuthner's work from this period, it is scarcely possible to throw any light on the artistic relationship between him and Fernkorn. In fact, the question of how far the rather older Preleuthner, who already had something of a reputation in Vienna, may have influenced his German junior has yet to be addressed.

The Heeresgeschichtliches Museum in Vienna possesses a series of bronze statuettes of the Babenberger margraves and dukes, one of which, depicting Duke Friedrich II *der Streitbare* ("the Valiant"), bears on the right-hand side of the socle a legend to the effect that it was "chased by Josef Selb: 1853." An artist of that name attended the Academy's school of engraving from 1826–28. Papers in the Heeresgeschichtliches Museum indicate that Selb worked for Preleuthner. Stylistically, the figures go back to the statues that Schwanthaler began in 1830 for the Bohemian Valhalla and that ushered in the artist's more animated late style, which was also characterized by much greater realism in detail.

Fernkorn moved to Vienna shortly after work had begun on the Bohemian Valhalla. Yet, after an interval of some ten years, ideas from that source were incorporated in his bronze statues of six heroes from the saga of the Nibelungs, exhibited at the Great Exhibition in London in 1851. But Ferkorn never achieved the much more strongly narrative manner of representation with its wealth of realistic accessories that characterized the work of Preleuthner and of Alexy as well, both of whom went far beyond Schwanthaler's late style. (Incidentally Preleuthner did statuettes of Hagen and Volker too.)

The statuettes of musicians designed by Preleuthner in 1843 (known only from a description) were already treated in this more realistic manner: "Gluck is standing at a music desk with a score on it, beating time—with the same expression of enthusiasm he used to wear when conducting his orchestra. Mozart is standing at a writ-ing desk, leaning on his right elbow and pensively holding a sheet of music in his hand. Joseph Haydn is standing in front of an organ with a roll of paper in his hand, and Beethoven is seen at a pianoforte, deep in thought, writing down in his notebook the gigantic ideas that come rushing in on him during his habitual walks and that can scarcely be checked at other times too."[12]

Fernkorn's *Archduke Charles Monument.norm*, the liveliest equestrian statue in Vienna, was designed during the years of his collaboration with Preleuthner. In 1847, Fernkorn made several versions of a statuette showing the archduke as commander of the Austrian troops at the Battle of Essling–Aspern in 1809.[13] In addition to a rearing, but riderless horse, there is a version in which the archduke has his hand outstretched, one in which he holds a flag, and a hitherto unknown bronzed plaster

221–23 Karl Alexy: three statuettes from a set of Austrian generals: *Count Rüdiger Salm, Wallenstein, Lazarus Schwendi*, 1844–45. Bronze, H. 47, 44.5, and 46 cm. Heeresgeschichtliches Museum, Vienna.
The clay models of Alexy's figures were completed in 1844. In the following year the Austrian diplomat Baron Karl von Hügel paid for them to be cast in bronze.

224–26 Franz Högler: three statuettes of Austrian generals: *Count Radetzky, Count Haynau, Prince Windischgrätz,* 1850–51. Bronze, H. 45 cm. Historisches Museum der Stadt Wien.

Small statuary, particularly the small bronze, has been popular with collectors since the Italian Renaissance. In the nineteenth-century, it provided middle-class collectors with an opportunity of purchasing works of art at prices that were within their means. We must not forget, however, that such sets also had a serious purpose, namely to educate people politically. This aspect is particularly clear in the case of Högler's three statuettes, which represent the military heroes of the Revolution of 1848–49 in Austria.

model, recently acquired by the Historisches Museum der Stadt Wien, in which the archduke is carrying a marshal's baton in his right hand. The socle bears the inscription: "A. Fernkorn fecit 1847." This is probably the earliest version, being based on the usual monumental equestrian treatment of the ruler with the marshal's baton.

In respect of this version particularly, it is possible to add the equestrian statue of Emperor Joseph II by Balthasar F. Moll (in the Franzensburg at Laxenburg) to the list of prototypes for Fernkorn's work given in the literature. The final form of the monument as eventually executed (with the flag), was arrived at toward the end of 1848 and submitted to the emperor for his approval. An interesting feature here is the design of the tall socle, very different from the one actually executed. The socle was decorated with four groups of figures: *Patriotism,* symbolized by a

militaman taking leave of his wife and children; *Loyalty,* with Andreas Hofer holding the flag and leading his Tirolese freedom fighters; *Compassion,* with an Austrian uhlan giving a wounded French cuirassier a drink; and *Valor,* with a fallen color–bearer handing the flag to a comrade. It was a program very much in line with the ideas of the time of the Wars of Liberation, ideas that had been taken up in the *Austria Fountain* as well.

Nor were these isolated cases, for in the same year (1847), Ramelmayr was commissioned to design an iron lion lying at the foot of a pyramid to mark the spot near Malborghetto where Austrian troops had offered fierce resistance to the French in 1809. Ten years later Fernkorn's *Lion of Aspern* was placed beside the church round which another battle had raged in 1809.

Apart from these individual monuments it was the Arsenal (built between

and not themselves vehicles of ideas. The figure of Andreas Hofer is a copy (made by Preleuthner in 1873) of Johann Nepomuk Schaller's figure in Innsbruck.

Lastly, in this context, we must look at the Heldenberg, the so-called Austrian Valhalla, in Klein-Wetzdorf, for which, starting in 1849, Ramelmayr created some 180 sculptures, including 150 busts; he was assisted by the sculptors Anton Dietrich and Johann Fessler. Originally the Heldenberg was meant as a memorial to the Austrian troops who had proved themselves in the revolutionary struggles of 1848–49; it was to be coupled with a tomb for the owner, the army supplier Joseph Pargfrieder, and for field marshals Radetzky and Wimpffen. This plan was modified in the execution. The addition of a part that did not really belong—to commemorate the deliverance of Emperor Francis Joseph I from the assassination attempt of 1853—had the effect of confusing the original intention. For example, the statue of the emperor does not occupy the center of the site (it is situated in a side avenue); moreover a crucifix stands beside a classical god of death. Parts are vaguely reminiscent of the nonchalance with which realistic figures are mixed with allegories and the world of men with the world of the gods in plays by Ferdinand Raimund. But if some of Ramelmayr's groups there, particularly the *Three Fates* and *Clio*, are examined closely we are forced to admit that there is nothing Biedermeier about their artistic content: the statuary is rooted in the soil of classical antiquity, and the composition of the groups is treated in a Romantic manner.

In 1860, when the *Archduke Charles Monument* was unveiled, the political situation already differed from the one prevailing at the time of its planning. The dream of the young Emperor Francis Joseph I of consolidating and maintaining Austria's position as the major great power in central Europe had been abruptly terminated in 1859 by Austria's crushing defeat at Solferino. A different, more realistic program—one based on the recollection of great deeds from the past rather than on dreams of power relating

1849 and 1856 as the pantheon of the Austrian army) that gave chiefly architectural, but also sculptural, expression to those ideas, with its statues of the principal commanders of the Austrian army. The statues, incidentally—and it is an early pointer to the major Ringstrasse projects undertaken in the years to come—were wholly subordinate to the architecture

227   Josef Selb and Johann Preleuthner: *Albrecht the Victorious of Babenberg.* Bronze, H. 16.5 cm. Heeresgeschichtliches Museum, Vienna.
One of a set of statuettes representing rulers of the Babenberg family, this is a good example of the way in which sculptors stimulated and influenced one another around the middle of the century. The almost floating quality of movement here, as well as individual details of the pose, are close derivations of Hanns Gasser's figure of *Comedy* for the Carl Theater. Fernkorn copied two other facade figures by Gasser, *Dance* and *Music,* in 1852; they can be seen today in the Auersperg Palace, Vienna.

228   Anton Dominik Fernkorn: *The Archduke Charles Monument* (model), 1847. Plaster, bronzed, H. 67.5 cm. Historisches Museum der Stadt Wien. Fernkorn made this first model for the future monument in Vienna's Heldenplatz in the same year as Eduard Duller published his biography of Archduke Charles. The monument recalls the archduke's most important victory, when he defeated the army of Napoleon at the Battle of Aspern. It shows him on the evening of that May 21, 1809, as he rode, yet again, alone at the head of his troops to urge them into the attack.

229 Adam Ramelmayr: *Knightly Armor,* 1849–56. Cast iron, life-size. Heldenberg, Klein Wetzdorf.
This portrayal of a medieval knight in armor, very much in the Romantic tradition of the first half of the century, stands for military heroism in general.

230 Hanns Gasser: *Legionary in the Academic Corps,* 1848. Plaster, H. 25 cm. Historisches Museum der Stadt Wien.
On March 14, 1848, a placard invited the students of the Academy of Fine Arts to join the Academic Corps. Under the command of Professor Perger the artists formed the Fifth Battalion of the newly constituted Academic Legion. A festive gathering was arranged in the council hall to celebrate the emperor's granting a constitution. It is here that Hanns Gasser is said to have first presented this figure, for which he had designed the uniform himself. The head is a self-portrait of the artist.

231 Joseph Klieber: *Frieze of Putti,* 1814–23. Sandstone against a gold-colored background. Annagasse, No. 14, Vienna 1.
This frieze is one of the finest examples of the kind of facade decoration that was usual on middle-class houses in Vienna in the first half of the century. The motifs are conventional and undergo little change. The subject of putti at the grape harvest goes back to the Belgian Baroque sculptor François Duquesnoy, who copied Classical models himself very often.

to the future—now determined the thematic content of public monuments. This is also the reason for the crucial difference between the small formats of the models and the large formats of the actual monuments. The true turning point, as we have seen, did not coincide with the "year of revolutions," 1848.

A further consequence of the defeat of 1859 was the loss of Lombardy and, with it, as far as the art world was concerned, the end of the preferential treatment hitherto meted out by the Austrian court to the sculptors of Upper Italy. Fernkorn's *Archduke Charles Monument* was followed by the equestrian monument to Field Marshal Schwarzenberg made by the Dresden sculptor Ernst Julius Hähnel in 1864–67. The last major monument by an Italian sculptor in Vienna was the marble monument to the poet Pietro Metastasio by Vincenzo Luccardi. It is located in the Minorite church (Minoritenkirche) and dates from 1854. This monument is also Vienna's earliest one to an artist. As far as Vienna's sculptors were concerned, 1848 and its aftermath meant a drop in the number of their commissions. Two reminders from this period are a statuette of a *Legionary in the Academic Corps* by Hanns Gasser and the oval portrait of Franz Bauer's wife who was killed on March 13, 1848, by a stray bullet. Do these two works mark the end of a stylistic epoch as well as the end of a political era? For sculpture, at least, this is not the case.

Selma Krasa

NOTES

1   For the general historical aspects, see R. Koselleck, *Vergangene Zukunft: Zur Semantik geschichtliche Zeiten,* 2nd ed., Frankfurt am Main, 1984; Baron E. von Feuchtersleben. "Rhapsodie über Monumente," in: *Sonntagsblätter,* 1846, pp. 621 ff. (the quotation occurs on p. 623). The only recent overview of nineteenth-century Viennese sculpture is M. Poch-Kalous, "Wiener Plastik im 19. Jahrhundert," in: *Geschichte der Stadt Wien, Plastik in Wien,* Vienna, 1970, new series VII/3, pp. 165 ff. On the sculpture of the second half of the century, see W. Krause, "Die Plastik der Wiener Ringstrasse, Von der Spätromantik bis zur Wende um 1900," in: *Die Wiener Ringstrasse—Bild einer Epoche,* Vol. IX/3, Wiesbaden, 1980.

2   S. Krasa-Florian, "Plastik," in: *Klassizismus in Wien* (cat. of the 56th special exhibition of the Historisches Museum der Stadt Wien), Vienna, 1978, pp. 73 ff.

3   S. Krasa-Florian, *Johann Nepomuk Schaller, 1777–1842: Ein Wiener Bildhauer aus dem Freundeskreis der Nazarener,* Vienna, 1977.

4   They are both in the Tiroler Landesmuseum Ferdinandeum, Innsbruck. See also *Die tirolische Nation, 1790–1820,* (exh. cat.) p. 446. nos. 13.182, 13.184.

5   A.G. Mayer, *Erinnerungen an Carl Rahl: Ein Beitrag zur Kunstgeschichte Wiens 1847–1865,* Vienna, 1882, p. 39.

6   A. Weissenhofer, "Die Wiener Akademie und das Kaiser-Franz-Denkmal," in: *Monatsblatt des Vereines für Geschichte der Stadt Wien,* Vol. 1, Vienna, 1919, pp. 1 ff.

7   G. Buser, "Über einige Darstellungen der Gebets– und Bildkunst des 19. Jahrhunderts," in: *Trivialzonen in der Kunst des 19. Jahrhunderts: Studien zur Philosophie und Literatur des 19. Jahrhunderts,* Vol. 15, Frankfurt am Main, 1971, pp. 131 ff.

8   F. Otten, *L.M. Schwanthaler, 1802–1848: Ein Bildhauer unter König Ludwig I. von Bayern* (*Studien zur Kunstgeschichte des 19. Jahrhunderts*), Vol. 12, Munich, 1970.

9   B. Prokisch, *Studien zur kirchlichen Kunst Oberösterreichs im 19. Jahrhundert* (thesis), Vienna, 1984, particularly pp. 12, 72.

10   Rudolf von Eitelberger, "Kunst und Künstler Wiens der neueren Zeit," in: *Gesammelte kunsthistorische Schriften,* Vol. 1, Vienna, 1877, pp. 158 ff.

11   J. Dürck-Kaulbach, *Erinnerungen an Wilhelm von Kaulbach und sein Haus,* Munich, 1918, p. 118.

12   *Allgemeine Wiener Musikzeitung,* Vol. III, nos. 14/15, Vienna, 1843, p. 62.

13   H. Aurenhammer, *Anton Dominik Fernkorn,* Vienna, 1959.

IX VIENNESE FASHION FROM THE CONGRESS TO THE REVOLUTION

Women's Fashion

The Congress of Vienna had made the city the political, cultural, and social center of Europe, the rendezvous of its crowned heads, its most beautiful women, and its aspirants in every sphere. Guided by Prince Clemens Wenzel Lothar Metternich, "Europe's coachman," the Hapsburg Monarchy was to assume a commanding role among the European states for decades to come.

Following the war years, entrepreneurs with plenty of capital and innovative spirit launched fresh economic initiatives that naturally found expression in the field of fashion as well. An important step in the dissemination of Viennese fashion was taken by Johann Schickh, the owner of a fancy-goods shop in the Kohlmarkt called At the Sign of the Three Graces *(Zu den drey Grazien)*.[1] In 1816 he founded the weekly *Wiener Modezeitung* ("Viennese Fashion Journal"), which ushered in a new era for Viennese fashion and for Viennese tailors and dressmakers, enabling the latter to publish their creations and so reach a wider potential clientele. More than 1,700 fashion prints, colored by hand, appeared in the thirty-three years from 1816 to 1848.[2] Today they provide us with an excellent survey of Viennese fashions of the period.

The men's fashion designs were by Josef Gunkel, the most celebrated gentlemen's tailor of the day, who was even immortalized by Johann Nestroy in his burlesque *Der Zerrissene* ("Man in Tatters").[3] The designs for the women's fashions were by Vienna's best-known dressmakers (Josef Georg Beer, Friedrich Bohlinger, and Thomas Petko); the hats, headdresses, and hairstyles were by Johann Langer, and later by the milliner Josefine Niederreiter.[4] In addition to its fashion supplements, the review also published prose, poetry, travel writing, theater criticism, and news from the worlds of literature, art, and music. Its contributors included such famous writers as Franz Grillparzer and Adalbert Stifter.[5]

In 1817 the *Wiener Modezeitung* became the *Wiener Zeitschrift für Kunst, Literatur, Theater und Mode* ("Viennese Review of Art, Literature, Theater, and Fashion")—the name it retained until it ceased to appear in 1848. When Johann Schickh died in 1835, the review was taken over by Friedrich Witthauer, who continued to run it successfully. In 1844 ill health forced him to relinquish control to Gustav von Franck. By that time the review's best years were already behind it; the reputation of Viennese fashion was on the wane, and for some time the leading custom tailors had once again been taking their cue from Paris. J.A. Bachmann attempted to keep the review going in 1847, but with the failure of the Revolution of 1848 its fate was sealed: it had sided too strongly with the revolution, and tighter regulations were being imposed on the press.[6]

The significance of this review's fashion prints lay in the fact that it deliberately published only Viennese fashions from original designs by Viennese tailors and dressmakers—unlike Bäuerle's *Theaterzeitung*, which presented Parisian fashions.[7]

The hand-colored copperplate engravings in the *Wiener Modezeitung* were among the finest in Europe. The painter Johann Nepomuk Ender and the costume director of both court theaters, Philipp von Stubenrauch, were engaged to draw the women's and men's fashions and the fashion accessories. The engraving was done by Franz Stöber. In addition to the fashion prints, other supplements featured furniture and interiors, the latest carriages, portraits (from 1840), as well as musical compositions by Franz Schubert and Konradin Kreutzer.[8]

How did the elegant Viennese lady or gentleman dress during this period? From the Congress of Vienna until about 1820, the lady would have worn a dress that conformed entirely to the Empire cut: high-waisted, with a fairly straight , slightly flared long skirt (gathered in the back only), and long, close-fitting sleeves that usually had a small puff at the shoulder. The neckline was often decorated with silk "blond lace" or vaporous cotton lace, embroidery, and openwork, as were the top, the cuffs, and the hem of the skirt.[9]

White was the fashionable color in those years, though blue-and-white and green-and-white combinations and delicate pastel shades were also employed.[10] From 1818, the fashion prints showed day dresses in checks,[11] for which the ladies of Vienna developed a particular predilection in the following years. The materials used were various cotton fabrics, silks, and sheep's wool.

The cut of women's coats corresponded to that of their dresses. The favorite color combinations for outerwear were green and white or blue and white, but checks and delicate stripes also found a place. The coats were usually trimmed with epaulettes and braid.

One of the most popular fashion accessories before and during the Congress of Vienna—and one that was to retain a firm place in women's fashion in the decades to come—was the cashmere shawl. The reason for its popularity with women was that its bright colors effectively set off the white and pastel shades of their dresses. Such a shawl was at stake in a wager made during the Congress—when politics did not entirely monopolize the scene!—between no less a person than Czar Alexander and Countess Flora Wrbna-Kageneck. After both had presented themselves in the most extreme negligee, it was a question of which of the two could first reappear in full evening dress. The countess apparently accomplished this feat in ten and a half minutes, with the czar (who was known for his gallantry and charm) following half a minute later. He presented the winner with a cashmere shawl, which suggests that at the time this was indeed a princely, not to say an imperial, gift.[12]

Further important accessories for women were a folding parasol to keep the sun off their faces, a fan, and gloves. The obligatory headgear was the *Schute,* or poke bonnet, a broad-brimmed hat made of satin or straw and, as a rule, trimmed with bows, lace, and flowers. Egon Friedell gave an apt, if hardly affectionate description of the poke bonnet: "....Like something designed for a horse, very large and extremely impractical, enveloping the face like blinkers so that the wearer's hearing and vision were impaired...."[13] But there was also the *Kopfmantel,* or head-wrap, "a most practical piece of headgear against the cold, which women use for promenades, the theater, etc. and which can be worn both over a hat and over the bare head, but is removed in company." The head-wrap was made of cotton lace and might measure as much as four Viennese ells (10 ft.) in length.[14] Women's dainty feet were shod in flat shoes with crossover straps.

A fashion novelty presented in the *Modezeitung* in 1817 was the first divided skirt, described as follows: "When the lady rides astraddle she wraps the sections round and buttons the same above the foot in such a way as to form trousers...."[15] This innovative garment, however, failed to find favor with the fashionable ladies of the day.

In the 1820s, Biedermeier women once again remembered that they had waists. The waistline accordingly slipped lower and lower, began to be laced in cor-

232 *Above*: Garters, ca. 1830. White silk with painted flower decoration and inscription: *Mein Wunsch—Ihr Glück* ("My desire—your happiness"), *Meine Bitte—Ihre Freundschaft* ("My plea—your friendship"). L. 8.9 cm. *Below*: Stockings, ca. 1830. Knitted white cotton yarn, decorated with various patterned rows and rose motifs made up of beads knitted in. L. 57 cm. Historisches Museum der Stadt Wien.

sets and emphasized with a broad belt; and around 1836, the waistline recovered its natural position. Since the part of the dress above the waist had to be close-fitting, the fashion-conscious Viennese woman was left with but one course open to her: she must force herself back into a corset. Evidently she suffered in the process, because various attempts were made at the time to render wearing a corset less of an ordeal. Johann Nepomuk Reithoffer made a breakthrough with his discovery that rubber could be combined with flax, wool, or silk to produce stretch fabrics, and he was marketing a seamless corset made of such fabric by 1828.[16] Patent corsets of the kind invented by August Piltz would, "in the event of the lady's feeling sick, after pulling on a small loop at the bosom fall away from the body instantly and without the help of another person."[17] All the associated discomfort notwithstanding, the corset was back—for whatever complex reasons—as an essential item in every woman's wardrobe.

In contrast to tops, women's skirts stood out in ever wider circles, and from the late 1820s until the mid 1830s, they left women's ankles free. Attention was drawn to this feature by white or cream-colored silk stockings with openwork round the ankle and over the instep. Knitted stockings of white yarn were also widely worn. These were sometimes decorated over the instep with a flower motif executed in colored glass beads. The same beads would then also fringe the stocking top.[18] Stockings were supported by often delightful garters made of silk or the finest buckskin, painted or embroidered, and bearing painted or embroidered inscriptions that made no attempt to conceal their (very discreet) eroticism. Some examples: "Walk upon roses and forget-me-nots," "My desire—your happiness," "My plea—your friendship," *De vous je suis amoureux* ("You I love"). [19]

Three-dimensional trimmings such as garlands, leaves, or little balls made of material, placed between the knee and the hemline, were very popular in the 1820s. Toward the end of the decade women liked to wear skirts with flounces.[20] Women also attached great importance to having their skirt and top harmoniously decorated.

Sweeping décolletés that left women's shoulders bare were not uncommon. Ball dresses combined them with short puffed sleeves, while day dresses of the late 1820s with the first leg-of-mutton sleeves ("ham" sleeves in German) were not uncommon. Broad-brimmed hats festooned with trimmings completed the woman's daytime outfit.[21]

For home wear, Viennese women chose a little cap as headdress, but for social occasions they preferred the turban. Intricate hairstyles with central partings (the hair waved on either side, and bound up on top of the head in a sort of loop adorned with artificial flowers, feathers, lace, or ribbons) delighted the beholder's eye at sumptuous balls.[22]

The 1820s saw the end of the colorless phase in women's fashions. A predilection for strong colors in checked, striped, and flowered fabrics became apparent.[23] The first checked creations, however, met with considerable misunderstanding if we are to believe what one contemporary wrote: "...the fashion for squared or checked patterns now increasingly prevailing in silk fabrics, merinos, and calicos, so deeply offensive to the eye accustomed to quiet highlights and folds, is a barbarous one...."[24] Designs for women's clothes in the late 1820s also showed a particular interest in animal and plant motifs.

Day dresses were made of percale and poplin, evening dresses of *pétinet*, a kind of tulle, and organdy.[25] The *Wickler*,[26] a sort of cloak, began its triumphal progress through the world of women's fashion in the mid 1820s. Ten years later it was giving way to a coat that emphasized the waist and was cut to accommodate the dress underneath it.

An event that gave a great stimulus to fashion designers in Vienna was the arrival of the first giraffe (in 1828). The city positively wallowed in *à la giraffe* fashions:[27] dresses, gloves, pins, rings, pendants, even tobacco pouches were inspired by the animal.[28] In the same year, the Austrian dancer Fanny Elssler's celebrated "Cachucha" costume, named for a folk dance, made its appearance in the ballrooms of Vienna. This creation in pink crepon, trimmed with black lace around the low neckline and the hem of the skirt, was made in various versions by Josef Georg Beer.[29]

In the early 1830s it was the Far East that inspired designers of women's clothing. Beer produced "mandarin-style" house-dresses with pagodas, birds, and imaginary flowers[30] and wide, loose coats made of Chinese cashmere with funnel-shaped Chinese sleeves and high collars.[31]

Sleeves underwent a special development in this period. At the beginning of the 1820s they were still close-fitting, but over the following years they started to swell up until the famous leg-of-mutton shape was achieved. Horsehair padding and whalebone produced positively balloon-like formations that not only graced women's daytime wear but were also to be found on the riding habits of fashion-conscious horsewomen.[32]

The problems of playing piano four-handed with a lady thus attired were described by a male sufferer as follows: "To make it possible, the sleeve had to be forced up with the steel spring and fastened with a pin at the shoulder, because otherwise her partner's arm was being constantly struck [by the sleeve]."[33] Such sleeves were the largest in the years 1835–36.[34] Then they suddenly disappeared from the fashion scene, and close-fitting, slightly puffed, or flounce-trimmed sleeves came back in fashion.[35]

The poke bonnet, with only a narrow brim framing the face and with fairly sparse trimmings of feathers and ribbons, regained its firm place in women's fashion during the 1830s, while shoes with crossover straps remained in vogue.

Strong colors were very popular in the mid 1830s; so were fabrics with varicolored stripes, tartan checks, stripes with woven flower motifs, and large checks, each bearing a single bunch of flowers.[36] Three-dimensional trimmings (modish in the 1820s) became less and less common during the following decade, until they disappeared altogether.

At the beginning of the 1830s the Far East had inspired the makers of women's clothing; toward the end of the decade clothesmakers (who still paid a visit to Paris before each season in search of fresh ideas)[37] began to flirt with a long-vanished epoch—the Rococo. In the following years, the lady of fashion had to attempt to appear as frail, graceful, and delicate as possible. No more for her the kind of dress that had dominated the scene until 1836, with its extravagant shapes and strong colors.

To comply with the new fashion, which to judge from the fashion prints of the day turned women into fragile "tea cozies," ladies wore a close-fitting top that curved down to a narrow waist. This was made to appear even narrower by a sweeping decolleté trimmed with lace and ribbons. Lace and ribbons reappeared on the sleeves and often also on the wide skirt, which was reinforced with horsehair padding and stood out in a circle, leaving only the toes visible.[38] The first crinoline was made by Josef Georg Beer in 1838.[39]

In the 1840s a plunging neckline was a feature of the Viennese beauty's day dress as well as of her evening dress, though in the case of the day dress the neckline was covered with a fichu. The day dress usually had long sleeves (close-fitting as far as the elbow, puffed below it) held in at the wrist with a narrow cuff.[40] A poke bonnet, trimmed inside the brim with bows and fabric flowers, a folding parasol, occasionally fingerless gloves, and shoes with crossover straps, which had been fashionable for years, were the principal accessories completing a woman's daytime wardrobe.

The necklines of ball dresses were very often adorned with a broad lace trimming, or bertha,[41] or laid in a fold that formed a wide collar and was fastened at the shoulders with clasps.[42] Women's evening dress was completed with half-length gloves, a fan, and a hairstyle with corkscrew curls or an elaborately plaited chignon at the nape of the neck.[43]

One is struck by the way in which the 1840s once again paid great attention to the decoration of skirts, while tops and sleeves were relatively neglected. For example, at the beginning of the 1840s, skirts with a middle section formed either by means of decoration or by an underskirt that showed through a frontal aper-

Following two pages: 233–50 Colored copperplate engravings from the *Wiener Zeitschrift für Kunst, Literatur, Theater und Mode* ("Viennese Review of Art, Literature, Theater and Fashion").

221

233 Day dress, 1816.

234 Coat, 1818.

235 Day dress, 1828.

236 *Wickler* ("cloak"), 1822.

237 House dress, 1831.

238 Riding habit and day dress, 1835.

239 Day dresses with leg-of-mutton sleeves, 1835.

240 Evening gown with crinoline, 1838.

241 Ladies' and gentlemen's evening wear, 1839.

242 Gentleman's evening suit with "floor-shy" trousers, 1819.

243 Ladies' and gentlemen's day wear, 1822.

244 Double frock coats, 1827.

245 Riding habit, 1828.

246 Riding habit and day suit, 1831.

247 Full evening dress, 1828.

248 Day suit, 1829.

249 Day wear, 1831.

250 House coat and day suit, 1830.

ture in the overskirt came into fashion; they remained fashionable until late in the decade.[44] Toward the end of the 1840s, this type of skirt was superseded by the flounced skirt,[45] which emphasized the circular shape even more and continued to dominate women's fashion until the late 1850s.

The fabrics used for women's clothes were also reminiscent of the Rococo: blends of silk and cotton, or organdy and chiffon for day wear; satin, moiré, brocade, damask, and tulle for evening wear. With the introduction of gas lighting, there was a noticeable increase in the use of shot fabrics with an iridescent effect.

Men's Fashion

For the elegant male, the years of the Congress of Vienna ushered in a crucial change. Pantaloons, or long trousers, became socially acceptable day wear. The most important thing about men's wear, according to that *arbiter elegantiarum* George Bryan Brummel, was that elegance consisted, not in being conspicuous, but in expressing oneself through superb cut and impeccable fit alone.[46]

A gentleman's outfit consisted of a dark frock coat, light-colored long trousers that reached down over ankle boots and had a strap at the instep, a waistcoat in a contrasting color to coat and trousers, with—until around 1820—a high collar, a white shirt with an elaborately knotted cravat, gloves, and a top hat.[47] For evening dress, however, men still wore knee breeches. These were not superseded by long black trousers until the late 1840s—and worn with black silk stockings and flat pumps.[48] In 1819, a sort of compromise between knee breeches and long trousers was brought in for evening wear: a three-quarter-length garment nicknamed "floor-shy" trousers.[49] The *Wiener Zeitschrift* began proposing long trousers for evening wear at the end of the 1820s, but they failed to gain acceptance at the time.[50]

Like that of the female sex, the fashionable male silhouette in the 1820s was slender—even if it meant resorting to a corset. Only men's sleeves showed a tendency to expand toward the end of the decade, like the sleeves on women's garments, though not to the same extreme degree, of course. For outerwear the fashion-consious man chose the double frock coat designed by Josef Gunkel. In the 1830s, additional skirts were added to the frock coat, and the waist was emphasized as it was in women's fashion.[51]

The cut of men's clothing changed little between the 1830s and the 1840s. Checked pantaloons were popular; so were frock coats in a different color, and waistcoats in brilliant hues. Checked pantaloons were readily combined with a checked waistcoat. The main colors used for frock coats for day wear were browns, blues, and greens; for evening dress the color preferred was blue, and by the late 1840s, black.[52]

The outerwear of the man of fashion was either an overcoat that matched the cut of his frock coat and was decorated with passementerie in imitation of Hungarian and Polish uniforms, or alternatively a kind of half-length cloak.[53]

At home, in imitation of Far Eastern fashion, the fashion-conscious man chose to wear a wide, loose morning coat of cashmere cloth printed with palmette motifs, comfortable trousers of light woolen cloth, slippers with curled-up toes, a shirt with a wide collar round which he would loosely wind a shawl; on his head he wore a little cap—rather like a fez—which might be trimmed with passementerie.[54]

The waistcoat was probably the most important piece of clothing worn by men in the Biedermeier era. Providing the principal color accent of male costume, it was either cream-colored with flowered embroidery, had a printed motif, or was varicolored. In the early part of the period, men often wore several waistcoats one on top of the other: for example, one in piqué and over it one in black silk which allowed the piqué to show through. Silk and velvet were the favorite fabrics for men's waistcoats.

Waistcoats were one of two items of clothing that permitted a man to develop a personal note, display his fashion know-how, and indulge in a little sartorial ex-

251 *Left*: Lady's dress, ca. 1817. Blue-and-white striped silk in the typical cut of the period, with the "Empire line" still in evidence. *Top*: Rounded neckline with three-dimensional decoration in white tulle and blue silk; high waistline emphasized by a belt, slightly gathered at the back; sleeves puffed at the shoulder, closer-fitting toward the wrist. *Skirt*: A-line, slightly gathered at the back; hem with three-dimensional decoration in white tulle and blue silk; pink silk shoes. L. (skirt) 124 cm. *Right*: Lady's dress, ca. 1840. Again the cut is typical of the period, showing how women's fashion was flirting with the Rococo. *Top*: yellow rep; close-fitting, curving down to a narrow waist; wide, rounded neckline; sleeves close-fitting over the upper arm, puffed from the elbow to the wrist and held in cuffs. *Skirt*: stands out in a circle; checked yellow silk with garlands of roses and scattered roses as decoration; black satin shoes with crossover straps. L. (skirt) 108 cm.
Historisches Museum der Stadt Wien: Fashion Collection.

travagance. Owning fifty waistcoats was not regarded as a luxury at the time. Morever, each of them must exhibit the very latest cut and precisely the right type and number of buttons.[55] The other item of clothing that expressed the wearer's individual taste was the necktie, or cravat. For day wear this was usually colorful and perhaps checked; for evening wear it was either white or black. There were many different ways of tying a cravat. In fact, the period saw a positive flood of literature on the "art of tying the cravat."[56] Even the great French author Honoré de Balzac, possibly driven by financial necessity, concerned himself with the cravat in his *Physiologie de la Toilette*. For Balzac, the whole *raison d'être* of the cravat lay in originality: it must be subject to no rules; its shape dictated by pure, spontaneous inspiration.[57] "The cravat is to a suit," he wrote, "what the truffle is to a dinner." Or again: "The art of tying his cravat is as important to the man of the world as the art of giving a dinner is to the statesman."[58]

The fashion accessories for men during this period were walking sticks or riding whips, short gloves, watch chains, and top hats. The top hat was the only admissible headgear for men. Though its shape changed frequently—in terms of height and brim width—it defended its position on the men's fashion scene for decades. In the Pre-March years, the top hat even succeeded in acquiring political significance: it was regarded as the headgear of the conservative citizen who was loyal to the state. In the 1830s, a soft felt hat with a broad brim, called a *Kalabreser*, was also worn.[59] The slouch hat came into favor with liberals, intellectuals, and artists in the 1840s. It was a visible sign of the independence of mind of its wearer and was considered the uniform of the revolutionary.

The way in which a man wore his hair and beard also played an important part in his life. [60] In the years following the Congress of Vienna, it was not fashionable to wear a beard, nor was it wise if one wished to avoid the risk of being regarded as a revolutionary. This attitude was slow to disappear. Side-whiskers and small moustaches came back into fashion in the 1820s and continued to be worn in the two following decades. In the 1830s, the goatee also returned. The full beard of the 1840s was, once again, seen as an expression of a liberal outlook on life and also as a symbol of political subversion. In general, however, men's fashion during the Biedermeier period was characterized by an "enforced simplicity resulting from an agreeable penchant for discretion."[61]

Regina Forstner

252 Anton Dietrich: Top hat, ca. 1830. Black-lacquered glazed cane, woven; tall crown with slightly curved brim; original label inside: "Royal Imperial, privileged, new, improved summer hats of whalebone and glazed cane by Anton Dietrich. Domiciled outside the Sack Gate No. 1016. Shop at Main Square No. 211 in Graz." H. 22.5 cm. Waistcoat, ca. 1830. Silk decorated with vertical stripes in purple and horizontal stripes in pale lilac with small black squares; cream, yellow, and olive green. Back and lining of natural-colored linen. Two rows of buttons, small round collar, and two side pockets. L. (back) 47 cm. Walking strick, ca. 1820. Black-lacquered wood, knob of embossed silver with floral decoration. L. 94 cm.
Historisches Museum der Stadt Wien: Fashion Collection.
The waistcoat was the most important item in a man's wardrobe in the Biedermeier period, while the top hat was the obligatory headgear. The waistcoat, preferably of silk or velvet, provided the color accent in male dress; it was either cream-colored with flowered embroidery, had printed motifs, or was varicolored.

1 Leopoldine Springschitz, *Wiener Mode im Wandel der Zeit*, Vienna, 1949, p. 83.
2 Hubert Kaut, *Modeblätter aus Wien*, Vienna, 1970, p. 49.
3 Johann Nestroy, *Der Zerrissene*, act 1, scene 5. Herr von Lips: "I've fourteen suits, some light, some dark [*dunkel*],/Tails and pantaloons, all by Gunkel...."
4 *Wiener Zeitschrift für Kunst, Theater und Mode*, lst–33rdyears, Vienna, 1816–48 [abbreviated as *WZ* hereafter].
5 *Ibid.*
6 Kaut (see above, note 2), p. 50.
7 *Wiener Allgemeine Theaterzeitung*, fashion supplements 1831–58.
8 See above, note 4.
9 *WZ*, May 22, 1816, pl. facing p. 220; Aug. 14, 1816, pl. facing p. 400. The two terms used in German are *Blonden*, a type of silk bobbin lace that was yellow in its unbleached state, thus its name—blond lace—in English; and *Vapeurspitze*, a type of cotton lace.
10 *WZ*, Jan. 15, 1817, pl. facing p. 40; Feb. 19, 1817, pl. facing p. 120; May 14, 1817, pl. facing p. 328.
11 *WZ*, July 9, 1818, pl. facing p. 668; June 29, 1820, pl. facing p. 636.
12 Lulu von Thürheim, *Mein Leben: Erinnerungen aus Österreichs grosser Welt*, Vol. 2, Vienna, 1913, pp. 117 f.
13 Egon Friedell, *Kulturgeschichte der Neuzeit*, Vol. 2, 4th ed., Munich, 1983, p. 1005.
14 *WZ*, Jan. 8, 1817, pl. facing p. 24. The Viennese ell measured 0.7792 m. (about 30 in.).
15 *WZ*, June 11, 1817, pl. facing p. 400.
16 Springschitz (see above, note 1), pp. 120 f.
17 *Ibid.*, p. 122.
18, 19 Historisches Museum der Stadt Wien: Fashion Collection.
20 WZ, Jan. 31, 1828, pl. facing p. 112; Feb. 7, 1828, pl. facing p. 136; Feb. 14, 1828, pl. facing p. 160; Apr. 24, 1828, pl. facing p. 404; May 15, 1828, pl. facing p. 476; July 3, 1828, pl. facing p. 656.
21 WZ, Apr. 24, 1828, pl. facing p. 404; May 15, 1828, pl. facing p. 476; July 3, 1828, pl. facing p. 656.
22 WZ, Jan. 31, 1828, pl. facing p. 112; Feb. 7, 1828, pl. facing p. 136.
23 WZ, Mar. 23, 1826, pl. facing p. 280; Apr. 27, 1828, pl. facing p. 400; July 13, 1826, pl. facing p. 668; Aug. 10, 1826, pl. facing p. 764; Dec. 21, 1826, pl. facing p. 1228; July, 1836, pl. facing p. 648; June 13, 1838, pl. facing p. 568.
24 "Über die herrschende Mode der gewürfelten Stoffe", in: *WZ*, Nov. 20, 1821, p. 1169; Nov. 24, 1821, p. 1189
25 Percale = a closely woven cotton fabric; poplin = a plain-woven cotton fabric; organdy = a very light cotton muslin.
26 WZ, Nov. 14, 1822, pl. facing p. 1112; Nov. 28, 1822, pl. facing p. 1160; Nov. 4, 1824, pl. facing p. 1152; Nov. 11, 1824, pl. facing p. 1176.
27 *WZ*, Nov. 8, 1827, pl. facing p. 1106.
28 Springschitz (see above, note 1), p. 131.
29 *WZ*, Sept. 27, 1827, pl. facing p. 962.
30 *WZ*, Apr. 7, 1831, pl. facing p. 336.
31 *WZ*, Oct. 23, 1831, pl. facing p. 1036.
32 *WZ*, Apr. 7, 1835, pl. facing p. 348.
33 Wolfgang Kudrnofsky, *Mode-Brevier*, Vienna, 1970, p. 99.
34 WZ, May 28, 1835, pl. facing p. 523; June 6, 1835, pl. facing p. 568; Sept. 1, 1836, pl. facing p. 840; Sept. 10, 1836, pl. facing p. 888.
35 WZ, Apr. 5, 1838, pl. facing p. 328; May 24, 1838, pl. facing p. 496; Sept. 13, 1838, pl. facing p. 880.
36 WZ, Feb. 1, 1838, pl. facing p. 112; May 24, 1838, pl. facing p. 496; July 19, 1838, pl. facing p. 688; Aug. 30, 1838, pl. facing p. 832; Sept. 27, 1838, pl. facing p. 928.
37 Springschitz (see above, note 1), p. 243.
38 See above, note 36.
39 *WZ*, Dec. 20, 1838, pl. facing p. 1216.
40 See above, note 36.
41 *WZ*, Jan. 19, 1837, pl. facing p. 69.
42 WZ, Jan. 24, 1839, pl. facing p. 88; Feb. 14, 1839, pl. facing p. 160; Feb. 21, 1839, pl. facing p. 184; Jan. 21, 1841, pl. facing p. 96.
43 WZ, Oct. 8, 1840, pl. facing p. 1288; Dec. 17, 1840, pl. facing p. 1608; Feb. 16, 1841, pl. facing p. 224.
44 WZ, July 7, 1836, pl. facing p. 648; Jan. 14, 1841, pl. facing p. 64; Mar. 4, 1841, pl. facing p. 288; Mar. 25, 1841. pl. facing 384; Nov. 27, 1847, pl. facing p. 940.
45 *WZ*, July 31, 1847, pl. facing p. 620.
46 Friedell (see above, note 13), p. 1005.
47 *WZ*, June 13, 1822, pl. facing p. 576; Dec. 12, 1822, pl. facing p. 1208.
48 *WZ*, Feb. 10, 1820, pl. facing p. 144.
49 *WZ*, Feb. 18, 1819, pl. facing p. 170.
50 *WZ*, Jan. 10, 1828, pl. facing p. 40.
51 *WZ*, Apr. 28, 1835, pl. facing p. 420; May 3, 1838, pl. facing p. 424.
52 WZ, Feb. 14, 1828, pl. facing p. 160; June 13, 1833, pl. facing p. 580; Aug. 17, 1837, pl. facing p. 784; Apr. 6, 1841, pl. facing p. 440.
53 WZ, Mar. 13, 1828, pl. facing p. 256; Apr. 11, 1833, pl. facing p. 364; Dec. 28, 1837, pl. facing p. 1240.
54 *WZ*, Mar. 11, 1830, pl. facing p. 248; July 29, 1841, pl. facing p. 960.
55 Springschitz (see above, note 1), pp. 100 f.
56 A. Varron, "Die Kunst seine Krawatte zu binden," in: *Ciba Rundschau*, 35, 1939, p. 1306.
57, 58 *Ibid., p.* 1304.
59 *WZ*, July 14, 1836, pl. facing p. 672.
60 *WZ*, lst–33rd years (1816–48).
61 Friedell (see above, note 13), p. 1004.

X LITERATURE IN THE BIEDERMEIER PERIOD

The Situation

Austrian Biedermeier literature is a highly imprecise classification at first glance. Despite all reservations about dividing history up into epochs—and one has to admit that is is necessary or at least useful to do so—such terms as Classicism, Romanticism, and Realism are associated with certain common criteria of substance and style that make it seem appropriate to subsume them under a generic heading. But is Biedermeier? Is one talking about a kind of "life awareness," perceptible in literature as elsewhere, that invites such attributes as bourgeois, sentimental, Weltschmerz, inner disintegration, a sense of order, harmless conviviality, or alternatively, Pre-March revolutionism? Or is Biedermeier simply the Age of Goethe, in which the radiance of that Weimar-based "prince of poets" was consciously or unconsciously the omnipresent reference point of all things literary?

Can one perhaps discover, in a countermovement to the actual course of historical and political events, a "rise of Austrian literature to European stature," appearing to compensate—at least in the intellectual sphere—for the decline of the Hapsburg Monarchy into provincialism and eventual political fragmentation? Or, given the right standpoint, does one also find here a long drawn-out Pre-March period of over thirty years, in which there is evidence everywhere—*ergo* in literature aswell—of a consistent thrust in the direction of the revolutionary events of 1848? The sheer number of possible approaches is an illustration of the problems of treating Biedermeier as an era.

On closer examination, the period from 1815 to 1848 is seen to be a period of transition, not decisively shaped by any one programmatic orientation. Despite certain ascertainable common features, which were not in fact exclusively confined to the period in question—I am thinking, for example, of *Ordnungsdenken* ("thinking in terms of order") handed down from the Baroque and extended under Josephine liberalism—the Biedermeier era was astonishingly varied and disparate in its literary manifestations. Both the cultivation and the rejection of Romanticism continued to exert a powerful influence on events. In keeping with the rise of nationalism, an increasing commitment to landscapes can be observed within German literature. The associated risk of partiality and narrowness of vision was obviated, at first, by liberalism (which remained effective until after the middle of the century), by political pragmatism, and by level-headed piety that, though privately binding, remained sceptical of creeds and churches.

It was a period of exceptionally richly talented individuals, whose processes of literary creation operated in a field of tension between the distinctly pro-writer mentality of old Austria, on the one hand, and what those concerned felt to be (and what posterity is still aware of as having been) an oppressive system of censorship on the other. The fact that censorship—like every other external pressure—can also be turned to good account in the creative process is no justification for its existence. Nevertheless, forgetting all its irony for a moment, Heinrich Heine's sarcastic remark in 1848 on the occasion of the abolition of censorship in Germany (where, in any case, it was much more restrained than in Metternich's Austria) needs to be examined in this respect too: "How, when a person has known censorship all his life, is he to write without it? All style will be at an end, all grammar, good usage!" In Austria Johann Nestroy said something very similar in his satire on the Revolution of 1848, *Freiheit in Krähwinkel* ("Freedom in Sleepytown"): "Writers have lost their favorite excuse. It wasn't a bad thing after all, when you'd run out of ideas, to be able to say to people: 'God, it's awful! They won't let you do a thing'."

Ever since the last years of the eighteenth century, writers had had to submit every book, before publication, to the Book Examination Office (*Bücherrevisionsamt*), and, above all, to police headquarters, where the notorious Count Sedlnitzky was in charge from 1815 onward. Here professional censors—usually men of considerable education—decided for or against the work submitted. The publicly spoken word (which covered everything from plays to sermons) was also subject to censorship in a modified form. There existed a third possibility in addition to approval or prohibition: the censor might mark individual passages of a work "dangerous" and make approval dependent upon their omission or alteration. There were also ways in which a book's distribution might be limited: advertizing might be banned, or would-be purchasers might have to produce a special certificate, which was available only to readers who were above suspicion, of course. Collected editions of a writer's work were usually treated less strictly; their high price was thought to prevent undesirably wide distribution.

The hazards to be negotiated by the author who was a prey to censorship were legion. Any criticism whatever of the state, the ruling dynasty, or the law was dealt with ruthlessly; foreign states and crowned heads enjoyed the same protection. In 1810 new censorship provisions

that appeared to be more liberal were passed, but the often-quoted sentence: "No ray of light, whatever its origin, shall in future go unheeded and unrecognized in the monarchy" was no more than a fancy form of words. As Metternich defined it, "censorship is the right to block the manifestation of ideas that confound the peace of the state, its interests, and its good order." It was the job of the police to keep the dreaded spirit of renewal, which was abroad in Europe, out of Austria; censorship was no isolated phenomenon but part of an extensive apparatus of political repression. It remained in effect until 1848; during the post-revolutionary restoration in Austria, it was resurrected with very little modification.

This is the background against which the work of the Austrian writers of the Biedermeier period must be considered. In their eyes and in the eyes of their public, playwrights enjoyed the highest esteem. Drama graced the stages of Vienna in a wide variety of forms. Some of the last examples of tragedies of circumstances were enacted alongside historical dramas, plays about artists, serious plays with a social message, and comedies of manners. The subjects for some plays were taken from fairy tales, myths, or legends; and finally there was an ever increasing amount of plays put on for pure entertainment, the kind that was mainly—though not exclusively—cultivated by the theaters in Vienna's suburbs. For the most part, narrative prose was directed at a very conventional reading public and even in its more outstanding manifestations came to be appreciated only gradually at its true value.

A major genre of the period was lyric poetry, which also played a crucial role in the period's many almanacs *(Musenalmanachen),* literary pocket-sized books, and calendars. Such publications as *Aurora, Gedenke mein* ("Remember Me"), *Huldigung den Frauen* ("Homage to Women"), and *Aglaja*, which also contained prose and were illustrated with etchings on literary themes, addressed an expanding, mainly middle-class readership. They represented a conservative element in literature, however—not least in their increasing tendency to trivia-

253 Ferdinand Georg Waldmüller: *Franz Grillparzer,* 1844. Oil on canvas, 69 × 55.5 cm. Historisches Museum der Stadt Wien. Franz Grillparzer, the "Austrian classic," was basically an unusually successful dramatist, whose plays—despite occasional brushes with the censorship authorites and the playwright's personal problems—were all performed.

lize—so that the more serious writers gradually began to dissociate themselves from such publications. Toward the end of the period and during the second half of the century, they were no more than albums of edifying verses for sensitive souls and well-educated young ladies: the literary equivalent of drawing-room music, or of the kind of shallow genre painting that suited the taste of a superficially cultured bourgeoisie. As such they helped to form a retrospective image of the Biedermeier years as a sort of golden age of improbably cozy domesticity.

The Theater

The most important literary figure of the period was Franz Grillparzer. Though a playwright first and foremost, Grillparzer made major or minor contributions to virtually every branch of literature. His work is astonishingly consistent, despite its author's deeply divided personality and the way in which he suffered, both on that account and at the hands of history. His poetic diction and creative genius were already fully developed in his earliest dramas. Grillparzer's gift for sympathetic observation, the psychological insight into the world around him that comes out so clearly in his diary, and his brilliant knack of translating situations from his own life into terms of theater brought characters of great suggestive power to the stage rather than mere skilfully crafted theatrical chessmen. Grillparzer's poetic ethos was rooted in lasting values. Writing was very much a part of his life, and his decision not to marry was much more than something dictated by his family background. There is an awareness of an immanent order of being which underpins Grillparzer's dramas; similarly, for the playwright personally, the heterogeneous elements of his environment were arranged into a self-contained world of the imagination by his writing.

Grillparzer's drama *Die Ahnfrau* ("The Progenitrix"), performed at the Hofburg Theater in 1817 and still, much to the author's later chagrin, classifiable as a tragedy of circumstances, already goes far beyond a mere depiction of blind, ineluctable destiny. Instead it develops the concept of personal freedom, which incorporates personal guilt as its negative component. *Sappho* (1818), a psychological drama about the Greek poetess, postulates the creative person's need to renounce bourgeois life and happiness to fulfill his or her mission. The trilogy *Das goldene Vlies* (1821, "The Golden Fleece"), which studies personal responsibility and the guilt arising out of the contradictions of existence, ends in the kind of resigned mood that was a crucial element in Grillparzer's own life.

Grillparzer had scarcely become known as a writer before he was in trouble with the censor. He had had problems with his poem *Campo Vaccino* (1819), but his problems coalesced, above all, around the tragedy *König Ottokars Glück und Ende* ("King Ottokar's Good Fortune and His End"), which was submitted for performance in 1823. His plea to Count Sedlnitzky not to rob him of "the fruit of years of work, my prospects for the future," was to no avail. Only the personal intervention of Empress Caroline Augusta made it possible for the play to be performed in 1825.

Although Grillparzer had studied the historical background in detail, he was not concerned here—nor later in *Ein Bruderzwist in Habsburg* ("A Fraternal Feud in Hapsburg") or in *Libussa* (about the legendary foundress of Prague)—with presenting dramatized history. Although the figure of Rudolf von Hapsburg, with its idealized traits, may correspond to what one might regard as a Biedermeier, people's emperor, and although the whole play—entirely in line with Grillparzer's personalist conception of the state and his concentration on the person of the monarch—may constitute a glorification of the dynasty and of Austria's mission; nevertheless, the dramatic conflict is sparked off primarily by a clash between power and order.

The concept of order (*Ordnungsgedanken*) can also be found in *Ein treuer Diener seines Herrn* (1828, "A Loyal Servant of His Master") and in a more sublime form in *Des Meeres und der Liebe Wellen* (1831, "Waves of the Ocean, Waves of Love"), a psychological drama that centers on the opposing claims of love and duty, and on the onset of passion. *Der Traum, ein Leben* (1834, "Dream, A Life") is also about passion and about reality and appearance.

Grillparzer's next work, the comedy *Weh dem, der lügt* (1836, "Woe Betide the Man Who Tells Lies"), precariously balanced between tragedy and comedy, examines the question of truth and falsehood. In it the writer contrasts the concept of truth as an absolute, removed from any kind of individual autonomy, with a deeper truth, which he postulates as committed to the ethos of personal responsibility. The play was a complete flop and the reason Grillparzer ended his public career as a playwright. It was not censorship that silenced Grillparzer, but the incomprehension of his audience.

255   *The Royal Imperial Court Theater beside the Castle, together with the Royal Imperial Riding School,* 1821–22. Copperplate engraving with watercolor, plate 16 × 21.4 cm, sheet 19 × 23.8 cm. Published by Tranquillo Mollo. Historisches Museum der Stadt Wien. The *Hoftheater* ("Court Theater") with its rich tradition occupied this building until 1888, when it moved into new premises on the Ring.

K·K·HOFTHEATER NÄCHST DER BURG, N⁰ 9. THÉATRE I·R·DE·LA·COUR PRÉS LE
NEBST DER K·K·REITSCHULE. PALAIS, AVEC LE MANÉGE I·R·

Vienne chez Tranquillo Mollo.

256 Franz Grillparzer: *Das goldene Vliess* ("The Golden Fleece"), drawing by the author for the last scene of the 4th Act of *Die Argonauten* ("The Argonauts"), 1819. Pen, 21 × 29 cm. Wiener Stadt- und Landesbibliothek.

Grillparzer could afford to give up writing for the stage because, in 1832, he had been appointed director of the Imperial Archives (*Hofkammerarchiv*). Life as a high-ranking civil servant—his job was more a sinecure than a serious hindrance to creative activity—enabled him to continue to write plays for his desk drawer, plays that he could invest with truth as he saw it, without having to make concessions to an audience.

The last three great plays by Grillparzer reveal his preoccupation with the concept of order. In *Die Jüdin von Toledo* ("The Jewess from Toledo"), the state embodies order amid the tensions of moral imperatives and individual intentions, freedom and commitment, inclination and duty. In the political drama *Libussa*, the fiction of a body politic based on shared humanity proves no match for the reality emodied in the male as the principle of organization and bonding, though a wide-ranging vision of the future leaves plenty of room for hope. Finally, in *Ein Bruderzwist in Habsburg* Grillparzer defines order as divine order:

"But order was established by God." It is the lodestar and corrective opposed to the inner chaos of man. In view of the danger of a new barbarism, which threatened to destroy that order, the writer tried to see through all distortions in his steadfast search for the image of true humanity.

Grillparzer's poetry—if, that is, we do not count the play *Der Traum, ein Leben* as a work of poetry—takes second place to his dramatic output. It is often matter-of-fact, deals with a particular subject, and is at its best in aphorisms and sarcastic polemics. His letters are remarkable, reflecting the writer's inner self searching for self-knowledge; his diaries and autobiography are also worthy of note. Of Grillparzer's shorter prose works, the novella *Der arme Spielmann* (1848, "The Poor Street Musician") is the most substantial.

Four years before Grillparzer abruptly quit the stage in 1836, his mentor at the Hofburg Theater, Joseph Schreyvogel, had died. Schreyvogel was a man imbued with the spirit of the Josephine Enlight-

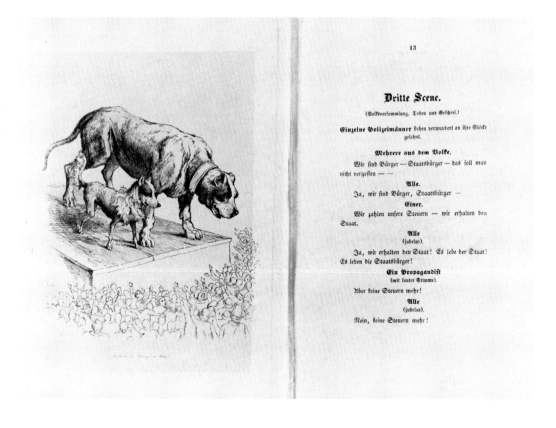

enment; he had also made a name for himself as a journalist, critic, and playwright, and had been secretary of the Hofburg Theater since 1814. As such he was responsible for reforming that institution. It had been a straight theater for only a short time (since 1810), and before Schreyvogel took charge it was dominated mainly by historical and Classicist dramas but also by tragedies of circumstances and their forerunners. The repertoire was composed of works by Iffland, Kotzebue, Collin, Zacharias Werner, and his imitator Adolf Müllner. With the advent of Schreyvogel, whose goal it was to reform the stage of the Hofburg Theater by giving it a European horizon (by presenting German classics and foreign-language classics in translation), that theater began to devote itself to producing the enduring works of world literature; current dramas were only given a place consistent with that scheme. Here was the foundation of this theater's outstanding importance in later years. Schreyvogel recognized the talent of the young Grillparzer and attracted

him to the Hofburg Theater. Following Grillparzer's departure, other authors stepped into the limelight, chief among them Friedrich Halm and Eduard von Bauernfeld.

Friedrich Halm (real name: Eligius von Münch-Bellinghausen) not only outdid Grillparzer at the Hofburg Theater; he later competed successfully with him for the post of First Keeper of the Court Library (1844). Halm's plays, most of which drew on medieval sagas for material, were imitative and superficial, the problems appearing to be artificially set up. They were enormously successful, however, particularly *Griseldis* (1835), *Der Sohn der Wildnis* (1842, "Son of the Wilderness"), and *Der Fechter von Ravenna* (1854, "The Swordsman of Ravenna"). Halm was better at writing comedy. His poetry is conventional, dry, and uninspired. His stories represent his best work; they are written in a prose full of psychological insights and characterized by realism, which looks forward to trends in the later decades of the century. Halm kept his distance from politics and from the outward circumstances of the life of his time, which spared him any close contact with the censor.

Eduard von Bauernfeld—an author already much played and much feted at the Hofburg Theater before Halm came along—was a very different case. Gregarious, partial to the atmosphere of the salon, a member of Schubert's circle, and a great friend of Grillparzer, Bauernfeld was possibly the most brilliant exponent of the bourgeois-liberal drawing-room comedy in his day. Skilled at handling fluent, elegant dialogue and with a great gift for humor, Bauernfeld also took unobtrusive pains to educate his audience to self-knowledge and to a rather more broadminded approach to the existing social order—which he accepted in principle. With his talent for ironic criticism, he was able to spot the shortcomings of the prevailing system very precisely, and to expose them. In *Der literarische Salon* (1836, "The Literary Salon") he focused his scorn on intellectual arrogance and corrupt theater criticism; in *Die Republik der Tiere* (1848, "The Animal Republic"), Bauernfeld mounted a direct attack on the Metternich system.

His diary, particularly where it becomes a sort of collection of aphorisms, is

an important literary document of the age. In it he noted, when the text of the projected Schubert opera *Der Graf von Gleichen* (1825) fell foul of the censor because of its portrayal of bigamy: "When, oh when will the devil take this accursed censorship?"

When even the Hofburg Theater showed a noticeable increase in the lighter kinds of theatrical entertainment, the suburban, or so-called low, theaters were staging them even more often. Classical drama did not reach its undisputed zenith in Austria until Grillparzer, but popular comedy could—in terms of quality and reputation as well—point to a tradition going back a lot farther. After Joseph II liberalized the provisions governing the theater in 1776, a number of new theaters were established in Vienna to meet the enormous popular demand. The Leopoldstadt Theater (opened in 1781) was and remained the most successful of the houses catering for the popular taste. The next to open—in 1788—was the Josefstadt Theater, which did sink to a fairly low level at times.

Then in 1801 the Theater an der Wien opened; it provided a lively and varied program of operas, concerts, dramas, symposia, and burlesques, until under the management of Karl Carl it became the foremost nursery of everything that we retrospectively bracket under the heading of "Viennese folk theater." Carl was an outstanding actor, director, and playwright himself besides being very good at engaging the most famous actors and writers to work for his theater. The favorite productions were burlesques, comedies of manners, parodies and travesties, and plays based on the traditional comic characters Hanswurst and Staberl. Major revues were produced as well as biblical and historical dramas, and even what was called "living theater," in which real trees as well as animals of all kinds were brought on stage. Folk plays drawn from everyday life in the city, mythological caricatures, and the ever-popular ballet completed the repertoire.

Until well beyond the middle of the century, the plot outlines continued to be taken from well-loved models, with French plays exerting a particularly pow-

258 Johann Christian Schoeller: *Staberl as a Wizard* (with a view of the Carl Theater), 1847. Watercolor, 14.3 × 11.2 cm. Historisches Museum der Stadt Wien.
This painting was a tribute to the director Karl Carl, who had succeeded in building his new theater in the space of seven months. Staberl was a constantly recurring comic figure in Viennese folk theater, related to Hanswurst. The former's chief characteristic was his ability to master every situation.

Meisl lay more in the direction of parody. He was responsible for a series of burlesques, comedies of manners, and village farces as well as for parodies of the current situation in Vienna and of the literary life of the city (an example was *Die Frau Ahndl* [1817, *Ahndl* is an Austrian dialect word for "grandmother"], a parody of Grillparzer's *Die Ahnfrau*).

Adolf Bäuerle's strong point was the local Viennese burlesque. In the long tradition of the hard-luck figure who is never at a loss for a joke, Bäuerle created the character of Staberl, who became one of the most popular stage personae of the period. *Die Bürger von Wien* (1813, "Citizens of Vienna"), *Die falsche Primadonna in Krähwinkel* (1819, "The Bogus Primadonna in Sleepytown"), and above all the fairy-tale opera *Aline oder Wien in einem anderen Weltteil* (1822, "Aline, or Vienna on a Different Continent") with the famous duet "*Ja, nur eine Kaiserstadt, ja nur ein Wien*" ("Yes, only one imperial city; yes only one Vienna") were among the most successful of his plays. (He wrote over seventy.) Morever, as the publisher of the *Wiener Allgemeine Theaterzeitung*, Bäuerle exercised great influence on theatrical life in Vienna generally.

Although the repertoires of Vienna's suburban theaters were completely dominated by the plays of Meisl, Gleich, and Bäuerle around 1820, the rising star of young Ferdinand Raimund was eventually to outshine them all. It was Raimund who became the true classic author of Biedermeier Vienna's folk theater. Raimund began his career as an actor, but he was dissatisfied with the existing repertoire and, from 1823 onward, produced plays of his own, nearly all of them at the Leopoldstadt Theater. In these he drew on elements of magic, fairy tales, allegories, and fantasies, always seeking to exert an educational influence. With the help of his highly poetical use of language, Raimund created theater of a very high standard. The Parnassus of the Hofburg Theater, however, always eluded Raimund. "I just haven't got all the fine words…. It's really too bad," he complained to Grillparzer. The latter saw that Raimund's great strength lay in his comic

erful influence. Original ideas were not yet as important as they were to become later, though subjects were being increasingly discussed. Material was still regarded simply as common property—and that went for the dramatic productions of the "literary" authors of the Hofburg Theater as well.

The leading authors at the suburban theater were Gleich, Meisl, and Bäuerle. In addition to a substantial body of horror fiction, Joseph Alois Gleich wrote more than 200 plays, most of which drew their material from myths and fairy tales. In the best of them he cultivated a kind of Viennese *Zauberspiel* (a magical extravaganza that borrowed elements of the moralizing village farce): man in himself is too weak and so must be educated to do better things; with the help of good spirits an ideal order is restored.

While Gleich was mainly interested in reforming people, the talents of Karl

DAS K.K.P. THEATER IN DER LEOPOLDSTADT. № 75. LE THEÂTRE I.R.P. DE LEOPOLDSTADT.

A Vienne chez Tranquillo Mollo.

260 *The Royal Imperial Private Theater in Leopoldstadt,* with a scene from Raimund's *Der Bauer als Millionär* ("The Millionaire Peasant"). Copperplate engraving, colored; plate 15.3 × 20.7 cm, sheet 18.2 × 22.5 cm. Published by Tranquillo Mollo. Historisches Museum der Stadt Wien.
The Leopoldstadt Theater was one of the great playhouses where the plays of Raimund and Nestroy were first performed and were constantly being reperformed.

Das Mädchen aus der Feenwelt oder der Bauer als Millionär
Zauberspiel von Raimund
Die Jugend. Alles hat man in der Welt! Jugend kriegt man nicht fürs Geld Brüderlein fein, Brüderlein fein, Mußt mir ja nicht böse seyn!

261 Johann Christian Schoeller: *The Girl from Fairyland, or The Millionaire Peasant, A Fairy-Tale Extravaganza by Raimund,* 1848. Copperplate engraving, colored, plate 21.4 × 27.3 cm, sheet 27.6 × 37 cm. Historisches Museum der Stadt Wien.

238

262   Glass showing Ferdinand Raimund as "Aschenmann" in *Der Verschwender* ("The Spendthrift"), ca. 1825. Cut glass, H. 14. cm, Diam. 9 cm. Historisches Museum der Stadt Wien. Besides writing their plays, both Raimund and Nestroy usually took the leading part in them as well.

talent and encouraged him to pursue this muse rather than to throw himself into great flights of poetry. Grillparzer felt that "the clash between the intuitively poetic and the vulgarly uncultivated" constituted "the chief charm of Raimund's creations" (1836).

Raimund was by no means deficient in humor, but he suffered from changing moods, which threatened to engulf him. Sentiment, naivety, and melancholy dominated Raimund's life, as they dominate his work, often forcing into the background the humor that is always to be found there. In images that he contrasted with the reality of everyday life, Raimund strove toward an ideal, toward a good that would not only prove victorious in the illusory world of the fairy-tale play but also find acceptance in a poetically transfigured daily round.

Der Barometermacher auf der Zauberinsel (1823, "The Weatherglass Maker on the Enchanted Island") was the first play Raimund attempted, a village farce set in the world of magic with numerous comic elements. *Der Bauer als Millionär* (1826, "The Millionaire Peasant"), with which Raimund achieved a sensational success, contrasted the materialist's pursuit of money with a modest but healthy and harmonious existence. The play's moral slant culminated in the improvement and cure of the leading character. The unpretentious tone of the songs—full of feeling and entirely free of false sentimentality—greatly contributed to the success of this and other plays by Raimund. In *Der Alpenkönig und der Menschenfeind* (1828, "The King of the Alps and the Misanthrope"), the central character's purification through self-knowledge communicated from an outside source was coupled with a hint of social criticism—albeit in poetic garb. *Der Verschwender* (1834, "The Spendthrift") is brought low by the lack of restraint that characterizes a person who lives by luck; the protagonist is saved by his own generosity, a quality he has always retained. However, he is saved only in the physical sense—true happiness and fulfillment in the domestically protected circle of a modest life are still denied him. Raimund's literary style

prevented him from attaining classic status. His attempts to achieve it—*Moisasurs Zauberfluch* (1827, "The Curse of Moisasur"), *Die gefesselte Phantasie* (1828, "Imagination Bound," poetry), and *Die unheilbringende Zauberkrone* (1829, "The Fateful Magic Crown")—failed at that level, throwing him back on his real and very personal achievement, which was to have brought poetic folk comedy to its apogee.

Raimund's writing appeared to conform to the system, though in fact it was a dream dreamt at a vast remove from the reality of the world of Metternich, and thus brought its author no problems with the censor at all. Raimund was able to state—as a recommendation in a letter to a Prague theater director—"My plays leave the hands of the censor almost unaltered, just as they were submitted" (1826).

It was a claim that could not be advanced by Raimund's great antipode, Johann Nepomuk Nestroy. Most unfortunately Nestroy was seen by Raimund, and has to an even greater extent been seen by posterity, as the older man's rival and, as it were, negative counterpart. Like Raimund, though with a superior educational background, Nestroy graduated to writing from acting. Quarrels with the censor dogged his career. He made his debut as a bass baritone at the Kärntnertor Theater in 1822. In 1823 he went to the German Theater in Amsterdam for two years, after which he worked in Brünn (now Brno in Czechoslovakia), where his engagement was terminated prematurely following difficulties with the censor.

By way of Graz and Pressburg (Bratislava), Nestroy returned to Vienna in 1831 and was engaged by Karl Carl at the Theater an der Wien. Until 1845 that theater, and the Leopoldstadt Theater from 1839 (also managed by Carl), constituted Nestroy's principal sphere of activity—apart from numerous tours as guest playwright and actor. From 1854 to 1860, Nestroy managed both theaters as Carl's successor. Nestroy had switched fairly early from singing to speaking roles, with comic roles soon predominating. Toward the end of 1827, he began to write plays himself—completing more than eighty in the course of his career—with the result that he became the most celebrated comic actor and playwright on the Viennese suburban stage.

Nestroy's plays, which can perhaps best be described as satirical burlesques, are hard to classify according to type. He showed as little scruple in his choice of outward forms as he did in his choice of models: Nestroy's work is usually classified as fairy–tale extravaganzas, parodies, burlesques, folk plays, and political comedies; yet these categories are hardly convincing when we look at specific instances. Nestroy's mind was always lively and perspicacious; the current forms, subjects, and circumstances he chose were filled with unmistakably trenchant characterizations, with his unique verbal wit, with a frequently pessimistic sarcasm, and with a satirical force that is both related to the subject and inherent in his language. The safe world of comedy is stripped of its illusions; the fairy-tale play is unmasked. The conciliatroy burslesque ending is used—sceptically—as a con-

ventional set piece, but at the same time it is exposed for what it is.

In *Der böse Geist Lumpazivagabundus* (1833, "The Evil Spirit Lumpazivagabundus," that being a humorous name for a vagrant or tramp) the fairy world is stripped of its ideal existence, as in all Nestroy's other fairy-tale plays. The fairies, wizards, and spirits that people the stage are anthropomorphic figures, behaving and thinking just like the characters in earthly comedies. Good fortune is incapable of reforming people and, in particular, stands no chance against reckless frivolity. Anyone who is nevertheless taken in by the conventional ending with the highly transparent promises of reform given by the "dissolute trio" is mercilessly enlightened in the sequel *Die Familien Zwirn, Knieriem, und Leim* (1835, "The Twist, Knee Strap, and Glue Families"). The good resolutions lie in ruins, and the marriages of our three heroes turn out to be disastrous. Some of the ideas that run through Nestroy's plays are:

263 Ferdinand Raimund: *Der Verschwender* ("The Spendthrift"), author's manuscript of the *Hobellied,* or "Plane Song," 1833. Wiener Stadt- und Landesbibliothek.
Two songs from plays by Raimund became enormously popular: *Brüderlein fein* from *Der Bauer als Millionär* (" The Millionare Peasant"), in which the rich man bids farewell to youth, and the *Hobellied* from *Der Verschwender* with the refrain "Fate applies the plane and planes us all the same."

264 Johann Christian Schoeller: *In Memoriam Ferdinand Raimund, who Died on September 5, 1836,* 1836. Watercolor, 21 × 24 cm. Historisches Museum der Stadt Wien.
Raimund in the role of "Valentin" in *Der Verschwender* ("The Spendthrift") is ferried across the River Styx. Vienna was shattered when his fear of being seriously ill caused the playwright to commit suicide.

DEM ANDENKEN
FERD. RAIMUND'S
GEST. DEN V SEPT.
MDCCCXXXVI.

marriage as "an institution for the mutual embitterment of existence" (*Der Färber und sein Zwillingsbruder* [1840, "The Dyer and his Twin Brother"]); the condition of being at the mercy of blind, unalterable fate ("It really is a luxury of fate that it flings arrows: one sees anyway from its dispositions that it didn't invent powder [i.e. is no great shakes"; *Mein Freund*, 1851); the vicissitudes of fortune (*Zu ebener Erde und erster Stock* [1835, 'Ground Floor and First Floor"]); and human weakness ("I think the worst of everyone, including myself, and I have seldom been wrong" [*Die beiden Nachtwandler*, 1836, "The Two Sleepwalkers"]). In the parody *Weder Lorbeerbaum noch Bettelstab* (1835, "Neither Laurels nor Beggary") the "middle way" is recommended as the best path through life, and in the same light, the playwright is justified in both entertaining the audience and earning his own living.

In addition to dealing with the unreliability of fortune whether for good or ill, *Zu ebener Erde und erster Stock* also contains some social criticism of the kind often found in Nestroy's plays. *Der Talisman* (1840, "The Talisman") takes a soberly satirical look at the different strata of society, denouncing prejudice and pil-

lorying selfish behavior. *Der Zerrissene* (1844, "Man in Tatters") caricatures the then current fashion for Weltschmerz and weariness of life, while *Der Unbedeutende* (1846, "The Man of No Consequence") makes an unsentimental plea for the honor of the little man.

When the revolution broke out in 1848, Nestroy seized on it as the subject of his burlesque *Freiheit in Krähwinkel* ("Freedom in Sleepytown"), in which he takes both the toppled system and the behavior of the revolutionaries to task. A prescribed order probably represented the ideal for Nestroy, too, given the enlightened liberalism of his views. Though to his satirical eye that order was now flawed, and he mercilessly put his finger on every fault and failing.

Nestroy took precautions, but they were not enough to save him from numerous difficulties with the censorship authorities. He practiced a kind of precensorship himself on the manuscripts of his plays, so that in the copies submitted to the censor the dialogue had already been toned down. For example, a piece of social criticism in *Zu ebener*

265 Johann Nestroy: *Self-Portrait,* with a dedication in his own hand, dated November 2, 1833. Pen and wash, 22 × 17 cm (oval). Wiener Stadt- und Landesbibliothek.

266 Johann Christian Schoeller: *Der Talisman*("The Talisman"), *Burlesque by Nestroy.* Copperplate engraving, colored, plate 20.9 × 26.6 cm, sheet 23 × 30.8 cm. Historisches Museum der Stadt Wien.
The "talisman" in question is a wig with which Titus Feuerfuchs ("Firefox") conceals his red hair. The play, based on a French prototype, is a parable about how easily people allow themselves to be deceived, and indeed clearly wish to be deceived, by appearances.

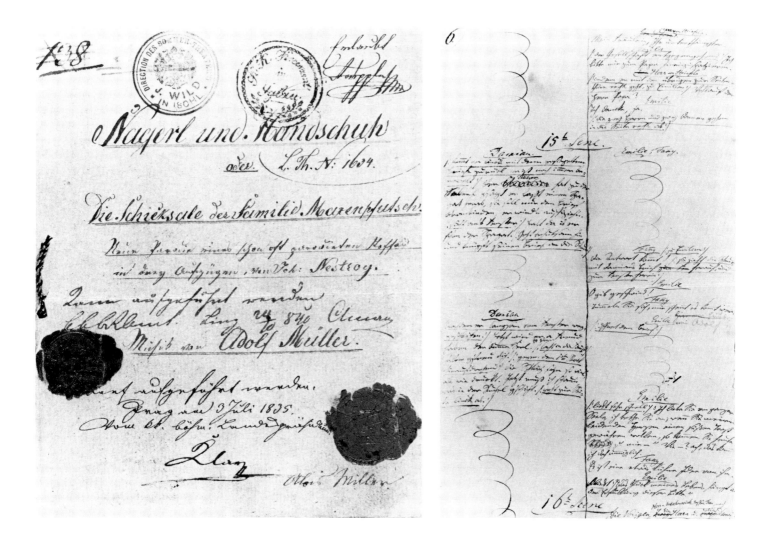

267 Johann Nestroy: *Nagerl und Handschuh,* theater manuscript and censorship authorization, 1835. Wiener Stadt- und Landesbibliothek.
No play could be performed unless it had been passed by the censor. However, Nestroy was a master at improvisation and usually managed to make up for what his seemingly innocent manuscripts omitted.

268 Johann Nestroy: *Zu ebener Erde und erster Stock* ("Ground Floor and First Floor"], author's self-censored manuscript, 1835. Wiener Stadt- und Landesbibliothek.

Erde und erster Stock—"If the rich didn't just invite other rich people but poor people instead, we'd all have enough to eat"—was watered down to the harmless: "They should have invited us." Nestroy was not able to give vent to his contempt for censorship from the stage until 1848: "A censor is a pencil in human form, or a human being in the form of a pencil, a line made flesh through the creations of the spirit, a crocodile lying in wait on the banks of the river of ideas to bite the heads off the writers swimming in it.... Censorship is the younger of two ugly sisters, the name of the elder being Inquisition. Censorship is the living admission by our rulers that they can only kick stupefied slaves, not govern free peoples" (*Freiheit in Krähwinkel*).

Poetry

The work of Nikolaus Lenau leads us into the completely different sphere of lyric poetry. This gained greatly in importance during the Biedermeier years, and among many talents great and small Lenau stands out as *the* Biedermeier lyric poet in Austria. A feeling for nature, a passion for travel, images from exotic spheres, love and friendship, Anacreontic motifs, and above all melancholy and Weltschmerz permeate Lenau's entire output. In fact, he wrote an "Ode to Melancholy": "You are my escort through life, brooding melancholy...." (*An die Melancholie,* 1830). Lenau's poems also have a very musical undertone. His view of nature arises out of a deep sensitivity and includes man as

243

269 Johann Nestroy as
"Sansquartier" in *Zwölf Mädchen
in Uniform* ("Twelve Girls in
Uniform"), ca. 1844. Plaster,
painted, H. 50 cm. Historisches
Museum der Stadt Wien.

Freiheit in Krähwinkel 1 Act. H. Nestroy. M. Schmid. D. Herzog und Scholz.

270 Johann Christian Schoeller: Scene from *Freiheit in Krähwinkel* ("Freedom in Sleepytown") with Johann Nestroy as "Eberhart Ultra," Jeanette Schmidt-Demmer, Katharina Herzog, and Wenzel Scholz, 1848. Watercolor, 11.2 × 14.2 cm. Historisches Museum der Stadt Wien. Nestroy was far too shrewd not to realize that the intoxication of the Revolution of 1848 could not last. Hence the—in places—highly sceptical tone of his "revolution play," *Freiheit in Krähwinkel.*

an essential component (*Schilflieder* [1832, "Reed Songs"]). One also senses Lenau's inner unrest.Weary of Europe, he set out optimistically for the New World. America disappointed him, however, and he soon returned to the old continent. No manifestation of existence, no framework of ideas, and no ideology was ever able truly to satisfy him. His verse epics in particular convey this poet's unremitting search.

Lenau's *Faust* (1836) is still a grand pantheistic design in which the hero turns his back on God and nature in profound scepticism, and even in the reconciliation of his death dream is simply a prey to self-deception. *Savonarola* (1837) is cast in the opposite mold: sustained by his love of a personal God, the hero develops his idea of a polity shaped by Christianity. In Lenau's curious allegories of *Die Albigenser* (1842, "The Albigenses"), the autonomous development of the mind and the positive power of doubt are once again portrayed in historical guise. *Don Juan* (1844), on the other hand, is filled with deep pessimism. In vain the hero tries to find emotional fulfillment and inner equilibrium through the opposite sex, eventually growing weary of life and disgusted with the world.

Lenau had no liking for political poetry, but his work does contain a scattering of comments on the situation in Austria, directed principally against the lack of intellectual freedom, of which he had personal experience. Such criticism was often veiled. "Oh do not think I feel no spark [of anger] ... whenever a ruler wantonly tramples his people," Lenau wrote in his notebook in 1833.

The plain, imitative poetry of Count Anton Auersperg (his real name, though like Lenau and Halm he chose a bourgeois pseudonym: Anastasius Grün) was markedly political but of inferior poetic power. The idea of freedom was the determining factor behind his entire poetic output. Particularly in his *Spaziergänge eines Wiener Poeten* (1831, "Walks of a Viennese Poet"), written under the influence of the revolutionary events of July, 1830, in Paris, he attacked the current deplorable state of affairs in Austria. This

271 Joseph Kriehuber: *Nikolaus Lenau,* 1841. Lithograph, 36 × 27.2 cm. Historisches Museum der Stadt Wien.

constitutes an outstanding example of the political poetry of the Biedermeier years. The collection was of course—like so many other works by Austrian writers during this period—printed in Germany, where censorship was far less strict than it was in Austria. It was the same with the verse epic *Schutt* (1835), based on a Christian legend, in which the poet celebrated the freedom of America. Grün occasionally made his escape from grueling struggles with the censorship authorities by retreating to his family seat in Croatia where—as he wrote in a letter to Lenau in 1836—life was quite tolerable "with my neighbors, the wolves and Croats .... They are honest fellows who at least do not go snuffling and sniffing at green Anastasius's [a play on his adopted pseudonym] poetic knapsack."

In comparison to Lenau's and Auersperg's work, the popular poems, songs, and ballads of Johann Nepomuk Vogl and Johann Gabriel Seidl enjoyed wide circulation. The self-tormenting Bohemian Ferdinand Sauter was a man who stood somewhat aloof from poetic fame, vacillating between a self-imposed solitude and a longing for company. At times

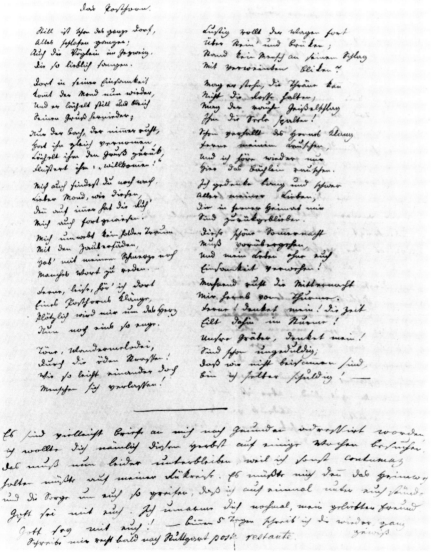

simple and full of feeling, at times sarcastic and cynical, Sauter's poetry is difficult to place in the overall poetic context of the period. Another rather special case is the poet, doctor, and philosopher Ernst von Feuchtersleben, whose thinking revolved around the moral purpose of mankind. In his *Diätetik der Seele* (1838, "Dietetics of the Soul"), a book that had a major influence on contemporaries, and of which Grillparzer thought highly, Feuchtersleben examines the interrelatedness of mind and body and attempts—in a period of intellectual repression—to set men free from their fear of existence. "Free resignation," or the composure of an inner equilibrium, is also the message that emerges from his aphorisms and his impressive contemplative poetry.

Poetry in dialect enjoyed growing popularity, particularly in the lyric field, though from the very outset there was a grave danger of shallowness and superficiality. Ignaz Franz Castelli, a kind of literary omnivore who tried his hand at everything yet was universally popular and respected as an author and who is inseparable from our image of the intellectual and social life of Biedermeier Vienna, published his "Poems in the Lower Austrian Dialect" in 1828. Franz Stelzhamer brought out the early volumes of his Upper Austrian dialect poems, characterized by sincere feeling, between 1837 and 1844. Others who followed in their footsteps were Josef Misson with the Lower Austrian verse epic *Da Naz* (1850) and Alexander Baumann with "*Singspiele* [light operas] from the Austrian Mountains in Folk Dialect" (1850).

Literary Societies

A feature of the period was the lively social life in which many of the abovementioned writers participated with a view to sharing ideas among themselves as well as with musicians, artists, actors, and generally with the intellectually aware of all classes. A particular meeting place of literary Vienna in the second quarter of the nineteenth century was the famous Silver Coffeehouse, on which the authorities accordingly kept a suspicious eye.

Ludlamshöhle, or "Ludlam's Den," which came into being in 1816–17 and counted among its members Castelli, Karl von Holtei, Moritz Gottlieb Saphir, and latterly Grillparzer himself, was a social club that gave itself a set of wittily nonsensical rules. Though nonpolitical, it was raided by the police during the night of April 18–19, 1826, for allegedly constituting a threat to the security of the state and indulging in revolutionary activities. Even Grillparzer had to submit to having his house searched. Scorning such adversities, in 1840 Friedrich Kaiser founded the Konkordia Society, of which Grillparzer was also a member. It failed to survive the revolutionary upheavals of 1848.

Friedrich Kaiser was the most successful author on the suburban stage after Nestroy, but he was always overshadowed by the latter. In addition to writing sentimental melodramas, Kaiser tried, by giving a positive portrayal of bourgeois life, to bring to the stage a genuine, that is to say realistic, kind of folk play. In certain respects he represented a bridge between the old Viennese folk comedy and the folk plays of someone like Ludwig Anzengruber, who had his heyday in the 1870s. However, the *Lebensbild*, or "picture of life," particularly advocated by Kaiser incurred the scorn of Nestroy: "If a play contains three jokes and otherwise nothing but corpses, the dead and dying, graves, and gravediggers, that's what they now call a picture of life" (*Der Talisman*, 1840).

Moritz Gottlieb Saphir, perhaps Nestroy's fiercest and most biased critic, essayed a sortie himself—albeit an unsuccessful one—into the dramatic sphere. Following earlier attempts, Saphir was active as a journalist in Vienna from 1834; and from 1837 he edited the review *Der Humorist,* which he used as a tribunal of literary criticism. He also wrote some unimportant but widely read poetry and organzied numerous declamatory symposia built around his own often very labored lectures.

Hard on the heels of the Konkordia Society, another social club called Soupiritum emerged with Castelli, Bauernfeld, and a number of former "Ludlamites" among its members. Soupiritum sought to continue the nonsense tradition of the earlier club. The "minutes" that were kept of its social gatherings include comic poems, rebuses, drawings, and epigrams that are often about as coarse and silly as possible. After 1848, the club continued in existence—with interruptions—as the Gnomes' Den or Baumann's Den (after the writer Alexander Baumann, at whose home it met for a while) until 1874.

Prose

Someone far removed from this kind of literary conviviality was Adalbert Stifter, the most important writer of the period and the author of some of the finest prose of the century. Between 1844 and 1850, he collected stories of his that had previously appeared in various publications into three volumes of "Studies" (*Studien*). These show Stifter as having been deeply imbued with bourgeois humanism, with profound religious belief, and with an unshakable faith in created being. Everything had its place in a preordained, God-given order; each tiniest fragment of the world faithfully reflected the whole, and the necessary march of time and change manifested the permanence of everything that exists. For Stifter, the perpetual self-renewal of nature ultimately demonstrated true greatness, as did dependence on *Heimat* (the place of one's birth), village, family, custom and religion, and feelings of inner calm and purity. It was this ideal of art and life, this morally conditioned fundamental order of the world which he sought unswervingly to convey so that it would have an educative, reformative effect on his readers. Derided as the "portrayer of bugs and buttercups," in 1852 Stifter used the Foreword of his volume of stories *Bunte Steine* ("Bright Stones") to formulate the ethical postulate underlying his writing—the "gentle law": "The blowing of the wind, the ripple of water, the growing of the corn, the heaving of the ocean, the green of the earth, the dazzle of the sky, the shimmer of the stars, these I regard as great.... As it is in the external world of nature, so it is in the inner world, the world of humankind. A whole life full of fairness, simplicity, self-control, the exercise of good sense, effectiveness in one's sphere, and admiration of the beautiful, coupled with a cheerful, unruffled death—these I regard as great; mighty stirrings of emotion, the terrible onrush of anger, the desire for revenge, the mind on fire that yearns for action, tears things down, makes changes, destroys and in its agitation often throws away its own life—these I regard not as greater but as smaller, for

these things are no more than the products of individual, unilateral forces, like storms, volcanoes, and earthquakes. Let us endeavor to catch a glimpse of the gentle law by which humankind is led. It provides forces that are directed at the continued existence of the individual. They take and make use of everything necessary to the continued existence and further development of the same. They ensure the continuance of the one and, through the one, of all.... It is...the law of justice, the law of custom, the law that requires that each man continues to exist, esteemed, honored, and unimperiled by his neighbor, that he is able to pursue his higher human career and gain the love and admiration of his fellow men, and that he is guarded like a jewel, as every man is a jewel for all other men."

Despite an increasingly pessimistic state of mind, Stifter never allowed himself to be diverted from his basic idea. Simplicity, tranquillity, and inner greatness as the determining forms of life, irrespective of historical or social contingencies, likewise characterize his great novel *Nachsommer* (1857, "Indian Summer"), about experiential and educational development, and the expansive pictorial narrative *Witiko* (1865), in which Stifter set his view of man against the trials and tribulations of his time.

Stifter's novellas were appreciated by his contemporaries, though perhaps not at their full value. The works of Charles Sealsfield (real name: Karl Postl), on the other hand, went virtually unnoticed. Postl, an ordained priest, fled from his monastery (the Kreuzherrnstift in Prague) in 1823 and went to the United States under an assumed name. Having returned to Europe, he lived more or less continuously in Switzerland from 1832, and it was only after his death that his true identity emerged. In *Austria As It Is* (1828), he criticized the political, social, and cultural situation in Austria unsparingly. From the literary point of view, however, his most important works are the great North American novels, which appeared between 1827 and 1836, and *Das Kajütenbuch* (1841, "The Cabin Book"). In formal terms these are travel

249

books, but behind the impressive descriptions of nature and the ethnographical details, at the center of his novels there is always a romanticized American people that often seems somehow unreal. At the same time, Postl's concept of order, which had a thoroughly religious motivation, and his leaning toward Puritanism and a patriarchal image of society led him into what the modern reader often feels to be an unacceptable glorification of the mentality of the American South.

The richness and variety of Biedermeier literature is also manifest in forms that lie outside the traditionally sacrosanct triple canon of drama, poetry, and prose, namely in gnomic poetry, aphorisms, and epigrams (Grillparzer, Feuchtersleben), historico-literary writing, autobiographical material such as diaries, letters, and memoirs, and in the extensive literature dealing with travel.

In addition to the autobiographical writings of Grillparzer and Bauernfeld, we must mention the *Denkwürdigkeiten aus meinem Leben* (1844, "Memorabilia from My Life") penned by the prolific Karoline Pichler, whose salon was frequented by the Viennese intelligentsia of her day, but whose novels have long since fallen into the oblivion they deserve. A vivid picture of the period is provided by Ignaz Franz Castelli's *Memoiren meines Lebens* (1861, "Memoirs of My Life"). Mention must also be made of the historical studies and descriptions inspired by Romanticism and its interest in the country's past. Here one thinks mainly of the works of Joseph von Hormayr. His monumental twenty-volume biographical opus, *Österreichischer Plutarch* (1807–14, "Austrian Plutarch") portrays generals and other figures not just in a strictly historical manner but with a substantial admixture of anecdote; it is not so much aimed at serving the needs of scholars as at providing a wider public with material for edification and emulation. Nor was Hormayr's work without effect on literary contemporaries, with Grillparzer chief among them.

However, during this period, the literary rendition of travel experiences was of especial importance—and here one is not just talking about Grillparzer, Lenau, or Postl (Sealsfield). The connection that Austria had enjoyed, since the mid-eighteenth century, with the Levant and regions even farther to the southeast also found expression in literature. Joseph von Hammer-Purgstall, in particular, probably the most important Orientalist Austria has ever produced, made a name for himself not only as the historian of the Ottoman Empire but also as a literary historian, linguist, poet, and translator of oriental verse. Everyone who was concerned at that time with the spirit and with the variety of forms of oriental poetry drew upon his works, not the least Goethe, Friedrich Rückert, and August Platen.

There were others, too, who wrote about their experiences of the East. Anton Prokesch von Osten, who served his country as a diplomat in Constantinople, Greece, and Egypt, published an account of a journey to the Holy Land and Egypt in 1829–31. Friedrich Schwarzenberg, cut off from his family and accepting only literary contacts in his voluntary solitude, described his war and travel adventures, which also took him to the Levant as well as to Algiers, in *Aus dem Wanderbuche eines verabschiedeten Lanzknechts* (1844, "From the Travel Diary of a Discharged Lancer"). A very different kind of author was Ida Pfeiffer, naive and and yet in her way impressive, with her *Reise einer Wienerin in das heilige Land* (1844, "A Viennese Woman's Journey to the Holy Land") and other travel books. And finally, still very much in the Baroque tradition, there was that outstanding stylist Jakob Philipp Fallmerayer, who visited Greece, the Near East, Palestine, and Egypt and described what he saw— he was profoundly impressed by the power of Byzantine-Russian Slavism—in his books, notably in *Fragmente aus dem Orient* (1845, "Fragments from the Orient").

Between 1815 and 1848, when they sought, each in their own way, to fashion universals, literary manifestations looked beyond the limitations imposed by attachment to a particular landscape or a particular age, and drew their creative power from problems other than those specific to their place and time. However,

275 Ida Pfeiffer: *Reise einer Wienerin ins Heilige Land* ("A Viennese Woman's Journey to the Holy Land"): frontispiece, 1844. Wiener Stadt- und Landesbibliothek.

276 *Aurora,* pocket-sized book for the year 1840: title page and frontispiece. Wiener Stadt- und Landesbibliothek.
Pocket-sized books and almanacs were a popular literary medium; the demands they made on the reader were usually not excessive.

251

that attachment always constituted the mainstay of their creative power.

Although the Revolution of 1848 may have brought no break in literary development, many of those concerned nevertheless experienced it as a turning point. Franz Grillparzer, deeply disturbed by the events of that October, made a will that opened on a note of resignation: "Since no one at the present moment, particularly no honest man, is safe from meeting a violent end...!" In the years that followed, he bound himself with a deeper conservatism to the historical and political situation of the day. Adalbert Stifter admitted, for his part, that the year 1848 had left him with an empty feeling. The presentiment that the new generation would demand new answers in terms of literature too, was already detectable in the attempts to preserve and to convey continuity in all domains—the literary sphere included.

Walter Obermaier

ys having to point out that ter-
classifications that have
emely useful and comprehen-
ition to other branches of the
be applied to music without
ous problems. This is certainly
gard to the cultural phenome-
ermeier. To speak of "Bieder-
c," for example, is to invent a
category, particularly since
features can be identified that
to characterize a Biedermeier
art. And yet there is a more or
formed section of the public
s it has a "good idea" of pre-
kind of music that most aptly
pellation "Biedermeier." The
eries of misinterpretations that
nong other things, to a glorifi-
-called Biedermeier culture.
the musical phenomena that
fore in the years between the
f Vienna and the Revolution of
so various and so multifaceted
eric term available will cover
ety, however, is not synony-
quality in this case, and one of
ing lessons that a study of the
he period has to teach is that
Vienna has little cause to pride itself on any particular brilliance in this field.

Beethoven and Schubert

From the usually reliable standpoint of the historian, much of importance can doubtless be ascertained that is capable of elevating Vienna to the status of a musi-cal center *par excellence* even in the years after 1815, but such an estimate must remain confined to names that did indeed make history. Invoking Beethoven and Schubert as two compos-ers who grew to substantial greatness in the musical life of the period, while it simplifies the task of passing judgement on an entire era that certainly made a major cultural contribution, at the same time introduces a serious distortion. For neither Beethoven nor Schubert—if, for the moment, we confine our attention to the first decade of the Biedermeier period—set his seal on his time, or even constituted a reflection of his time.

Beethoven in his day was admired as one might admire a monument, though only a small, elite circle had access to—rather than simply respect for—his "great-ness," which was a quality that even the musically less cultivated attributed to him without envy. However, it was not until generations later that Beethoven's true importance was discovered, and even then people could not agree about whether to call him a Classical or a Ro-mantic composer.

As a person Beethoven bore no resem-blance to the common conception of a Biedermeier man; on the contrary, handi-capped by a hearing disorder, the com-poser was brusque in his dealings with his fellow men, avoided company—supposedly the breath of life to Bieder-meier man, who is invariably described as gregarious—and worked like one pos-sessed. There was nothing pleasant (in the sense of agreeable or likeable) about the music of Beethoven's mature years; it was quite unsuitable for social occasions, made intellectual demands that were well beyond the range of any kind of domestic musicmaking, and indeed had no place in that context. His works came into being quite uninfluenced by the circumstances of his time. Most of them received immediate publication—often helped along by some rather rough treatment meted out to the publisher by the composer himself—but they were dreadfully expensive to produce and sold because of the composer's name rather than because of their playability. People went in awe of Beethoven, and one of the reasons was simply that they failed to understand him. (Later, when musicologists got to grips with the man, his method of composition was grasped more quickly than Schubert's. Beethoven's musical thinking, based on rigorous thematic work that sought to explore all possibilities, became a model for subsequent generations of composers and was adopted not only by Johannes Brahms but also by Arnold Schönberg, among others.)

It was different with Schubert. People thought—indeed, some still think—that he was the prototype of the Biedermeier artist. One explanation for this distorted picture of Schubert the man as well as Schubert the composer may be that his personality has eluded the grasp of academically oriented biographers. Very few facts about Schubert's life have survived and even fewer truly conclusive utterances. On the other hand a so-called Schubert circle made itself distinctly heard—but, for the most part, not until long after Schubert's death, when its members were interrogated about the composer. The result was a spate of "reminiscences" by friends who were probably not particularly concerned with establishing the truth.

Undoubtedly one discerns a Biedermeier side to Schubert, but even this cannot be understood without some comment. There is, on the one hand, the Schubert who readily "struck up a waltz" at the urging of his friends and also committed to writing a large number of dance compositions; on the other hand, there is the much sought-after musical centerpiece of the so-called *Schubertiades*. So-

cial gatherings, though a thorn in the flesh to "Metternich's men," were a favorite means of communication, particularly in the period after 1815, and musical entertainment was often regarded as an important ingredient of such occasions. The *Schubertiades*—it is not possible to establish who invented the term— were no different in this respect. We must beware, however, of jumping to the conclusion that these were gatherings of artists, writers, and suchlike people held in honor of Schubert and for the purpose of enjoying a bit of harmless fun.

Schubert, though he may well have given his name to these events, was far from being the center of attention as far as the

277 Ludwig van Beethoven: Manuscript letter to an unknown addressee, Vienna, November 6, 1821. Wiener Stadt- und Landesbibliothek.

278 Josef Willibrord Mähler: *Ludwig van Beethoven,* 1804–5. Oil on canvas, 117.5 × 90.5 cm. Historisches Museum der Stadt Wien: Beethoven apartment. Ludwig van Beethoven owned this painting himself and took it with him whenever he moved. It eventually passed to his heir, his nephew Karl; and through Karl's descendants it came into the possession of the city of Vienna.

entertainment was concerned. He was, above all, a useful musician who could not only play but also sing, if necessary. Granted, many of his songs and dances were first performed on such occasions, but hardly any of his major chamber-music works were. From this somewhat one-sided relationship one can speculate as to the true purpose of the "Schubert circle."

It is possible that Schubert (who on some evenings did not even attend) merely provided a cover for meetings that were not without a certain intellectual and political explosiveness. After all, the circle did include such leading intellects of the day as Eduard von Bauernfeld, Leopold Kupelwieser, Moritz von Schwind, Franz von Schober, and Franz Grillparzer, to name only the best known. The documents make no men-

tion of irate discussions concerning the political pressures that were a burden to them all, but perhaps that obdurate silence is proof enough in itself. In fact, Schubert the artist was little understood and even less appreciated by the self-styled "Schubertians." Nowhere do we find any indication that they really regarded him as one of the greatest composers of all time. Moreover, in the works of his mature period, Schubert reached far beyond Biedermeier. Whether we take the example of his "Great" Symphony in C Major, or the string quintet, or the last great piano sonatas—everywhere we encounter a powerful and highly original personality colored by an often tragic element that is perhaps more of an enigma than ever today. Particularly in the instrumental sphere, this Schubert fashioned sounds that did not really come into their

279 Johann Peter Leyser: *Beethoven Out Walking.* Lithograph, 26.2 × 22.4 cm. Historisches Museum der Stadt Wien.

280 Johann Nepomuk Höchle: *The Room in Black Spaniard House Where Beethoven Died,* 1827. Ink-brush drawing, 25.8 × 21.1 cm. Historisches Museum der Stadt Wien.
This drawing was made shortly after Beethoven's death. Originally there were two pianos in this room in the composer's apartment; clearly one of them was sometimes moved into the adjacent room.

281 Moritz von Schwind: *A Schubert Evening at the House of Josef von Spaun,* 1868. Pen and pencil and wash, 55 × 93 cm. Historisches Museum der Stadt Wien. This drawing, made long after Schubert's death, was a preliminary design for a Schubert Room planned by Moritz von Schwind, which was never executed.

own until toward the end of the nineteenth century. His contemporaries—even the critics, who unfailingly presented him as "the prince of song"—knew next to nothing of this side of the composer. Occasionally one has the impression that people were actually unwilling to attempt to measure his instrumental compositions against the works of Beethoven, who was already famous in his lifetime. What is certain is that contemporaries would not have succeeded in any such attempt, caught up as they were in a musical aesthetic that simply did not permit them access to different stylistic trends.

Not that a comparison between Schubert and Beethoven brings anything very meaningful to light, since in terms of artistic potency the two have little in common. The differences are perhaps most striking where we have works by both in the form of sketches. By the time a work of Beethoven's reached a coherent form, he had covered a great deal of paper. Schubert completed these preliminary stages—in so far asthey existed for him—in his head, for what he set down on paper was already virtually definitive. Where Beethoven "chiseled out" his form, Schubert cleared formal hurdles with brilliant ease, carried along by his exuberant musical imagination. (Robert Schumann could only speak admiringly in this context of Schubert's *himmlische Längen* [his "divine longueurs"].)

After their deaths both composers suffered a common fate in Vienna: they were forgotten, and it was years before one could once again speak with any justification of a sustained interest in their work. So if Beethoven and Schubert owed little to the Biedermeier mentality—and with regard to the latter we also have to adjust our traditional image of the man, in so far as he was a highly educated artist with a particularly well-developed interest in literature, and not the rather helpless

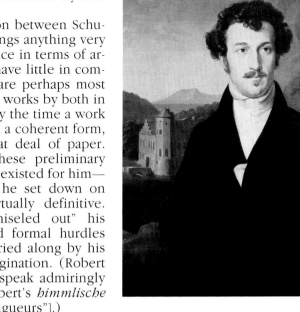

282 Leopold Kupelwieser: *Franz von Schober,* 1822, Oil on canvas, 75.2 × 60 cm. Historisches Museum der Stadt Wien: Schubert's birthplace.

257

283 Franz Schubert: Octet in F. Major, D. 803; manuscript in the composer's own hand. Wiener Stadt- und Landesbibliothek.

284 Franz Schubert: *Erlkönig* ("Erl King") set to music for solo voice with pianoforte accompaniment, 2nd edition, Vienna, published by Anton Diabelli. Wiener Stadt- und Landesbibliothek.

285 Wilhelm August Rieder: *Franz Schubert,* 1825. Watercolor, 19.8 × 24.5 cm. Historisches Museum der Stadt Wien.
Apparently this watercolor was painted on a day when Schubert sought shelter during a downpour at his friend Rieder's house.

286 Leopold Kupelwieser: *The Schubertians on an Outing in the Country from Atzenbrugg to Aumühl,* 1820. Watercolor, 23.7 × 38.9 cm. Historisches Museum der Stadt Wien.

Schwammerl (literally "mushroom"; the equivalent English nickname would be "tubby") that he pretended to be—the question we have to answer is: what musical fruits of Viennese provenance does the Biedermeier era have to show?

The Heyday of Musical Arrangements

The altered structure of society after 1815 had a quite decisive effect on the musical life of the time. Patronage in the old sense ceased to exist, with the result that musicians (whose position had always been a subordinate one) were no longer able to find employment at court and had to look elsewhere for their income as free-lance—which usually meant out-of-work—artists.

Schubert was one of the first well-known composers to find himself confronted with this, initially, almost insoluble problem. Only a few of the innumerable composers resident in Vienna contrived to make a living at their trade. If they were not employed in an "official" function, they were financially dependent on the sale of their works. Although contemporary music was played almost exclusively (exceptions were the works of Mozart and Haydn), this did not prove sufficiently lucrative.

For many, the only way of making money was to acquire a share in the successes of other—mostly foreign—composers by making arrangements of their works. The law of copyright was far from clear as yet—in 1818 people began thinking about it, and around 1823 they started to take energetic steps to stem the flood of arrangements and piratical editions of the same—so that publishers and arrangers contrived to do very well out of individual "hits" of the period.

One man who kept the heads of composers and publishers above water for a long time was Gioacchino Rossini, whose star began to rise in Austria from about 1816, and who was eventually to throw Vienna into a scarcely comprehensible Rossini frenzy. So it was that the Italian composer rapidly became the prey of Viennese publishers as they competed with one another by every available means, legal and illegal. In their search for marketable products, they came up with every imaginable form of adaptation.

287 *Franz Schubert's Grave in Währing Cemetery.* Lithograph, plate 24.9 × 19.9 cm, sheet 45.8 × 32 cm. Historisches Museum der Stadt Wien.

288 Joseph Kriehuber: *Anton Diabelli,* 1841. Lithograph, 62.5 × 45.5 cm. Historisches Museum der Stadt Wien. Anton Diabelli was the principal publisher of Schubert's music.

Musikalisch-declamatorische Privatunterhaltung,

gegeben von

C. F. Müller

am 12ten März 1818 Mittags

in dem unentgeldlich überlassenen Saale des Hôtels zum römischen Kaiser.

Vorkommende Stücke sind:

1. Ouverture auf zwey Fortepiano, jedes zu 4 Hände, von F. Schubert, vorgetragen von den Fräulein Therese und Babette Kunz, den Herren Schubert und Hüttenbrenner.

2. Berg und Thal, Gedicht von J. F. Castelli, vorgetragen von dem Concertgeber.

3. Variationen für die Violine von Rovelli (mit Quartettbegleitung), gespielt von Herrn B. Molique.

4. Sprache der Blumen, Gedicht von Ch. Schreiber, gesprochen von Mad. Gottdank, Mitglied des k. k. priv. Theaters an der Wien.

5. Adelaide von Mathisson mit Musik von Beethoven, gesungen von Herrn Jäger, Mitglied des k. k. priv. Theaters an der Wien.

6. Des Kaisers Albrecht Hund, Gedicht von H. J. v. Collin, vorgetragen von Herrn F. Demmer, Mitglied des k. k. priv. Theaters an der Wien.

7. Variationen für die Guitarre, von Giuliani (mit Quartett-Begleitung), gespielt von Herrn Mendl, Schüler des Herrn Giuliani.

8. Der geplagte Bräutigam, Gedicht von Theodor Körner, gesprochen von dem Concertgeber.

9. Grand Rondeau brillant à 4 mains für das Fortepiano, von Moscheles, gespielt von den Fräulein Therese und Babette Kunz.

Sämmtliche Damen und Herren haben aus besonderer Gefälligkeit gegen den Concertgeber die Ausführung der obengenannten Stücke übernommen.

289 Invitation to a "musical-recitational private entertainment given by C. F. Müller on March 12, 1818, at noon." Wiener Stadt- und Landesbibliothek.

Rossini's *Barber of Seville*, for example, was published in arrangements for two flutes, for two violins, for a string quartet, and even for the czakan—a flutelike instrument that fitted into a walking stick.

The market must have been a substantial one, because otherwise there would be no accounting for publishing houses as large as P. Mechetti, T. Mollo, and T. Haslinger simultaneously offering such a wealth of arrangements—usually of the same works, at least in the case of the most salable pieces. Clearly this music was eminently suitable for domestic performance, and publishers were good at addressing the swelling numbers of amateur musicmakers and encouraging them to purchase "easy-to-play" arrangements.

Whole series of such arrangements were published, and publishers were never at a loss for a tempting title. There was a "Musical Bee," for example, and "Recreations on the Way to Parnassus"; there was also a "Shortest Route to Parnassus," while other titles were "Musical Entertainment," "Olympiade: A Series of Brilliant New Compositions," "The Musical Collector," or "Polyhymnia: Suite of Pieces Chosen for the Physharmonica."

Granted, these series also contained some original works by such composers as Abbé Joseph Gelinek, Max Josef Leidesdorf, Mauro Giuliani, Johann Peter Pixis, Count Robert Gallenberg, Josef Kinsky, Anton Diabelli, Stefano Pavesi, Nikolaus Krufft, Carl Blum, Leopold Jansa, and Johann Pensel, among others. But such pieces—usually short variations, polonaises, marches, duets, or divertimenti—were merely further instances of the taste of the period. They were works in vogue, and their musical quality was often poor. Schubert himself complained of what he felt to be an appalling decline in taste in the early 1820s. There was very little interest in works that also made intellectual demands on players, and if a publisher offered editions of works by Mozart, or even compositions by Beethoven, it was only in order to improve the look of his list.

This decline in taste was an inexorable tendency of the period. The Metternich system, with total state control of all intellectual activity, had the effect not so much of reducing the scope of artistic expression as of diluting its quality. People retreated within their own four walls, the better to escape notice. There, in the domestic circle, a favorite pastime was music, which, when it was not associated with "revolutionary" lyrics, was quite beyond the philistine comprehension of the censorship authorities, though there was the—no doubt unusual—case of a purely instrumental work of Schubert's having to be passed by the censor!

At home, doubtless without any expenditure of effort on practicing, people consumed everything that was musically in vogue at the time. The result was a prodigious spread of amateurism during this period. Already around 1818, Vienna is believed to have boasted something like two thousand amateur musicians who, while certainly not lacking in enthusiasm, were sorely lacking in musical training. Had they been at all interested in the truly great works of the Classical composers, the Conservatory (founded by the Society of Music Lovers in 1817) would have been besieged by impossible numbers of applicants. History shows that this did not happen.

The amateur musicmakers of Biedermeier Vienna found their needs supplied by the kind of thing we know to have filled the various music publishers' lists. Let us not forget, however, that printed sheet music, despite new and cheaper methods of production (such as Senefelder's invention of lithography), was still an extremely expensive luxury that only the better-off bourgeois could afford without making considerable sacrifices. As a result, trade in manuscript music was still flourishing; some of it was produced by professional copyists, while some was the work of rather less skilled hands.

With the exception of a very few musical circles (one of them was the musical salon organized by the Sonnleithner family, which Schubert himself frequented for a short while), mediocrity prevailed in the private musical life of the age. While Beethoven and Schubert were alive, it was possible to point to them—even knowledgeable critics did so—as "evidence" that the musical city of Vienna had not yet become mired in provincialism. After their deaths, it became all too evident that an era which their two names had sustained was now over. What followed, however, was not a collapse of taste, as is often claimed, but simply the continuation of an attitude of mind that had long since settled happily for the banal in art.

The musical poverty of the years leading up to 1848 became manifest only because Vienna was without a major resident composer at that time. Partly because of that lack, the center of gravity of musical life in Europe shifted—"officially"—from Vienna to Paris, with Vienna being reduced to a mere transit station for many composers and interpreters who had achieved European fame.

Robert Schumann, who flirted with the idea of moving to Vienna, might possibly have imparted a fresh stimulus to the musical life of the city and woken it from its long sleep. His plans to move failed to materialize, however, and for years—if we except, for the moment, the whole area of dance music—Vienna was condemned to insignifiance as far as musical creativity was concerned.

The Concert Scene

After the *Gesellschaft der Musikfreunde* ("Society of Music Lovers") was founded in 1812, as the result of an initiative on the part of a body of serious amateurs who wished to restore symphonic music to its proper place in public life, the next noteworthy effort in this direction came in 1819, with the inauguration of the *Concerts spirituels* ("religious concerts"). The intention was to provide a framework for the performance of sacred music— oratorios and the like—and for the symphonies of the Classical masters. The basic idea (some serious cultivation of music in the public sphere to balance the great increase in private musicmaking) was universally applauded. The people in charge of organizing these concerts, however, were themselves amateurs, and they proceeded to justify their poor reputation in full measure. The programs they put together in the early years looked absolutely magnificent and would have merited the highest praise. Unfortunately the picture was rather different in practice.

They usually set out to realize their exalted goals without benefit of rehearsal (a piece of nonsense that was laid down in the statutes of the society), so that what they actually put on was a public *prima-vista* performance. Beethoven himself was obliged to submit to this misguided conception of the musician's art, apostrophizing the result as *Winkelmusik* (perhaps "back-of-beyond music" best conveys Beethoven's contempt). The organizers showed proof of courage, and the programs—which we can no longer take at face value—offer glowing testimo-

290 Friedrich Rehberg: *Antonio Salieri,* 1821. Lithograph, 44.5 × 31.4 cm. Historisches Museum der Stadt Wien.

291 Joseph Kriehuber: *Niccolò Paganini,* 1828. Lithograph, 44.5 × 32 cm. Historisches Museum der Stadt Wien.

ny to the high level of public music-making. However, testimony we cannot ignore—not just fromcritics, but also from "lay" contemporaries—tells a very different story.

The Society of Music Lovers likewise had great plans, but there too it became unfortunately clear that the group of people who had a hand in organizing the concerts complacently took their cue from the prevailing taste of the time: there can be no question of considering them as a supreme musical court handing down exemplary judgements. Those organizers also felt that, having once hit on a pattern for the evening's program, they must stick with it—year in, year out. The program was set up as follows: a symphony (or rather extracts from a symphony) to begin with, then an aria in the Italian style, which became an inevitable feature of these concerts; the main body of the proceedings was an instrumental concerto, and the evening was rounded off with an overture and a solemn conclusion, for which hymns or oratoriolike compositions were felt to be eminently suitable. In other words, it was a good mixture, and although the naive listener doubtless got plenty of variety, the accomplished musician was less well served.

After 1830 things became even worse. The concert organized by the society on the occasion of the opening of its new concert hall in the Tuchlauben (1831) was symptomatic of this "development": the program was made up of works by Franz Lachner, Ignaz Franz von Mosel, Gioacchino Rossini, and Johann Nepomuk Hummel. "This insipid program," the critic Eduard Hanslick was later to write, "with its positively glaring absence of Haydn, Mozart, Beethoven, and Schubert, was scarcely a brilliant omen for the future activities of the 'Austrian Music Lovers' in their new concert hall. Instead it appears eloquently to prefigure the 1830–48 concert period and its characterless superficiality." Such, indeed, was the musical insensitivity of the organizers that at one concert the famous "mad aria" from Donizetti's *Lucia di Lammermoor* was performed between the first and second movements of Schubert's "Great" Symphony in C Major.

The society's record was no more felicitous in the case of the faltering music festivals, and again it fell to Hanslick to reproach Vienna with "sins of tardiness" over Felix Mendelssohn's great oratorios (*St. Paul,* for example). It was not as if the society had had any competition to contend with, for before the *Concerts spirituels* disappeared completely in 1848 they presented a pretty sorry picture. It

292   Franz Liszt: Bravura studies based on Paganini's Caprices, 1838. Manuscript in the composer's own hand. Wiener Stadt- und Landesbibliothek.

was not until 1842 that things began to change for the better in terms of orchestral playing, with the inauguration of the Philharmonic Concerts by Otto Nicolai. Suddenly Viennese audiences discovered to their astonishment what a really well-rehearsed orchestra sounded like. The performance of Beethoven's Ninth Symphony in 1843 was very much a star turn in this respect.

Until Nicolai introduced this kind of intensely rehearsed orchestral playing, raising the standard of orchestral concerts to an unprecedented level, Viennese audiences had clung to other well-loved institutions besides the concerts of the Society of Music Lovers and the *Concerts spirituels*. There were the charity "academies," and there were the various "morning, midday, and evening entertainments," all of which were probably innocent of any serious preoccupation with art. At them virtuosi, amateur musicians, and promoters busily shook hands while an orchestra played as if it already had its mind on the next engagement.

The brilliant critic and composer Friedrich August Kanne, appalled by this

form of concert life—in addition to the music, the program was often "enriched" with a gratuitous recitation—denounced it in the *Wiener allgemeine musikalische Zeitung*, where he worked as editor-in-chief: "But who can contain his displeasure when the most curious juxtapositions of musical compositions and poetic recitations give the whole concert the appearance of a *ragoût mêlé* [mixed stew]? In principle virtuosi and composers are urged to ring adventurous changes in their choice of masters or musical genre or the character of the same...but the clashing contrasts and the glaring differences are made even more apparent by this admixture of recitation. One leaves the concert hall with a motley picture."

A "motley" program was also what the almost countless numbers of virtuoso concerts offered. Arias, male-voice quartets, recitations, overtures, and sometimes even a movement from a symphony framed the virtuoso recital and gave the performer time to recover his breath. Among pianists it was Johann Nepomuk Hummel and Ignaz Moscheles who represented the virtuoso type *par excel-*

293 Wilhelm Rolling, after Josef Danhauser: *Ignaz Schuppanzigh*. Lithograph, 22.9 × 15.2 cm. Historisches Museum der Stadt Wien.

294 F. Wolf, after Georg Decker: *Wenzel Müller,* 1835. Lithograph, 48 × 34.6 cm. Historisches Museum der Stadt Wien.

lence, and a whole host of lesser players attempted—unsuccessfully—to match their achievements. Pianos were now more robustly built (thanks mainly to the firm of Conrad Graf) and usually stood up to the often violent treatment they received on these occasions. Nor was musical virtuosity confined to the piano; violinists, flutists, French horn players, harpists, and others all contributed, performing either their own works or arrangements. Toward the end of the 1820s, just as audiences and critics were beginning to show signs of becoming weary of virtuosity, Niccolò Paganini burst upon the Viennese musical scene, rekindling the old debate about virtuosity and demonic possession.

What Paganini performed on the violin in 1838 was echoed on the piano ten years later by Franz Liszt (who had actually made his Viennese debut in 1822). Liszt, whose success in Vienna in 1838 encouraged him to take up a career as a virtuoso, differed from Paganini in being a deeply thoughtful musician. Both as an interpreter and as a composer he left traces that

reach into the twentieth century. This also distinguished him from his rival Sigismund Thalberg, the chief feature of whose playing was its flawless technical brilliance. Liszt was an important figure in the musical life of Vienna in several ways, most notably as an interpreter of Classical works for the piano. It was Liszt who "rediscovered" Beethoven's late piano music, performing it with an attack far superior to that of Clara Wieck, who made her Viennese debut in 1837 playing Beethoven, among other composers. Clara Wieck and her interpretations were much admired; Liszt's, on the other hand, carried conviction. Then there was the way in which he championed Schubert. Whatever we may think today of Liszt's arrangements of Schubert's songs—the Haslinger editions were hugely successful—the fact remains that it was Liszt who first made Schubert's name known throughout Europe. Liszt's great virtuosity made it hard for a musical world—critics included—that judged by outward appearances to appreciate him at his true worth. Whatever the man did, he

265

did with utter commitment and with convincing artistic seriousness.

The same could have been said of only very few Viennese composers and interpreters in the Pre-March years. One who had scant regard for public opinion and behaved in a positively elitist manner was Ignaz Schuppanzigh. the quartet productions he launched were a unique feature of the Viennese musical scene. The very fact that he played almost exclusively Beethoven (with some Schubert, too) raised him above the rest of the city's musicmaking in a way that received far too little appreciation from a society that strove to avoid musical individuality. We can believe the reviewers who wrote that Schuppanzigh's accomplishments were rated more highly by foreigners than by native audiences and that, once again, the Viennese were unaware of what a jewel—in terms of the cultivation of Classical music—they had in their midst.

One of those reviewers wrote as follows: "Foreign artists, connoisseurs, and lovers of art, after attending a performance by one or another of these quartets, averred that they had never, anywhere, heard anything so perfect in this type of performance. Perfection was indeed the word for the majority of these productions. Here there was no pushing to the fore, no trying to be heard, none of the singling out of particular passages and particular voices that mars most performances of this kind; all four musicians had but one aim and worked toward it with an authentic, concentrated virtuosity that found expression in subordination to the whole, and with a clear awareness and unwavering attention. It is this that makes these quartets a veritable tutorial in taste and performance."

Schuppanzigh's death in 1830 marked the beginning of "most miserable days" for chamber music in Vienna, as Hanslick remarked in his *Geschichte des Concertwesens* ("History of the Concert"). Foreign quartets visited the city, and only Leopold Jansa, a member of the court orchestra, tried to take Schuppanzigh's place. Jansa's personality was clearly not equal to the task, and he soon gave up the attempt.

Music and the Theater

Between the congress and the revolution, Vienna offered all sections of its population ample opportunity to express their passion for the theater to the full. There were some noted playhouses at their disposal—the two court theaters, and three major theaters in the suburbs. For years on end, however, repertoires were selected almost exclusively in accordance with audience requirements, which led to an inevitable decline in taste. The suburban theaters were always having to struggle to survive: the Theater an der Wien, for example, was disposed of in a lottery in 1819 to meet the debts of Count Palffy, and in 1826 was eventually sold at public auction. Probably this state of affairs prevented the suburban theaters from risking any long-term planning involving artistic aspects. One might, however, have expected the Kärntnertor Theater, which was responsible for operatic productions, to open its doors to composers of a variety of tendencies, but here too the dictates of success appear to have forced all other considerations—notably artistic ones—into second place.

Opera in the Pre-March years was dominated basically by the Italians, about which there would certainly be nothing shameful had experiment with German opera or the *Singspiel* ("light opera") been taken rather further than it was. The canny businessman Domenico Barbaja, who acquired the lease on the opera house in 1821, did mount a successful production of Weber's *Der Freischütz* but he took the failure of the same composer's *Euryanthe* (occasioned mainly by its disastrous libretto) as a pretext for canceling Schubert's *Fiërabras* and for turning his back on the whole development of German–language opera.

Henceforth Rossini was king—indeed his reign had begun back in 1816, though the Rossini frenzy did not break out properly until Barbaja invited the composer to Vienna for a *stagione*, or "season," in 1822. Rossini was eventually supplanted by the early successes of Donizetti and Bellini, which meant that the Italians continued to call the tune at the Kärntnertor Theater right up to the first performance of an opera by Verdi (*I Lombardi*, in 1846).

The suburban theaters, on the contrary, were haunted in the main by writers and composers who had little to offer that was not routine, and who usually scored only ephemeral successes with their divertissements, burlesques, and farces. Adolf Bäuerle, Karl Meisl, Joseph Alois Gleich, and Ignaz Franz Castelli were some of the writers who used to produce work for several theaters simultaneously, and Franz Volkert, Vincenz and Ferdinand Tuczek, Franz Roser, and Franz Gläser were among the composers who set mostly rather fatuous texts to equally undemanding music.

The Josephstadt Theater, which was reopened in 1822 at enormous expense, never really managed to find a consistent line—a failure it probably owed to its resident conductor, Franz Gläser, who did not shrink from using the most scurrilous arrangements (as witness a performance of Weber's *Oberon* in a form of doggerel known as *Knittelversen*—irregular, four-foot rhyming couplets). The two other major suburban theaters, however, were in the fortunate position of being able to call upon the services of people who, in their way, made theatrical history.

The Leopoldstadt Theater took on Ferdinand Raimund as an actor in 1817. In 1823, exasperated by the kind of trash he was being asked to perform, Raimund took up writing himself. The composers available to him were the old hand Wenzel Müller (who had done long service with the Leopoldstadt Theater) for *Der Barometermacher auf der Zauberinsel* ("The Weatherglass Maker on the Enchanted Island") and for his further successes, *Der Diamant des Geisterkönigs* ("The Ghost King's Diamond") and *Das Mädchen aus der Feenwelt* ("The Girl from Fairyland"), and a man called Joseph Drechsler, who was not only a thoroughly sound composer, the author of a theoretical work on harmony and figured bass, but also a conductor with plenty of theatrical experience. Raimund himself had an excellent feeling for music; with him, musical folk comedy—to use a generic term for the then prevalent fairy-tale extravaganzas, burlesques, and parodies—entered a new and fruitful phase of development. Music took on a more important role; it was no longer relegated to the purely accessory character that had been assigned to it by the entertainment plays with which theaters had been inundated hitherto.

At the Theater an der Wien the pendulum also began to swing in a more positive direction when Adolf Müller Sr. was appointed conductor and resident composer there in 1826. His first production, a parody of Boieldieu's *La Dame blanche* ("The White Lady"), was a big success. Müller, who had a solid grounding as a composer and a good deal of theatrical experience behind him—he had even held the post of conductor at the court opera house for a short while—subsequently wrote the music for the principal plays premiered at the Theater an der Wien. Altogether Müller composed for some five hundred plays. Yet he only became a kind of institution, if not a celebrity, as a result of his close collaboration with Johann Nestroy, of whom he already had a high opinion as a singer. (Nestroy was among those most in demand for performances of Schubert's male-voice quartets.)

Nestroy made his debut at the Theater an der Wien in 1832 and put his fruitful collaboration with Müller very successfully to the test. Between them, they made the Theater an der Wien the principal venue for musical folk comedy, a position it managed to retain for many years to come. A further indication of the positive attitude toward art that prevailed there is the fact that both Albert Lortzing and Franz von Suppé received engagements at the theater. Suppé, who, a year after it was commissioned, scored a notable artistic success with *Dichter und Bauer* (1846, "Poet and Peasant"), subsequently ushered in the incredibly successful Viennese operetta era at the same theater.

Church Music

It was characteristic of the Biedermeier period that, in the field of music, people wasted little time in looking back at the great works of the past but were keen to be involved in the events of the present. Printed music not issued as "new publications" hardly sold at all. (This was the reason why publishers soon hit upon the device of leaving printed matter undated. The consequence for later musical research was that it began by getting its dates all wrong before, by dint of hard work and with the help of publishers' catalogs and public announcements, it managed to arrive at dates that were approximately reliable.) The greatest awareness of tradition existed in the field of church music. Certainly there were enough composers in the Pre-March years who enjoyed not only an excellent reputation as church musicians but also a stable position, and whose works were performed repeatedly. They included Joseph Preindl, Ignaz Assmayer, Simon Sechter, Joseph von Eybler, and Ignaz Seyfried. (There were also various lesser composers of church music—Schiedermayer, Blahack, and others—whose fame did not extend beyond the boundaries of a particular parish. Presumably, too, the pressure of the "great" composers was so powerful that even Schubert could only get a hearing with minor contributions, and hardly at all with masses.)

Apart from the above-named church composers, whose renown depended on their influence, church music was in practice confined to a stock repertoire that was the same in virtually every parish. Mozart, Joseph and Michael Haydn, and Johann Georg Albrechtsberger were the composers most frequently performed. Performers sang and played from manuscript copies for the most part, and in the 1830s especially, copyists had to work nonstop, often for several parishes at the same time, in order to keep up with the growing demand. Copyists were not inhibited by any feeling that they must be particularly faithful to the original work being copied. If a conductor had a larger body of instrumentalists at his disposal, masses by Haydn and Mozart, as well as lesser works of church music, would be unhesitatingly expanded to include horns, trombones, and other parts not written for in the original. So despite its preference for the great classics, church music of the Biedermeier era offered a lively illustration of the musical practice of the period.

Dance Music

Pre-March Vienna did rise to a position of unrivaled dominance in one genre, and that was in dance music. There was nothing accidental about this phenomenon, the mentality of the inhabitants of the metropolis on the Danube having been such as to make them highly partial to all kinds of dissipation—and even to excess, as in the days of the Langaus dance. There were plenty of opportunities for enjoying oneself in Vienna, and people were inventive when it came to taking advantage of them. Vienna, then, proved fertile soil for a branch of music that, for the first time, turned dancing into a real pleasure. What is so inexplicable and at the same time so stimulating about the positively revolutionary development of dance music in Vienna is that it was a case of talents coming together in the same place at the same time—and hence setting up in competition. Without that, such sublime achievements could scarcely have materialized. In this context, it is quite irrelevant that the waltz—the dance mainly concerned here—did not actually have its roots in Vienna; as a process of assimilation, it was certainly a successful one.

It fell to Joseph Lanner to pick up certain ideas—and there were many of them, from many different sources—and to pave the way for other men to follow. For a long time, however, Lanner's importance was by no means so self-evident. A lot of the groundwork, it is true, had been done by Michael Pamer, who through leading small—tiny, to begin with—orchestras in public houses first appropriated to himself that popular sound which eventually achieved what became a specifically Viennese quality. Initially, however, it was probably untypical of Vienna (for both Bavarian and Czech elements undoubtedly went into the early waltz forms). Two rising musicians in Pamer's orchestra were Lanner and Johann Strauss

295 *Modern Love Waltzes for the Pianoforte*: a collection of dances, 1826. Historisches Museum der Stadt Wien. The man standing on the left is supposedly Franz Schubert.

296 Philipp Steidler: *Joseph Lanner.* Oil on canvas, 158 × 111 cm. Historisches Museum der Stadt Wien.

297 Joseph Lanner: *Zeisel-Jux-Ländler for the Pianoforte,* Lanner's first published work. Published by Tobias Haslinger, Vienna. Wiener Stadt- und Landesbibliothek.

298 Joseph Kriehuber: *Johann Strauss the Elder,* 1835. Lithograph, 33.5 × 24 cm. Historisches Museum der Stadt Wien: Wurzbach Collection.

the Elder—two very different characters, whose artistic ambitions later turned their rivalry almost into enmity.

Curiously it was not Strauss but the sensitive and melodically gifted Lanner who cast the waltz in a form that tightened up its melodic invention. He was inspired by Carl Maria von Weber's *Aufforderung zum Tanz* ("Invitation to the Dance"), which was reedited in Vienna in 1824. (Weber's composition utilized the introduction and coda that were later to characterize the waltz.) Lanner had already asserted his artistic independence with a five-part waltz sequence entitled *Mitternachts-Walzern* (Op. 7, "Midnight Waltzes") and given the waltz its distinctive shape as a musical type. Lanner was a successful composer in his day, and as Musical Director of the Royal Imperial Ballrooms he also achieved social respectability, yet it was Johann Strauss the Elder who constituted the bigger attraction.

From 1827 onward, beginning with his first appearance at the Two Doves *(Zu den zwey Täuberln)* and subsequently at the Sparrow *(Sperl)*, Strauss quite literally put himself on show. To borrow a modern term, he knew precisely how to sell himself: he organized festive occasions in magnificent style, played in Baden (Vienna's health resort) in the summer months before the emperor and his court, and lived like a lord. He also made a great name for himself as a touring conductor with his own orchestra, which was something quite new at the time. Strauss's concert tours to Budapest, Berlin, Holland, France, and England made him a European celebrity. And the success he achieved was not merely personal; his efforts made the Viennese waltz and Viennese dance music generally, an Austrian export item that was in demand all over Europe. Strauss was undoubtedly one of the most popular musicians ever to have lived and worked in Vienna. At his funeral 100,000 Viennese thronged the streets—a fifth of the entire population.

His only real rival (apart from the modest Lanner) was his own son, who, on his debut in Dommayer's Casino in Hietzing in 1844, earned an ovation that must have sounded as if it would go on for ever. Johann Strauss the Elder was well aware of the extraordinary talent of his son, the man who eventually "sold" the Viennese waltz to the entire world in its final, definitive form (with introductions that were conceived almost symphonically).

Ernst Hilmar

299 Invitation to a *soirée dansante* ("an evening of dancing") in Dommayer's Casino on October 15, 1844. Wiener Stadt- und Landesbibliothek.
This was the first public appearance of Johann Strauss the Younger.

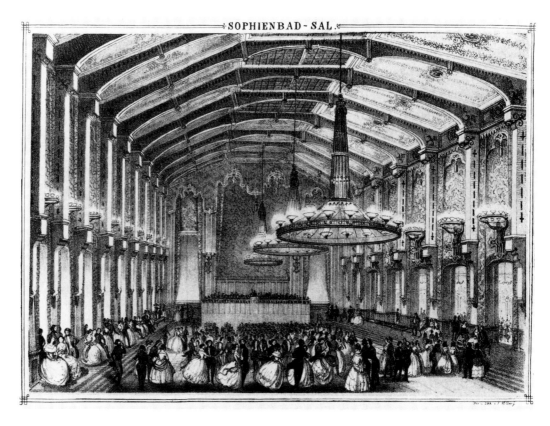

[14161]

Einladung
zur
Soirée dansante
welche Dinstag am 15. October 1844,
selbst bey ungünstiger Witterung in
Dommayer's Casino
in Hietzing Statt finden wird.
Johann Strauss
(Sohn),

wird die Ehre haben, zum ersten Mahle sein eigenes Orchester-Personale zu dirigiren, und nebst verschiedenen Ouverturen und Opern-Piecen, auch mehrere seiner eigenen Compositionen vorzutragen. — Der Gunst und Huld des hochverehrten Publicums empfiehlt sich ergebenst

Johann Strauß jun.

Eintrittskarten zu 20 kr. CM. sind in der k. k. Hof-Musikalienhandlung des Pietro Mechetti und Comp. in Stierböck's Kaffehhaus in der Jägerzeil, in Gäbesam's und in Puth's Kaffehhäusern in Mariahilf zu bekommen. Eintrittspreis an der Cassa 30 kr. CM. Anfang um 6 Uhr.

[2]

--- SOPHIENBAD-SAL ---

300 *The Sophienbad Hall,* 1848. Lithograph, 14.3 × 19.2 cm. Historisches Museum der Stadt Wien.
Invitation card to an inaugural festival ball on January 12, 1848, at which the Musical Director of the Royal Imperial Court Balls, Johann Strauss the Elder, performed his latest compositions.

GUIDE TO PERSONS MENTIONED IN THE BOOK

ALBERT KASIMIR OF SAXE-TESCHEN, DUKE (Moritzburg) 1738–1822 (Vienna): his art collection formed the basis of the Albertina collection of graphic art in Vienna

ALBRECHT, J. active in Vienna ca. 1840–50: lithographer

ALBRECHTSBERGER, JOHANN GEORG (Klosterneuburg) 1736–1809 (Vienna): composer, conductor, and court organist at St. Stephen's Cathedral, Vienna

ALEXANDER I PAVLOVICH (St. Petersburg) 1777–1825 (Taganrog): czar of Russia, 1801–25

ALEXY KARL (Poprád) 1823–1880 (?): sculptor

ALT, FRANZ (Vienna) 1821–1914 (Vienna): painter of architectural and landscape watercolors

ALT, JAKOB (Frankfurt a. M.) 1789–1872 (Vienna): watercolorist and lithographer

ALT, RUDOLF VON (Vienna) 1812–1905 (Vienna): architectural and landscape painter; important watercolorist

AMERLING, FRIEDRICH VON (Vienna) 1803–1887 (Vienna): painter

ASSMAYER, IGNAZ (Salzburg) 1790–1862 (Vienna): organist and composer of church music

AUBER, DANIEL FRANÇOIS ESPRIT (Caen) 1782–1871 (Paris): opera composer

BACH, CHRISTOPH DE (Mittau) 1768–1834 (Vienna): equestrian and circus director

BAUER, FRANZ (Vienna) 1798–1872 (Vienna): sculptor

BÄUERLE, ADOLF (Vienna) 1786–1859 (Basel): theater manager and novelist

BAUERNFELD, EDUARD VON (Vienna) 1802–1890 (Oberdöbling): writer, chiefly for the stage

BAUMANN, ALEXANDER (Vienna) 1814–1857 (Graz): dialect poet and playwright

BEER, JOSEF GEORG b. 1803: middle-class tailor, women's fashion designer

BEETHOVEN, LUDWIG VAN (Bonn) 1770–1827 (Vienna): composer

BITTNER, NORBERT (Vienna) 1786–1851 (Vienna): etcher and architectural painter

BLUM, CARL (Berlin) 1786–1844 (Berlin): composer and theater director

BÖHM, JOSEPH DANIEL (Wallendorf) 1794–1865 (Vienna): sculptor and medallist

BÖHM, W. active in Vienna ca. 1844: engraver

CALAFATI, BASILIO (Trieste) 1800–1878 (Vienna): entrepreneur in the Prater

CANOVA, ANTONIO (Possagno, near Bassano) 1757–1822 (Venice): sculptor

CARL, KARL [real name: Karl Bernbrunn] (Cracow) 1787–1854 (Ischl): theater manager, director, and actor

CASTELLI, IGNAZ FRANZ (Vienna) 1781–1862 (Vienna): lyric poet and playwright

CASTLEREAGH, ROBERT STEWART, VISCOUNT (Mont Stewart) 1769–1822 (North Cray Farm): marquis of Londonderry and a British statesman who played an important part in the Congress of Vienna

CHARLES [KARL], ARCHDUKE (Florence) 1771–1847 (Vienna): army commander, the victor of Aspern

COSTENOBLE, KARL LUDWIG (Herford) 1769–1837 (Prague): actor and writer

COURIGIER, JOSEF ANTON (Einsiedeln) 1750–1830 (Paris): sculptor and goldsmith

DANHAUSER, JOSEF (Vienna) 1805–1845 (Vienna): historical and genre painter

DIABELLI, ANTON (Mattsee, near Salzburg) 1781–1858 (Vienna): composer and music publisher

DIALER, JOSEPH ALOIS (Imst) 1797–1846 (Vienna): sculptor

DIETRICH, ANTON (Vienna) 1797–1872 (Vienna): sculptor

DRECHSLER, JOSEPH (Wällisch-Birken) 1782–1852 (Vienna): composer, taught Johann Strauss

ELSSLER, FANNY (Gumpendorf, Vienna) 1810–1884 (Vienna): dancer

ENDER, JOHANN NEPOMUK (Vienna) 1793–1854 (Vienna): portraitist and historical painter

ENDER, THOMAS (Vienna) 1793–1875 (Vienna): painter, chiefly of watercolors

ENDLICHER, STEPHAN (Pressburg/Bratislava) 1804–1849 (Vienna): Orientalist

EYBL, FRANZ (Vienna) 1806–1880 (Vienna): portrait and genre painter

EYBLER, JOSEPH VON (Schwechat) 1764–1846 (Schönbrunn): composer of church music

FALLMERAYER, JAKOB PHILIPP (Tschöch, near Brixen/Bressanone) 1790–1861 (Munich): travel writer and historian

FENDI, PETER (Vienna) 1796–1842 (Vienna): painter and graphic artist

FERDINAND I (Vienna) 1793–1875 (Prague): emperor of Austria, 1835–48

FERNKORN, ANTON DOMINIK (Erfurt) 1813–1878 (Vienna?): sculptor

FERTBAUER, LEOPOLD (Vienna) 1802–1875 (Vienna): painter

FESSLER, JOHANN (Bregenz) 1803–1875 (Vienna): sculptor

FEUCHTERSLEBEN, ERNST VON, BARON (Vienna) 1806–1849 (Vienna): author, doctor, and philosopher

FISCHER, JOHANN MARTIN (Bebele) 1740–1820 (Vienna): sculptor

FISCHER VON ERLACH, JOHANN BERNHARD (Graz) 1656–1723 (Vienna): the most important Baroque architect in Austria

FISCHHOF, ADOLF (Buda) 1816–1893 (Emmersdorf): politician, doctor, and writer

FÖRSTER, CHRISTIAN LUDWIG FRIEDRICH (Ansbach) 1797–1863 (Gleichenberg): architect

FRANCIS [FRANZ] I (II) (Florence) 1768–1835 (Vienna): Holy Roman Emperor, 1792–1806; emperor of Austria, 1804–35

FRANCIS CHARLES [FRANZ KARL], Archduke (Vienna) 1802–1878 (Vienna): father of Emperor Francis Joseph I

FRANCIS JOSEPH [FRANZ JOSEPH] I (Vienna) 1830–1916 (Vienna): emperor of Austria, 1848–1916

FREDERICK WILLIAM [FRIEDRICH WILHELM] III (Potsdam) 1770–1840 (Berlin): king of Prussia, 1797–1840

FRIEDELL, EGON [real name: Friedmann] (Vienna) 1878–1938 (Vienna): writer, cultural historian, and actor

FÜHRICH, JOSEF VON (Kratzau, Bohemia) 1800–1876 (Vienna): painter and illustrator, chiefly of religious subjects

GALLENBERG, WENZEL ROBERT, COUNT (Vienna) 1783–1839 (Vienna): composer and music theorist

GASSER, HANNS (Eisentratten) 1817–1868 (Budapest): sculptor

GAUERMANN, FRIEDRICH (Scheuchenstein, near Miesenbach) 1807–1862 (Vienna): painter and graphic artist

GAUERMANN, JAKOB (Öffingen) 1773–1843 (Miesenbach): painter and graphic artist; painter to Archduke Johann

GEIGER, PETER JOHANN NEPOMUK (Vienna) 1805–1880 (Vienna): lithographer and etcher

GELINEK, JOSEPH (Selez) 1758–1825 (?): composer

GERHARDT, HEINRICH living in Vienna around 1849: lithographer

GLÄSER, FRANZ (Obergeorgenthal) 1798–1861 (Copenhagen): composer and conductor

GLEICH, JOSEPH ALOIS (Vienna) 1772–1841 (Vienna): writer, civil servant, and assistant theater manager

GRILLPARZER, FRANZ (Vienna) 1791–1872 (Vienna): author and dramatist

GRÜN, ANASTASIUS [real name: Count Anton Alexander von Auersperg] (Laibach/Ljubljana) 1806–1876 (Graz): author, chiefly of poetry

GUNKEL, JOSEF : the most famous men's tailor in nineteenth-century Vienna

GURK, EDUARD (Vienna) 1801–1841 (Jerusalem): painter and copperplate engraver

HÄHNEL, ERNST JULIUS (Dresden) 1811–1891 (Dresden): sculptor

HALM, FRIEDRICH [real name: Baron Eligius von Münch-Bellinghausen] (Cracow) 1806–1871 (Vienna): writer and playwright

HAMMER-PURGSTALL, JOSEPH VON, BARON (Graz) 1774–1856 (Vienna): Orientalist and diplomat

HASLINGER, TOBIAS (Zell, near Zellhof) 1787–1842 (Vienna): music publisher, publishing chiefly the Viennese classics

HIRSCHHÄUTER, JOSEPH (Vienna) 1801–1859 (Vienna): sculptor

HÖCHLE, JOHANN NEPOMUK (Munich) 1790–1835 (Vienna): genre painter and lithographer

HOFBAUER, ST. CLEMENT MARY [KLEMENS MARIA] (Tasswitz) 1751–1820 (Vienna): Roman Catholic priest, paved the way for the establishment of the Redemptorists in Vienna; canonized in 1909

HOFFMANN, JOSEF (Pirnitz) 1870–1956 (Vienna): architect and designer, cofounder of the Wiener Werkstätten, founder of the Österreichischer Werkbund

HÖGER, JOSEF (Vienna) 1801–1877 (Vienna): painter

HÖGLER, FRANZ (Vienna) 1802–1855 (Vienna): sculptor

HOHENBERG, JOHANN FERDINAND VON (Vienna) 1732–1816 (Vienna): architect, built the Gloriette at Schönbrunn

HORMAYR, JOSEPH VON, BARON (Innsbruck) 1781–1848 (Munich): historian, biographer, and diplomat

HORNBOSTEL, CHRISTIAN GEORG (Vienna) 1778–1841 (Vienna): manufacturer in Leobersdorf, the first man in Europe to produce silk fabrics on machine looms

HUMBOLDT, WILHELM VON, BARON (Potsdam) 1767–1835 (Tegel): scholar and statesman

HUMMEL, JOHANN NEPOMUK (Pressburg/Bratislava) 1778–1837 (Weimar): composer and piano teacher

JANSA LEOPOLD (Wildenschwert) 1797–1875 (Vienna): violin virtuoso and musical director

JOHANN, ARCHDUKE (Florence) 1782–1859 (Graz): the most popular archduke of Austria

JOSEPH II (Vienna) 1741–1790 (Vienna): Holy Roman Emperor, 1765–90

KÄHSMANN, JOSEPH (Windischfeistritz) 1751–1837 (Vienna): sculptor

KAISER, FRIEDRICH (Biberach) 1814–1874 (Vienna): playwright, founder of the Konkordia Society, a writers' club in Vienna

KALIWODA, FRANZ active in Vienna ca. 1820–59: painter and lithographer

KANNE, FRIEDRICH AUGUST (Delitsch) 1778–1833 (Vienna): author, critic, and composer

KININGER, VINCENZ GEORG (Regensburg/Ratisbon) 1767–1851 (Vienna): graphic artist, watercolorist, and miniaturist

KINSKY, JOSEF (Olmütz) b. ca. 1789: composer and theater conductor

KLIEBER, JOSEPH (Innsbruck) 1773–1850 (Vienna): sculptor, head of the Vienna School of Engraving

KOLLARZ, FRANZ (Nory Slovnik) 1825–1894 (Maria Lanzendorf): illustrator and lithographer

KOLOWRAT-LIEBSTEINSKY, FRANZ ANTON, COUNT (Prague) 1778–1861 (Vienna): statesman, an opponent of Metternich

KORNHÄUSEL, JOSEF (Vienna) 1782–1860 (Vienna): architect; his buildings are regarded as typical of the Biedermeier era

KOSSUTH, LAJOS (Monok) 1802–1894 (Turin): leader of the Hungarian independence movement, 1848–49

KOTHGASSER, ANTON (Vienna) 1769–1851 (Vienna): the most famous glass painter of his day

KOTZEBUE, AUGUST VON (Weimar) 1761–1819 (Mannheim): writer and Russian councilor of state; he was stabbed to death as an enemy of German unity and freedom by a student from Jena named K.L. Sand

KRAFFT, JOHANN ADAM active in Vienna around 1826: painter

KRAFFT, JOHANN PETER (Hanau) 1780–1856 (Vienna): painter belonging to the transition from Neoclassicism to Biedermeier

KREUTZER, KONRADIN (Messkirch) 1780–1849 (Riga): German composer of operas, *Singspiele*, and theater music

KRIEHUBER, JOSEPH (Vienna) 1800–1876 (Vienna): portrait and landscape painter, lithographer

KRUFFT, NIKOLAUS VON, BARON (Vienna) 1779–1818 (Vienna): composer

KUNZ, CARL active in Vienna around 1840: painter

KUPELWIESER, LEOPOLD (Piesting) 1796–1862 (Vienna): painter, influenced by the Nazarenes

LACHNER, FRANZ (Rain) b. 1804: composer
Lampi the Elder, Johann Baptist (Romeno) 1751–1830 (Vienna): painter, chiefly of portraits and historical paintings

LANNER, JOSEPH (Vienna) 1801–1843 (Oberdöbling): violinist, conductor, and composer for dance orchestras; one of the fathers of the Viennese waltz

LANZEDELLY THE ELDER, JOSEPH (Meleris) 1772–1831 (Vienna): lithographer and miniaturist

LENAU, NIKOLAUS [real name: Nikolaus Niembsch von Strehlenau] (Csatád) 1802–1850 (Oberdöbling): author, chiefly of poetry

LEOPOLD II (Vienna) 1747–1792 (Vienna): Grand Duke of Tuscany (as Leopold I), 1765–92; Holy Roman Emperor, 1790–92

LEYBOLD, CARL JAKOB THEODOR (Stuttgart) 1786–1844 (Stuttgart): lithographer, historical painter, and portraitist

LISZT, FRANZ (Raiding) 1811–1886 (Bayreuth): Hungarian composer, conductor, and piano virtuoso

LODER, MATTHÄUS (Vienna) 1781–1828 (Vordernberg): painter and illustrator

LOOS, ADOLF (Brünn) 1870–1933 (Kalksburg, near Vienna): architect and writer on modern art

LOOS, FRIEDRICH (Graz) 1797–1890 (Kiel): painter and graphic artist

LÖSCHENKOHL, JOHANN HIERONYMUS (Elberfeld, near Cologne) 1754–1807 (Vienna): wood carver, publisher, art dealer, and "photojournalist"

LOUIS XVIII (Versailles) 1755–1824 (Paris): king of France, 1814/15–24

LÖWE, JOHANN MICHAEL SIEGFRIED (Königsberg) 1756–1831 (Berlin): miniaturist and copperplate engraver

LUX, JOSEPH AUGUST (Vienna) 1871–1947 (Anif, near Salzburg): writer

MÄHLER, JOSEF WILLIBRORD (Ehrenbreitstein) 1778–1860 (Vienna): portraitist

MAHLKNECHT, CARL (Vienna) 1810–1893 (Vienna): copperplate engraver

MALECK, FRANZ VON 1787–1849: painter and copperplate engraver

MANSFELD, HEINRICH AUGUST (Vienna) 1816–1901 (Vienna): painter

MARCHESI, POMPEO (Saltrio) 1789–1858 (Milan): sculptor; made the *Emperor Francis Monument* in Vienna

MARIE LOUISE VON HAPSBURG-LOTHRINGEN (Vienna) 1791–1847 (Parma): eldest daughter of Emperor Francis I; second wife of Napoleon I

MAŘIK, THOMAS (Pisek) 1810–1855 (Vienna): sculptor and painter

MEISL, KARL (Laibach/Ljubljana) 1775–1853 (Vienna): playwright

MENDELSSOHN-BARTHOLDY, FELIX (Hamburg) 1809–1847 (Leipzig): composer, pianist, and conductor

METTERNICH, CLEMENS LOTHAR WENZEL VON, PRINCE (Koblenz) 1773–1859 (Vienna): Austrian statesman; chancellor, 1821–48

MISSON, JOSEF (Mühlbach am Manhartsberg) 1803–1875 (Vienna): dialect poet and priest

MOREAU, KARL VON (Paris) 1766–1840 (Vienna): architect and painter

MOSCHELES, IGNAZ (Prague) 1794–1870 (Leipzig): composer, pianist, and piano teacher

MOSEL, IGNAZ FRANZ VON (Vienna) 1772–1844 (Vienna): composer and writer on music

MÖSSMER, JOSEF (Vienna) 1780–1845 (Vienna): painter and graphic artist, chiefly of landscapes

MÜLLER, ADOLF [real name: Schmid] (Tolna) b. 1801: composer

MÜLLER, WENZEL (Turnau, Moravia) 1767–1835 (Baden, near Vienna): conductor and theater composer

MURAT, JOACHIM (La Bastide) 1767–1815 (Pizzo): French marshal, 1804; king of Naples, 1808–15

NAPOLEON I (Ajaccio) 1769–1821 (Longwood, St. Helena): emperor of the French

NAPOLEON II (Paris) 1811–1832 (Schönbrunn): sole legitimate son of Napoleon I; king of Rome, duke of Reichstadt

NEDER, MICHAEL (Vienna) 1807–1882 (Vienna): genre and portrait painter

NESTROY, JOHANN NEPOMUK (Vienna) 1801–1862 (Graz): actor and playwright; perfected the folk theater of old Vienna

NEUKOMM, SIGISMUND VON (Salzburg) 1778–1858 (Paris): composer; a pupil of Michael and Joseph Haydn

NICOLAI, OTTO (Königsberg) 1810–1849 (Berlin): composer and conductor; initiated the Philharmonic Concerts

NIGG, JOSEF (Vienna) 1782–1863 (Vienna): painter

NOBILE, PETER VON (Campestro) 1774–1854 (Vienna): architect; head of the architectural department of the Vienna Academy

NÜLL, EDUARD VAN DER (Vienna) 1812–1868
(Vienna): architect; built the court opera house
in Vienna together with Sicard von Sicardsburg
NUSSBAUMER, MICHAEL (Schörstadt, Carinthia) 1785–
1861 (Rome): sculptor

OPITZ, GEORG EMANUEL (Prague) 1775–1841
(Leipzig): illustrator, etcher, and copperplate
engraver

PAGANINI, NICCOLÒ (Genoa) 1782–1840 (Nice):
violin virtuoso and composer
PAMER, MICHAEL (Vienna) 1782–1827 (Vienna):
theater conductor and composer
PENSEL, JOHANN 1794–1828 (Vienna): dance composer
PERGEN, JOHANN P. ANTON, COUNT (Vienna) 1725–
1814 (Vienna): minister
PERGER, SIGMUND FERDINAND VON (Vienna) 1778–
1841 (Vienna): painter and porcelain painter
PETROVITS, DEMETER (Baja) 1799–1854 (Vienna):
sculptor
PETTENKOFEN, AUGUST XAVER VON (Vienna) 1822–
1889 (Vienna): painter, illustrator, and lithog-
rapher
PFEIFFER, IDA (Vienna) 1797–1858 (Vienna):
explorer and travel writer
PICHL, ALOIS (Milan?) 1782–1856 (Vienna):
architect
PICHLER, KAROLINE (Vienna) 1769–1843 (Vienna):
short-story writer; in her day a central figure on
the Viennese literary scene
PIXIS, JOHANN PETER (Mannheim) 1788–1874
(Baden-Baden): composer and pianist
PREINDL, JOSEPH (Marbach) 1756–1823 (Vienna):
church musician, conductor at St. Stephen's
Cathedral, Vienna
PRELEUTHNER, JOHANN (Vienna) 1807–1897
(Gloggnitz): sculptor
PROKESCH VON OSTEN, ANTON, COUNT (Graz) 1795–
1846 (Vienna): diplomat, travel writer, and
historian

RAIMUND, FERDINAND (Vienna) 1790–1836
(Pottenstein): playwright whose fairy-tale ex-
travaganzas are still regularly performed today
RAMELMAYR, ADAM (Vienna) 1807–1887 (Vienna):
sculptor
RANFTL, JOHANN MATHIAS (Vienna) 1805–1854
(Vienna): painter, chiefly of portaits and histor-
ical paintings
RASUMOVSKY, ANDREAS KYRILLOVICH, PRINCE (St.
Petersburg) 1752–1836 (Vienna): Russian
ambassador to Austria; a patron of Beethoven
RAUCH, CHRISTIAN DANIEL (Arolsen) 1777–1857
(Dresden): sculptor
RAULINO, TOBIAS DIONYS (Mainz) 1785–1839
(Vienna): painter and watercolorist
REBELL, JOSEPH (Vienna) 1787–1828 (Dresden):
painter and etcher, chiefly of landscapes
REHBERG, FRIEDRICH (Hanover) 1758–1835
(Munich): painter, lithographer, and etcher
REIM, VINZENZ 1796–1858: graphic artist
REMY, LUDWIG VON (Reichshoffen, Alsace) 1776–
1851 (Vienna): architect; head of the
Hofbaudirektionskanzlei ("Imperial Construc-
tion Ministry")

RIEDER, WILHELM AUGUST (Döbling, Vienna) 1796–
1880 (Vienna): historical, genre, and portrait
painter; painted portraits of Franz Schubert
ROSER VON REITER, FRANZ (Naarn) 1779–1830:
composer
RÖSNER, CARL (Vienna) 1804–1869 (Steyr):
architect
ROSSINI, GIOACCHINO (Pesaro) 1792–1868 (Ruelle,
near Paris): composer
RUGENDAS, JOHANN LORENZ (Augsburg) 1775–1826
(Augsburg): graphic artist and engraver

SALIERI, ANTONIO (Legnano) 1750–1825 (Vienna):
Hofkapellmeister ("Court Conductor") and
composer
SAND, KARL LUDWIG (Wunsiedel) 1795–1820
(Mannheim): the student who stabbed August
von Kotzebue on August 23, 1819
SAPHIR, MORITZ GOTTLIEB(Lovas-Bereny) 1795–1858
(Baden, near Vienna): critic and journalist
SAUTER, FERDINAND (Werfen) 1804–1854 (Vienna):
poet; a master of the impromptu
SCHALLER, JOHANN NEPOMUK (Vienna) 1777–1842
(Vienna): sculptor
SCHALLER, LUDWIG (Vienna) 1804–1865 (Munich):
sculptor
SCHÄRMER, JOHANN MARTIN (Nassereith) 1785–1868
(Vienna): sculptor
SCHEMERL VON LEYTENBACH, JOSEPH (Laibach/
Ljubljana) 1752–1837 (Vienna): architect and
writer
SEYERER, FRANZ (Prague) 1762–1839 (Vienna):
painter
SCHICKH, JOHANN proprietor of a fashion shop;
founded the weekly journal Wiener
Modezeitung, in 1816
SCHINDLER, CARL (Vienna) 1821–1842 (Laab im
Walde): painter and watercolorist, nicknamed
Soldaten-Schindler ("Soldier Schindler")
SCHNORR VON CAROLSFELD, JULIUS (Leipzig) 1794–
1872 (Dresden): historical painter and illustra-
tor
SCHOBER, FRANZ VON (Torup, near Malmø) 1796–
1882 (Dresden): art lover and writer
SCHOELLER, JOHANN CHRISTIAN (Rappoltsweiler,
Alsace) 1782–1851 (Vienna): illustrator and
caricaturist
SCHOLZ, WENZEL (Brixen/Bressanone) 1787–1857
(Vienna): actor
SCHÖNLAUB, FIDELIUS [JOHANN] (Vienna) 1805–1883
(Munich): sculptor
SCHREYVOGEL, JOSEPH (Vienna) 1768–1832
(Vienna): journalist, critic, playwright, and
manager of the Hofburg Theater
SCHUBERT, FRANZ (Vienna) 1797–1828 (Vienna):
composer; the "prince of song" whose sympho-
nies and chamber-music works only gradually
came to be appreciated at their full value
SCHUPPANZIGH, IGNAZ (Vienna) 1776–1830
(Vienna): musician and conductor
SCHÜTZ, JOSEPH active in Vienna from 1784 until
after 1815: painter
SCHWANTHALER, LUDWIG MICHAEL VON (Munich) 1802–
1848 (Munich): sculptor
SCHWARZENBERG, FRIEDRICH VON, PRINCE (Pressburg/
Bratislava) 1800–1870 (Vienna): travel writer,
short-story writer, and officer

SCHWIND, MORITZ VON (Vienna) 1804–1871
(Munich): painter and illustrator
SEALSFIELD, CHARLES [real name: Karl Anton
Postl] (Poppitz) 1793–1864 (Solothurn):
narrative writer
SECHTER, SIMON (Friedberg) 1788–1867 (Vienna):
composer, music theorist, and court organist
SEDLNITZKY, JOSEPH VON, COUNT (Troplowitz) 1778–
1855 (Baden, near Vienna): Vienna's chief of
police and head of the censorship office
SEYFRIED, IGNAZ (Vienna) 1776–1841 (Vienna):
composer, pianist, and conductor
SICARD VON SICARDSBURG, AUGUST (Budapest) 1813–
1868(Weidling, near Vienna): architect;
codesigner of the court opera house in Vienna
SPRENGER, PAUL (Sagau) 1789–1854 (Vienna):
architect
STADLER, JOHANN (Vienna) 1804–1859 (Vienna):
lithographer, portraitist, and genre painter
STEIDLER, PHILIPP (Vienna) 1817–1879 (Vienna):
portrait painter
STEINFELD, FRANZ (Vienna) 1787–1868 (Pisck,
Bohemia): landscape painter, etcher, and
lithographer
STELZHAMER, FRANZ (Grosspiesenham, near Ried i.
I.) 1802–1874 (Henndorf): dialect poet
STIFTER, ADALBERT (Oberplan) 1805–1868 (Linz):
narrative writer
STÖBER, FRANZ (Vienna) 1795–1858 (Vienna):
copperplate engraver and etcher
STRAUSS THE ELDER, JOHANN (Vienna) 1804–1849
(Vienna): composer and conductor
STUWER, ANTON d. 1858: pyrotechnician
SUPPÉ, FRANZ VON (Spalato) 1819–1895 (Vienna):
conductor and composer of operettas

TALLEYRAND-PÉRIGORD, CHARLES MAURICE DE,
PRINCE (Paris) 1754–1838 (Paris): French
statesman who played an important part in the
Congress of Vienna
THALBERG, SIGISMUND (Geneva) 1812–1871
(Naples): piano virtuoso and composer
THORVALDSEN, BERTEL (Copenhagen) 1768(?)–1844
(Copenhagen): sculptor
TREML, JOHANN FRIEDRICH (Vienna) 1816–1852
(Vienna): painter; a pupil of Peter Fendi

VASQUEZ, CARL, COUNT 1798–1861: publisher of a
series of plans of Vienna
VOGL, JOHANN NEPOMUK (Vienna) 1804(?)–1854(?)
(Vienna): author

WALDMÜLLER, FERDINAND GEORG (Vienna) 1793–1865
(Hinterbrühl): painter; his portraits and land-
scapes have led to his being regarded as *the*
typical Biedermeier painter
WEBER, CARL MARIA VON (Eutin) 1786–1826 (Lon-
don): composer and opera conductor
WIECK, CLARA (Leipzig) 1819–1896 (Frankfurt a.
M.): piano virtuoso; married Robert Schumann
in 1840
WIGAND, BALTHASAR (Vienna) 1770–1846
(Felixdorf): painter
WOLF, FRANZ (Vienna) 1795–1859 (Vienna): li-
thographer and painter

ZAUNER, FRANZ ANTON (Untervalpatann) 1746–1822
(Vienna): sculptor; the principal exponent of
Austrian Classicism
ZIEGLER, JOSEPH (Vienna) 1774–1846 (Vienna):
architect
ZUTZ, JOSEF active in Vienna around 1820: painter
and graphic artist

PHOTO CREDITS

Index

This book was printed and bound in August, 1986, by Ueberreuter Korneuburg, Austria.
Setting: Allprint AG, Zurich.
Photolithographs: Cliché + Litho AG, Zurich.
Coordination: Hubertus von Gemmingen.
Editorial: Barbara Perroud-Benson.
Index: Christiane Gäumann.
Design and Production: Emma Staffelbach.

Printed in Austria